TRANSFORMING STUDY ABROAD

TRANSFORMING STUDY ABROAD

A Handbook

Neriko Musha Doerr

berghahn
NEW YORK · OXFORD
www.berghahnbooks.com

First published in 2019 by
Berghahn Books
www.berghahnbooks.com

Library of Congress Cataloging-in-Publication Data
A C.I.P. cataloging record is available from the Library of Congress

British Library Cataloguing in Publication Data
A catalog record for this book is available from the British Library

ISBN 978-1-78920-115-4 hardback
ISBN 978-1-78920-756-9 paperback
ISBN 978-1-78920-116-1 ebook

For Benedict Anderson, John Borneman, and Elizabeth Povinelli,
the teachers who changed my life

Contents

Acknowledgments

I am grateful for Rotarians and fellow students in Tokyo and Aotearoa/ New Zealand who made my study abroad year in Aotearoa/New Zealand a wonderful one; my teachers and fellow students at Cornell University's anthropology program and government program; researchers and practitioners in the field of study abroad who taught me and supported me over the years, especially Tamar Breslauer and Caroline Donovan White who let me get involved in NAFSA; and students, chaperons, and program directors who participated in my research on study abroad trips. I also thank Jaime Taber and Kristyn Sanito, who copyedited the manuscript, and three anonymous reviewers who gave me constructive comments. The text's deficiencies are wholly my responsibility.

Introduction

I clearly remember the shock of seeing a wall-mounted rotary telephone with the handset set at the bottom part of the phone. I was used to a phone module with a metal cradle for the handset at the top and a rotary dial or push buttons on its face below. However, the handset was at the bottom of the phone in front of me, as was the metal pick-up/hang-up cradle, with the rotary dial above it.

That telephone turned my world upside down, shattering my worldview of what is "normal." I was eighteen years old, attending a local high school while on a yearlong stay in Aotearoa/New Zealand as a Rotary Club International Youth Exchange student. By making me realize that things do not have to be one way, this deep shock captured the essence of my study abroad experience: what you take for granted as the only way—the way you are used to—is challenged by a totally different yet similarly effective way of doing the same thing. This is the power of study abroad: small, everyday items and activities can trigger a grave new understanding that stays with you the rest of your life.

Yet, on a detailed examination, a more complex picture emerges. This "life-changing" year triggered me to travel to Aotearoa/New Zealand many times afterword, doing ethnographic research and seeing other aspects of the country. As I got to know more about the country as an anthropologist, I started to reframe my year there as an exchange student. As I became familiar with the field of study abroad and its theories and practices, this reframing of my year in Aotearoa/New Zealand made me think that some key notions used in study abroad could be revisited.

This personal endeavor became a cautionary tale, which then pushed me to write this book. Study abroad can be a double-edged sword: it can be a life-changing experience that makes you rethink your worldview, but it can also lead you to interpret it in superficial or even inaccurate and dangerous ways. This book seeks to start up conversations for overcoming this risk and argues, with careful reframing of some key notions, that study abroad can become an occasion for learning how the world works: how sociocultural, economic, and political structures

Figure 0.1 An "upside-down" wall-mounted phone (© User: Diamondmagna via Wikimedia Commons, CC BY-SA 3.0).

shape our daily lives and how we can become active agents in transforming them. Through transforming study abroad, we can transform ourselves as well as the world.

Eric Wolf (1994) once said that theories are just "takes" on phenomena. Some capture what is happening better than others do. My theoretical exploration of study abroad boils down to a search for "takes" that help us understand what happens in study abroad. This book is an attempt to ferret out takes that can explain it to us so that we can build on it.

Written for study abroad practitioners, as well as for those interested in the working of the field, this book introduces takes from various disciplines that may help to expand our understanding of study abroad experiences. However, there is no end to it: the diversity of ways of seeing, feeling, and understanding experiences means that we will always find more ways to view things and develop new ways to understand them. This book is part of that never-ending endeavor. And as I invite others into this endeavor, I hope that together we can find ways to grasp, explain, and understand the sensations that the students experience during study abroad—like my shock of seeing an upside-down phone—and capitalize on it as meaningful experience that can benefit them for the rest of their lives.

Three Study Abroad Experiences

I studied abroad three times. To be sure, not all of my study abroad experience induced world-shattering shock, nor did all of it inspire me to analyze world around me and what I had taken for granted. In hindsight, what made the difference was not the length of stay, or staying with a host family, or engaging the "locals," or the amount of reflection, as often suggested in study abroad literature as important factors. Instead, it was my analytical lens developed during my third study abroad experience, when I stayed in the dorm and mixed less with the locals than I had on my second experience as a student abroad.

What made the difference—theoretical frameworks by which to understand my experience—were gained while I participated in a graduate program in cultural anthropology during the third study abroad experience. With rigorous and critical theoretical frameworks, I was able to think and make sense of my experience during and outside study abroad with greater clarity than at any other time or through any other reflection. This book seeks to share this experience and such frameworks by introducing what I started to learn in graduate school and continue to learn to this day, namely, theories in cultural anthropology, political science, linguistics, and other fields of social science and humanities.

What I learned in my third study abroad experience can actually occur anywhere, including at students' home institutions (my fellow students were domestic students) and before (as well as during and after) studying abroad. However, I will argue throughout this book that study abroad has something specific to offer—attention to daily activities—that is conducive to inspiring and applying such a rigorous analytical lens. This book aims to be of some use in that process.

In short, although study abroad experience can provide world-shattering moments, for it to become a meaningful learning experience about the world, we need rigorous analytical frameworks. I will illustrate this in a more concrete way by introducing my three study abroad experiences that would exemplify different types of study abroad: short-term study abroad with little preparation, long-term study abroad with much preparation though in terms of learning "culture," and long-term study abroad with the subject content that provides analytical frameworks.

My First Time Studying Abroad: New Experiences without Interpretive Framework

I was born and raised in Japan. My first study abroad experience, which was also my first experience abroad, took place when I was eleven; I stayed with a host family for three weeks in a port town in the United Kingdom. My father's work took him to Manchester, and my sister, brother, cousin, and I were put in a summer study abroad program in a nearby city and housed by different host families. We attended school in the morning and did extracurricular excursions at the YMCA in the afternoon. Most of the other students were from France; some were from Spain. The only British people I got to know were my host family and the teacher, and I spent most of my time attending school with my sister, cousin, and French students. I remember strange feelings of awkwardness attached to being in one group of loud "foreigner" adolescents on an extended, controlled vacation. Unburdened by regular serious life routines of study or work, we spent carefree days with some light experience of "studying language."

I was entirely unprepared for this study abroad experience. I knew hardly any English (it was a compulsory school subject from seventh grade in Japan, but I was only in sixth grade at the time) and did not know what to expect. Despite seeing, experiencing, and interacting with people whom I would not have encountered had I stayed in Japan, I did not have tools to interpret or understand them.

For example, one day during this study abroad stay, a cashier at a store gave my sister and me the wrong change. We noticed it and told her. I thought the discrepancy reflected anti-Asian racism. My sister, however, told me she had overheard the cashier telling another store person that the cash register was not working properly. I had grown up as a mainstream Japanese, and had a very naïve interpretation of inter-racial relations. For the first time in my life, I realized what it is like to anticipate victimization and also erroneously read things into others' actions. However, beyond that, that experience did not lead to anything meaningful.

I was surprised to see that many of my fellow students were dark-skinned people from France, as this defied my then stereotype of French as "white." Only later did I realize that France has many immigrants, that this has to do with France's former colonies in Africa, and that people in former colonies tend to migrate to former colonizers' countries mainly because they have some familiarity with the languages and various social systems imposed on them by the colonizers. At that time, though, nobody explained this to me, and there was no occasion to discuss it. Regardless of the novelty of this initial experience outside Japan, it was not as impactful as my second trip.

My Second Time Studying Abroad: Knowledgeable about Home and Host Countries without Critical Interpretive Frameworks

I studied abroad for the second time as a Rotary Club International Youth Exchange student seven years later, as mentioned. It was a year-long experience with much preparation and follow-up. After passing a written test and then an interview, I was one of the thirteen high school students chosen from one Rotary Club district of Tokyo to study abroad. Everything but the airfare was paid for; I even received a weekly stipend. The selection took place a year before our departure, and we (the program's outgoing students) met for workshops and retreats (pre-trip meetings) every month before the trip. We learned Japanese things, such as how to put a kimono on, so that we could "introduce Japan" while abroad. We also learned things like "Western table manners" to enable us to adjust better while abroad (destination countries for the students in our group were the United States, Canada, Australia, Aotearoa/New Zealand, and Brazil). Several sleepover retreats were organized for socializing with program alumni and students who had come to Japan from abroad on the same program. Of all these activities, it was our trip to Hiroshima, where we visited the Hiroshima Peace Memorial Museum, that made the deepest impression. They tried to train us to be Japanese ambassadors, as it were.

When I was in Aotearoa/New Zealand, I had one "counselor family" and lived with four host families, three months each (to reduce the burden on each host family, who host without compensation), which allowed me to see how different each family is. Once a month there was a retreat and/or get-together with other Rotary exchange students from around the world. I attended a local high school with my host siblings, as all host families had children who attended the same high school. I observed different lifestyles (e.g., one host family had a swimming pool, which is unthinkable in Japan), different ways of thinking (e.g., people cared about social life as much as about school achievement, in stark contrast to what I knew in Japan, where schoolwork was prioritized over everything), and different sensibilities (e.g., walking in pouring rain without an umbrella or walking down on the street barefooted). But what shocked me the most was the realization that, above and beyond what we would usually think of as "cultural difference," there are different ways of doing things, symbolized by that upside-down phone mentioned at the beginning of this chapter.

Upon returning to Japan, I attended several post-trip meetings (though not as many as some of my fellow students in the cohort), offering guidance to prospective students and socializing with my cohort as well as alumni and students currently studying abroad in Japan. Comparisons of experience abounded between students who had gone to different places—Australia, the United States, Canada, Brazil. The friends I made then—both in my cohort and in classrooms and host families in Aotearoa/New Zealand—have become lifelong friends with whom I have kept in touch, at first through yearly Christmas cards and occasional visits and now also via social media.

In my second study abroad experience, I was in a program that study abroad literature would praise as preparing us students well. Besides the workshops and retreats mentioned earlier, the program promoted learning about Japan: we were given a book about "Japanese culture" and encouraged to learn things like Japanese "traditional dance" (*nihon buyou*), flower arrangement, and tea ceremony, which most of us did. I took flower arrangement classes and did use that skill a couple of times while in Aotearoa/New Zealand. By regularly interacting with study abroad alumni and students from abroad studying in Japan, we learned what to expect, what to watch out for, and how to prepare ourselves for the experience.

Nonetheless, we were not provided with rigorous theoretical frameworks to understand the interactions that occur during study abroad. We viewed "Japanese culture" in terms of the safe diversity of tea ceremony, Japanese dance, and food. We had an essentialistic view of Japan that was promoted at the time by quasi-scholarly genre of *Nihonjinron*, or Japanology, which presents a static, homogenized image of Japan based on the viewpoint of Tokyo's privileged middle class. We did not realize the cultural politics informed by relations of power—for example, that what is considered "Japanese culture" is really Tokyo-centered middle-class practices derived from practices of the Samurai caste and imposed everywhere as the norm, marginalizing other practices within Japan.

My view of the destination, Aotearoa/New Zealand, was similar. Staying with four host families and having another family as a counselor allowed me to see diversity among Aotearoa/New Zealand households, but all their members were Pākehā (white) New Zealanders from affluent backgrounds. Though I did talk with some students from Māori, Samoan, and Fijian backgrounds, most of my school friends were Pākehā New Zealanders, and I was not exposed to other viewpoints—especially those of indigenous Māori, who together with Pākehā constitute the "bicultural" nation of Aotearoa/New Zealand.

As the arrangement of this year was what would be considered a model case according to study abroad discourses—detailed preparation, full "immersion" in local life, and follow-ups—this brief examination challenges "common sense" of study abroad. Calling my year a "cross-cultural" experience would have ignored the complexity of each society by rendering it internally homogeneous. I learned to speak English during this year, yet learning to speak with "native speakers" actually meant getting used to each person's way of speaking— I often had to start over when I met a new person—until I gained enough repertoires of decoding skills. Describing my experience an "immersion" created an illusion that I lived like most New Zealanders, which was hardly true (I lived like a daughter/guest in affluent Pākehā households). Calling my stay there crossing the "border" is to ignore other borders within Japan or Aotearoa/New Zealand—ethnic, class, regional, generational, and even between those who love rugby (Aotearoa/New Zealand's national sport) and those who do not. And, though it did transform me, it was one of many transformations I experienced throughout my life, including when I first found out at a young age my family rules (e.g., no "bad" words can be used) that I thought were universally applied to all children were not, or when I found out that, for doing the same work, I was paid double the wage of old women from northern Japan working with me at a ski hotel because the employer thought Tokyo college students would not work for a lower wage, which shattered my belief in the existence of egalitarianism and fair labor relations in Japan.

The difference is, I was asked about self-transformative experiences during studying abroad much more than about self-transformative experiences in other contexts. Study abroad then does not specifically offer transformative experiences in itself, as is often believed (see chapter 7 for the review of this discourse); rather, we make it seem that way by constantly asking students for examples of such experiences. In short, though I was well trained in a setup that study abroad discourses would highly recommend for my second round of study abroad, the framework I used was not rigorous enough to understand the relations of power involved in social configurations in either Japan or Aotearoa/New Zealand.

My Third Time Studying Abroad: Critical Interpretative Frameworks of Cultural Politics

My third study abroad experience was all about academics. I came to the United States to attend graduate school and gain a PhD in cultural anthropology at Cornell University—in other words, as a degree-seeking study abroad student. I lived on campus in Ithaca, New York, taking classes for three years, during which I married an American and decided to stay in the United States. After finishing my course work, I went to Aotearoa/New Zealand for nine months for fieldwork and, one and a half years after my return to the United States, received the doctoral degree with a dissertation based on that fieldwork.

There was no talk of "immersion" or "learning culture." I studied and worked side by side with other American students, and although I did make friends with other international students from around the world—Thailand, Japan, Korea, China—it did not seem to matter as much as it does in study abroad discourses, which often concern whom students should spend time with while studying abroad. At a college that attracted not just students but also professors from all over the world, being an international student was not a remarkable fact but just another anecdotal item about oneself. It was very common for any students to share in class their viewpoints shaped by their different backgrounds and upbringing.

This study abroad experience—my third—focused on academics, as mentioned. I learned theoretical viewpoints—not because my program was study abroad but because they were the subject content of the program. I learned to revisit and question taken-for-granted notions around us as something constructed in relations of power at particular historical moments. I learned about objectification of "culture" and its political uses. I also learned about diversity and power relations within Japan and about negative parts of Japanese history—for instance, a student from Korea told me in class discussions about the many Korean people living in Japan who were scapegoated and killed in the chaos of a big earthquake in Tokyo region in the 1920s, and a student from Malaysia spoke of atrocities committed by Japanese soldiers that tended not to be discussed explicitly in Japan. It was, however, framed not as "cultural difference" in viewpoints but rather as historical documentation, as well as what public schools in Japan do not teach their students.

Armed with these theoretical understandings, I started to make sense of my first and second study abroad experiences. It was no longer about "the encounter between two different cultures"—how I, a Japanese, went to the UK and Aotearoa/New Zealand and learned about these "cultures"—but about understanding encounters with various people with multiple subject positions and diverse perspectives informed by broader sociocultural, economic, and political forces in Japan, the UK, and Aotearoa/New Zealand.

What These Three Study Abroad Experiences Tell Us

Every study abroad experience is different, even for the same person. One's stage in life, destination, the goal of the stay, the context of the stay, the group one goes with—all these affect the experience. In trying to make sense of these diverse experiences, however, I found I was pulled by existing discourses. Ken Plummer (1995) argues that existing narratives provide not only the grammar, vocabularies, and sequences of our own stories but also recipes for structuring our experience and directing our lives. Finding that someone else's narrative describes our own experience also comforts us, assuring us that our experience is not anomalous but has a name, turning fragmented parts into a coherent story, and providing a community to belong to.

Such narratives are like theoretical frameworks or "takes" on the experience. And when compared, my three study abroad experiences show that these narratives are the most important piece of the puzzle of making study abroad experience meaningful. Study abroad provides narratives to examine our daily experiences and mundane encounters, like trying new foods and meeting new people, and allows us to analyze and express what they mean. Such narratives can be based on concepts that may need revisiting, as this book seeks to do, or on theoretically rigorous, well-thought-through notions.

Take the upside-down phone, for example: it was not merely a "cultural difference" of Aotearoa/New Zealand as I first thought and as conventional study abroad discourses would have it. The particular model of phone comes from the UK, the former mother country of Aotearoa/New Zealand, as do much of the infrastructure and institutions in Aotearoa/New Zealand. Having gained independence in 1947, Aotearoa/New Zealand is now a former British settler colony, but the UK's influence on Aotearoa/New Zealand remained strong, at least until the 1970s, when the country's character started to change from "England of the South Seas" to a bicultural "Pacific country" (of descendants of British settlers, called Pākehā, and indigenous Māori) seeking ties with other Pacific nations. This shift emerged out of Māoris' intensifying protests against their marginalization and from changes in alliances as the UK transferred its focus from its former colonies (in the British Commonwealth) to Europe by joining the then European Economic Community (Belich 2001; Walker 1990). Against this backdrop, the existence of this upside-down phone in Aotearoa/ New Zealand can be understood as the legacy of British colonialism and by extension a sign of Pākehā New Zealanders' continued dominance over indigenous Māoris in the 1980s.

In short, what we consider "culture" is not ways of doing things specific to a group of people that happen to be shaped that way or that have been passed down from ancestors (let alone transmitted by genes or blood). "Culture" relies not on mere static "difference" but on results of historical and current social, economic, and political institutions, arrangements, and interactions, which are connected throughout the world in uneven, constantly shifting ways. Through the upside-down phone, my second study abroad experience allowed me to relativize the "normal," but it was the theoretical frameworks I discovered during my third study abroad experience that allowed me to understand the phone's meaning as a legacy of British colonialism. Thus, my second study abroad experience gave me a shock, whereas my third provided explanation and understanding. The former left me an observer of the world, but the latter allowed me to be inside the world, because understanding how the world works made me part of its construction and transformation.

To clarify, I am using my personal trajectory as a way to explain how learning critical theories helped me understand my prior study abroad experiences. That they were both study abroad was only a coincidence: as mentioned, learning theoretical frameworks during my third experience of studying abroad did not have to happen "abroad": I could have learned it in my home country, as was the case for many of my fellow students in the program who were domestic students. Also coincidental was the fact that I learned critical theories in my third round of study abroad; they just happened to be in my subject area. Not all graduate-level study abroad involves learning critical theory—it may be absent from engineering work, for instance. I take advantage of this coincidence, however, and suggest how such theoretical frameworks not only help us analyze study abroad experiences but also transform them.

What this book suggests, then, is to make such critical theoretical frameworks available to all study abroad students via study abroad practitioners. These theories are useful in analyzing any occurrences and events. What I ultimately suggest in this book is to then turn study abroad experience as a meaningful intellectual training of analyzing daily life that can become useful even after these students return home (as the notion of "global" came to be increasingly questioned, as will be discussed in chapter 1). Because of its focus on daily life through the notion of "immersion," study abroad is best suited for such a job, and such training can be study abroad's major contribution to the field of education. The next section elaborates on this point.

Regimes of Experience and Nurturing Analytical Eyes for Daily Practices during Study Abroad and Beyond

Critical theoretical frameworks enable students to interpret and understand why "difference" exists, how the difference emerged and is sustained, and how they come to notice that difference but not others so that they can take part in those processes as active agents. If we incorporate such theoretical frameworks, study abroad as an educational endeavor can become a good site to engage students in thinking about how and why difference occurs and is noticed in daily life because study abroad pushes students to pay close attention to their daily activities through the "immersion" concept.

Framing and attention matter in what we notice and highlight (McDermott and Varenne 1995). For example, as mentioned, although we have transformative experiences in various contexts, we tend to highlight those during studying abroad because self-transformation is expected to happen there, and thus many occasions to talk about it are offered (see chapter 7). I call this gap "regimes of experience"—where we only notice certain experience and ignore other similar experience not because of their degrees of importance but because of the ways in which we privilege certain context as the space of that particular experience: because we privilege study abroad as the occasion for self-transformation and thus inquire often whether it happened, we ignore self-transformation occurred in other contexts.

Regimes of experience do have effects on students. I have argued elsewhere (Doerr 2017c) that the concept of "global learner" can include not only study abroad students but also English as a Second Language (ESL) students who learn about their host society's lifestyles and students in bilingual Māori-English classes in Aotearoa/New Zealand who learn about issues facing indigenous peoples around the world (see also chapter 1). One of my students who had read the article told me that, growing up in a white, middle-class suburb, he thought he never had any "global learning" experience. However, after reading the article, he realized that he has had "global learning" experience all along: his family had always hosted relatives from Venezuela for three months every year while they worked and sent remittance home, which involved him adjusting to their lifestyles and speaking Spanish with them. Without a suggestion that global learning can happen outside study abroad, he would not have even thought to look into his daily life, he said (Jon Hernandez, personal communication). In this way, new ways of framing can change students' perceptions.

From this understanding, as mentioned, I suggest focusing on our daily acts and experiences with the same rigor as we do during study abroad—asking questions about them, reflecting on them, and so on—and connect such mundane experiences in our daily life to wider structural and institutional arrangements, viewing the former as effects of the latter and vice versa. For example, the price of a T-shirt is related to the labor conditions and wage structure of the country where the T-shirt was made, as well as the trade regulations and national and local legislations that allow such items to be circulated and sold in our country. As consumers, we can affect that practice by buying T-shirts of the brand that has good labor relations or boycott ones that do not, voting with our money. We can do so by being aware of how our daily life is shaped by global structural arrangements and how we are complicit in that global structural arrangement as voters, consumers, and marchers and social media participants who voice opinions and spread awareness.

A Handbook for Transforming Study Abroad

The aim of this book is to take the first step toward incorporating critical theoretical frameworks into discussions of study abroad. Written for study abroad practitioners, the book is meant to help them guide study abroad students toward various theoretically informed critical perspectives from which to interpret their study abroad and post–study abroad experience and make the most of it. It can also benefit students who are interested in deepening their study abroad and other experience on their own.

To structure the book's relevance to study abroad practitioners and students, I will revisit nine key terms in study abroad—the global (chapter 1), the national (chapter 1), culture (chapter 2), native speaker (chapter 3), immersion (chapter 4), host society (chapter 5), host family (chapter 5), border crossing (chapter 6), and self-transformation (chapter 7)—and frame them in terms of current theoretical discussions. In each chapter, I suggest sample activities and questions for implementing such frameworks; asked before, during, and after their study abroad stay, these questions can engage students in such discussions.

I need to note here that, although this book deals with many concepts that are relevant to diverse types of study abroad programs (as my three study abroad experiences show: they were a three-week summer intensive language program for secondary school students, a one-year exchange student program for high school students with no subject content focus, and a study abroad stay through direct enrollment at a graduate school), some of its discussions are more geared toward credit-seeking (rather than degree-seeking) study abroad programs for American students. This is partly because credit-seeking programs are increasing, especially in the United States (Chieffo and Griffith 2004) and partly because my research is based on such programs. Credit-seeking programs often take the form of a semester-long program, an intensive summer program that lasts four to six weeks, or an "island-type" program with a group of students led by professors from the student's home institution that lasts one to two weeks and stays together as a group throughout their sojourn as in a field trip. These programs, though they often have subject-content focus, tend to include "learning the culture of the destination" as an important part of the program. In contrast, degree-seeking programs tend to last more than a year and focus more on learning the subject area than "the culture of the destination."

Implementing Theoretical Viewpoints: Encouraging Students to Ask Questions

This book is designed to introduce current theoretical discussions to study abroad practitioners so that they can pass these latest understandings of key terms on to study abroad students, as mentioned. I have sometimes wondered if these theories that challenge current study abroad discourses may put off students and discourage them to study abroad. However, when I cover these issues in my college classes with theoretical readings I introduce in this book, students usually respond to this question with a "no," further saying that they would rather know about these issues before they study abroad so that they know what to avoid and thus have peace of mind that they are well informed about current discussions. Though it does make sense in this light to focus on pre-trip orientations to inform students about these theoretical issues, I do believe in reminding them during and after their stay as they have their own concrete experiences to further apply and digest these theoretical arguments.

Students' involvement in this critical revisiting of key terms is also an important part of their study abroad experience. To recapture, it helps them develop critical, deep understanding of their own study abroad experiences and cultivates a habit of seeing the complexity of social practices and questioning the dominant ideologies behind activities. Students learn to question taken-for-granted ideas, to look deeper into how relations of power structure our daily lives, how our subject positions influence our perceptions and experience of the world, and how we can change the world for the better.

Though my task is to introduce existing theories that show how various key terms in study abroad are constructed, I will still have to retain some of these terms because there are no good alternatives and because offering alternative terms for concepts such as "culture," "nation," and "language" reproduces the very effect I am critiquing: that they imply internally homogeneous, bounded unit. Nonetheless, awareness of the power politics and ideological natures behind these terms is important. Stuart Hall discusses something similar regarding notions like "identity": after deconstructing such notions, Hall argues, we still must think with them because there are no good concepts to replace them with; we just have to use them differently, "now in their detotalized or deconstructed forms, and no longer operating within the paradigm in which they were originally generated" (1996: 1). That is, we can continue to use the notions we critique but with clear awareness of their biases, their ideological underpinnings, and the effects of their uncritical use.

I encourage study abroad practitioners not to lecture the students about these latest understandings of key terms but instead to ask students questions that push them to consider their own concrete experiences in light of these understandings. The sample activities and questions suggested for each chapter model such practices, which can be modified to fit the particular contexts of study abroad under question. Also, some questions are left vague on purpose. It is not to keep discussions abstract but to avoid restricting kinds of answer students come up with. If students have difficulty understanding the intent of the question, the study abroad practitioners can supplement with further explanations and concrete examples to facilitate the discussion and connect the questions ultimately to concrete experiences of the student.

There are three rationales for this approach that focuses on students' concrete experiences. First, this focus helps students reflect on how their own specific subject positions have influenced their experience. Second, thinking about and through one's own concrete experiences is usually conducive to grasping difficult theoretical ideas. This is the basis of Freirean pedagogies, including critical pedagogy, as will be discussed further in chapter 4. The third rationale concerns the need to lessen the impact of the "symbolic violence" of education that imposes a "correct" viewpoint onto others, backed up by the teacher's position as the "expert" (Bourdieu and Passeron 1977). Open-ended self-reflection guided by questions allows educators to avoid imposing their viewpoints to some degree, despite a lingering risk that students will be led toward certain worldviews.

Sections at the end of each chapter suggest topic-focused examples of questions that can get students thinking about the issues raised in each chapter. However, some questions—especially those about the heterogeneity of society and its continuing portrayal as homogeneous—can be asked under many headings. To avoid repetition, the questions are numbered throughout, and I will refer to these numbers when the same questions can be asked in different contexts. Besides questions about the focus of each chapter, four kinds of questions should be asked no matter what the topic is. The first kind of questions (marked with "W") concerns how students' own subject positions shape their perceptions and experiences. We can foster awareness of this by asking them how their perceptions and experiences compare with other students' and how their subject positions affect differences.

The second point that students should always be encouraged to examine is the relations of power involved in what they experience and observe (question series marked with "X"). We can develop the above questions (W) about how people's diverse viewpoints follow from their subject positions by further asking which of these diverse viewpoints tend to be privileged as "regular" viewpoints and which ones are marginalized and erased, for example, in study abroad promotional materials. In this way, students can not only recognize where their views are located and become self-aware of their positions but also (if their viewpoints are privileged and normalized) start applying cultural relativism—a belief that no "cultural" beliefs and practices is better than others and that we should understand others' practices in their own context instead of from our own viewpoint—in their interpretations of things and events they encounter.

The third question (question series marked "Y") we can always ask students relates to the issue of change. We can always caution students not to "freeze" what they see during their study abroad stay by perceiving it as something that has been happening for many centuries. We can prompt them to imagine what it was like, for example, a hundred years ago, as well as fifty, twenty, ten, and five years ago, so that they can relativize what they saw as a snapshot of that society in a particular time period. We can then suggest that they think about what caused the changes and how we could be part of further changes to improve the conditions of people.

This question leads to the fourth question (marked with "Z") we can encourage students to always consider: how their home society and the host society are connected. That is, instead of viewing the home and host societies as two separate, distinct "cultures" that happen to have many differences, and the student as jumping into "another culture" by studying abroad, I encourage students to understand how what they see in the host society may to various degrees be an effect of what is happening directly and indirectly in their home society. For example, the behavior of consumers in a student's home society could be affecting the industry of the host society (including students visiting the host society as study abroad students), or political relationships and various trading regulations between the students' home and host countries could shape both societies. For example, American students studying abroad in Guatemala need to understand that the United States intervened in Guatemala in the 1950s with a CIA-sponsored military coup that toppled its democratically elected president and established an authoritarian government, which led in turn to a long civil war that devastated the country; otherwise, they would understand what they see in Guatemala as a distinct "culture" that happens to be very different from that of the United States. This understanding of home-host society relationships also helps students understand what they see in their home society—for instance, that immigrants from Guatemala had to seek a "better life" outside their homeland—and why. As such relations can be ongoing, participating in changing the host society's situations can take the form of acting to pressure one's own government, which can lead to discussions with students about intervention and issues of ethnocentrism and cultural relativism.

Though the example questions will not be repeated in each chapter, I encourage they be asked for various items in combination with the specific questions being asked no matter what topic we are focusing on. For example, when the study abroad practitioner is asking the student about the media representation of people in the host society, they can add questions regarding whose viewpoint gets privileged and how the students' subject position is affecting their view. And study abroad practitioners can use or modify these example questions to fit each situation. These questions can be asked on various occasions as seen in the examples below.

Before the Students Study Abroad

(1) in orientation sessions
    (a) with questions posted on screen so that students can think of answers themselves or have discussions in a large group or small groups
    (b) in survey forms in which students write down answers that they then keep or give to practitioners who hold them until the students return from the study abroad trip
(2) in small group discussions with practitioners or study abroad alumni when they are getting ready to study abroad
(3) in a one-on-one conference with a practitioner
(4) on a handout listing questions, on which students can write answers in their own time; they can then keep it themselves or hand it in to practitioners
(5) online, where they can be posted as one of the mandatory/ optional assignments students complete before studying abroad

During Students' Study Abroad Stay

(1) in classes or general meetings
    (a) with questions displayed on screen so that students can think of answers themselves or have discussions in a big group or small groups
    (b) in survey forms in which students write down answers that they then keep or give to practitioners to make the survey more official
(2) in small group discussions or one-on-one conferences with practitioners
(3) in an office or study room where the list of questions is displayed on the wall, allowing students to answer in their own time; they then keep the answers or hand them in to practitioners
(4) online, where answers can be posted as one of the mandatory/ optional assignments students complete before going home

After Students Return from Their Study Abroad Stay

(1) in reentry sessions
    (a) with questions displayed on screen to let students think of answers themselves or have discussions in a big group or small groups

    (b) in survey forms where students write down answers that they can keep, or else give to practitioners to make the survey more official

(2) in small group discussions with practitioners

(3) in a one-on-one conference with a practitioner

(4) on a handout listing questions that students can answer in their own time; they can then keep it to themselves or hand it in to the practitioners

(5) online, posted as one of the mandatory/optional assignments students complete for a grade or credit.

Some of the activities suggested can be done as appropriate for these activities as specified, including with students who are not planning to study abroad. Some of the activities can be done for general student body regardless of their plan to study abroad as well.

Structure of the Book

Each chapter in this book discusses one key term or set of terms from the field of study abroad as mentioned. After reviewing how it is usually used in study abroad literature, each chapter introduces current discussions of the term(s) in various disciplines—cultural anthropology, political science, educational studies, linguistics, critical literacy, and so on—and makes suggestions about how these understandings can be incorporated into study abroad practices by asking questions to students. Each chapter ends with an annotated list of recommended readings.

    In chapter 1, I discuss the notions of the "national" and "global" together, because the term global relies on the notion of the national as the unit of difference, which it claims to overcome and connect. One stated goal of study abroad—the nurturing of students' "global competence" and their transformation into "global citizens"—relies on the existence of cultural difference, which overlaps with national difference, as implied in the understanding that students need to go "abroad" to experience cultural difference. Yet students do not need to go abroad to learn about cultural difference firsthand: they can do so from the diversity that already exists within the nation. Though the emerging notion of "study away" is starting to correct the neglect of intranational diversity, study abroad discourses still tend to rely on and perpetuate the ideology of nation-state. Based on this understanding, this chapter examines nation-state ideology and criticism of it so as to incorporate that understanding into study abroad practices and avoid perpetuating the ideology of the nation-state as consisting of a homogeneous "culture."

The notion of the global, built on the notion of the national (also explained in chapter 1), is a key concept in study abroad. After showing how it is used in study abroad discourses—from "global competence" to "global citizenship"—this first chapter also introduces discussions of globalization in cultural anthropology, geography, and political science. The latest argument on the topic is that such discussions tend to be ideologically "globalist" in their valorization of global flows and connections. The chapter then discusses three problems of this globalism— (1) it masks the unevenness of inclusion in the category of the global because of regimes of mobility that mark some mobility "global" and desirable while other mobility is seen as criminal and suspicious; (2) it renders those who do not move deficient; and (3) it revives the ideology of nation-states as bounded unit that is internally homogeneous by focusing only on the crossing of national borders—and suggests ways of engaging students in understanding these aspects of the term global. Because the notion of the global is commonplace in study abroad, it makes for many promising opportunities for educators to engage students in thinking about the notion critically.

Chapter 2 covers the notion of "culture," which study abroad literature tends to see as a homogeneous and bounded unit of difference. This literature focuses on two types of "culture"—"high culture" and "exotic culture," depending on the destination—and in both cases, it depicts "culture" as a fully knowable pool to immerse oneself in. Drawing on theories from cultural anthropology and educational studies, I first introduce five frameworks of "culture" to further situate the notion of "culture" in study abroad. The first is the culture-as-problem (normal-versus-deficient) framework, which situates difference in terms of hierarchy: what dominant group members do is considered "normal," and what marginalized group members do is considered "deficient" rather than viewed as "cultural difference." The second is the culture-as-division-to-be-ignored (color blindness) framework that avoids seeing "cultural difference" because it views it as divisive and thus upholds the dominant practices as the default "norm." These two approaches can be seen in the study abroad context when students carry out community service, especially done in developing countries, where what is considered desirable in the students' home country (thus, the "norm") gets imposed on the community under question in the name of "development." The third, the culture-as-safe-difference framework, decontextualizes, depoliticizes, and domesticates difference into "safe" differences in realms like cuisine, art, and fashion. Study abroad promotional materials tend to use this framework. Fourth, the culture-as-political-resource framework focuses on objectified "culture" as serving political purposes, based on a preconceived notion of a link between "a culture" and a group. Study abroad discourses often use this "culture"-group linkage for commercial purposes but overlook its political aspect as a strategy for mobilization.

The fifth framework, the culture-as-constructed-difference framework, views "culture" as constructed as the unit of difference in relations of power and reveals how particular sociocultural environments make us notice certain differences and not others as meaningful. By viewing "culture" as a folk term, not an analytical term, this framework adopts what is currently the most accepted standpoint in anthropology. Study abroad, on the other hand, typically views "cultural difference" as preexisting rather than constructed in relations of power. I suggest four ways of engaging students in thinking about their study abroad experience in this framework: challenging the view that "culture" is a homogeneous bounded unit; gaining an idea of the complexity inherent in any society, the students' home and host societies included; viewing "culture" as merely a way to divide people into groups; and analyzing how "culture" is mutually constructed in relation to other "cultures" positioned in relations of power.

Chapter 3 unpacks the term "native speaker" as it is used when study abroad students are learning the language of the destination, and the common assumption that students automatically gain proficiency by being immersed among "native speakers" of the language. By examining three assumptions behind the notion of the "native speaker"—its link to the ideology of the nation-state, the notion of language as an internally homogeneous unit, and belief in the innate competence of "native speakers"—and exploring how the term has been treated in linguistics, especially in Second Language Acquisition (SLA) theories, this chapter suggests ways to involve study abroad students in critical understanding of the notion of the "native speaker," language, and linguistic competence. The suggestions target the diversity of language and the political nature of the assumption that it is homogeneous (which simultaneously marginalizes those who do not speak the "standard" variety and forces them to assimilate), as well as the notion of linguistic competence, which creates a hierarchy of "native" and "non-native" speakers. They are meant to engage students in thinking about the political implications of judgments we make about "learning the language of the study abroad destination," whereby they can come to a deeper understanding of the notion of the "native speaker," "language," "correctness," and "competence."

Chapter 4 revisits the notion of immersion, one of the most consequential terms in study abroad. I first review several critiques of the idea, noting especially its effects: it constructs the view that the host society and students' home society are fundamentally different and internally homogeneous, and from this assumption, it places at the top of a hierarchy of experience the direct enrollment in long-term study abroad combined with a focus on out-of-classroom experience, maximal interaction with locals, and staying with a host family. I call for avoiding such constructions based on the view that study abroad is an encounter of two distinct, homogeneous "cultures"; instead, I call for viewing study abroad experience as something constantly co-constructed by both study abroad students and people in the host society along with other diverse peoples who exist in the space of the host society.

I then show how labeling certain acts as immersion is a commentary on the social positions of those involved. Calling an act "immersion" constructs study abroad students as seeking luxurious enrichment practices and intending to go home eventually (as opposed to immigrants), the people they interact with as legitimate members of the society, and these groups as separated by great social distance. I call for urging students to be aware of these effects of the notion of immersion, but I also seek ways to capitalize on the attention to daily life that the notion of immersion encourages, as I have suggested in this introduction, and ways to get students to analyze the processes of othering that occur during and outside of study abroad and connect their daily experiences to the wider sociocultural, economic, and political structures so as to understand how these structures shape their lives and how to act on them to create social change. I also suggest a workshop to apply this idea.

Chapter 5 examines the notion of host society and host family. As discussed in chapters 2 and 4, a host society is often viewed as homogeneous, and staying with a host family is usually portrayed as the best way to immerse oneself in the host society because it means "living like a local." I first point out the contradiction of two coexisting views of the host society's space-time here: (a) homogeneous insider space-time where host society is seen to be occupied only by "local" people; and (b) heterogeneous space-time where insider space-time as described above and outsider space-time filled with study abroad students and tourists (i.e., "outsiders") coexist. Whereas homogeneous insider space-time (a) is talked about when students were describing their immersion experience, heterogeneous insider/outsider space-times (b) are mentioned when claiming one's "good study abroad student" status as someone who avoids outsider space-time.

I then introduce critical discussions about this notion by examining four problematic assumptions (researchers' arguments against them are in parentheses): (1) staying with a host family is the best way to learn about the host society (no, it depends on the amount of engagement with the host family and the attitudes of those involved); (2) the host family represents the entire host society (no, host families are specific types of people in that they have spare time and money and are willing to live with a stranger); (3) the host family provides "authentic" experience of the host society (no, their daily routines are modified to accommodate the students' needs); and (4) the host family and the study abroad students are very different (no, difference and similarity are negotiated and sanctioned variously, depending on whether the difference is viewed as culturally inspired). From these understandings, I go on to challenge the view behind the notion of "living *like* a local," which is that two distinct and internally homogeneous "cultures" encounter each other as the student joins a static host society life represented by the host family. Instead, I suggest viewing life in the host society as constantly constructed by the diverse people who reside there, including study abroad students who also influence it, albeit only a little (as the host family modifies its lifestyle for the students), and are influenced by it as students adjust to the life there. Staying with a host family is thus about "living *with* locals," I suggest.

Chapter 6 discusses the notions of border crossing in study abroad, and volunteer/service work and its increasing incorporation in study abroad. In study abroad, border crossing is celebrated and relies on the existence of difference, as discussed in chapters 1 and 2. It is highlighted by a view of study abroad as (1) "adventure" that relies on the existence of something new and unknown; (2) a disorienting experience, which by creating cognitive dissonance supposedly produces a particular sensibility toward difference; and, (3) an immersion experience, in which noticing difference is inherent in learning. As for volunteer/service work, its merit for students is increasingly held to lie in their crossing a border into a community of lower socioeconomic status (often implying difference in race) and learning to empathize with those who are "different" from you.

This chapter argues that the difference that is recognized is constructed through our own actions: framing study abroad as adventure, expecting cognitive dissonance while in the study abroad destination, recognizing the moment of learning when encountering difference, and calling our act of helping volunteer/service work for "others." I encourage making students aware of this constructive process while also discouraging study abroad and volunteer/service work to be framed as border crossing so that we can frame these experiences differently—as enjoying life in the host society without framing it as disorienting or different, and working with people, not as an outsider "helping" them but as a collaborator working for the same goal.

Chapter 7 investigates the ways in which study abroad discourses expect study abroad to result in particular types of student self-transformation. This chapter traces two ways of talking about such self-transformation: outcome assessment and students' self-narratives, which respectively derive their desirable learning outcomes and desirable transformations from the views of the dominant group. While the former sets a goal against which students' aptitude and attitudes are measured, the latter provides narrative structures that shape not only students' ways of narrating but also their experiences. And both ways assume that study abroad students are monocultural, monolingual, white, middle-class youth, limiting ways to express or even erasing minority students' learned outcome and that experiences can be measured and narrated. For these reasons, I argue that these desired learning outcomes and desired kinds of self-transformation should be more inclusive so as to reflect the diversity of the student body and the things they would learn, based on their specific backgrounds. I also suggest highlighting self-transformation in daily life as well.

The conclusion reviews and summarizes the discussions in the book and suggests ways to incorporate the theoretical insights introduced in this volume into actions. It also suggests new frameworks for understanding study abroad.

Study Abroad for Action

Study abroad is uniquely valuable in that it pushes us to recognize areas of experience—daily life—that, though usually overlooked, remain significant. John Dewey called for "education of, by, and for experience". (1938: 29), encouraging it as an alternative to more "oppressive" styles of teaching associated with lecture-based formats in which students passively memorize what the teacher tells them. Later, David Kolb (1984) theorized experiential learning by combining the theories of John Dewey, Kurt Lewin, and Jean Piaget to link experience to abstract conceptualization. Scott Wurdinger and Julie Carlson (2010) identify five types of experiential learning: project-based, problem-based, service, place-based (i.e., focused on the local community and environment), and active (i.e., interacting with peers and materials in the classroom).

Whereas these approaches are categorized as experiential learning and tend to focus on the process of learning by a hands-on, learning-by-doing method, critical pedagogy focuses on students' lived experience as resource to understand social theories and put them in action. Lived experience is significant as a site where sociocultural, economic, and political structures intertwine and manifest themselves, shaping our lives. It is at this "innocent level" of daily life that the most harmful work of domination is done (Kincheloe and Steinberg 1997), which makes it all the more important for everyone to examine them critically. To do so, we need theoretical frameworks and informed discussions.

In this spirit, this book introduces some key concepts and discusses the ways in which they relate to wider social structures so that study abroad practitioners can ask students critical questions and lead them to think and act critically from their own experience. The habit of questioning "common sense" in this way can then become a good starting point for thinking about various other phenomena in the world beyond study abroad.

◀◎ Sample Questions

W: How Students' Own Subject Positions Shape Their Perceptions and Experiences
W1: How do you think your own racial, socioeconomic, regional, and other backgrounds influenced the way in which you experienced and interpreted your life in the host society?
W2: How do you think someone with racial, socioeconomic, regional, and other backgrounds different from yours experienced and interpreted life in the host society?

X: The Relations of Power
X1: Whose view is privileged, and whose view is marginalized?
X2: Who benefits and who gets marginalized by this?

Y: The Issue of Change
Y1: Do you think this has changed? If so, what caused the change?
Y2: What do you think the host society was like ten years ago, twenty years ago, fifty years ago?
Y3: How can we change it?
Y4: How else can we imagine the culture to be?

Z: Connections between the Students' Home Society and the Host Society
Z1: How do you think the policies, regulations, and practices in your home society have influenced what you are seeing in the host society now?
Z2: How do you think the policies, regulations, and practices in the host society have influenced what is happening in your home society?

1

THE GLOBAL AND THE NATIONAL

Does the Global Need the National, and If It Does, What's Wrong with That?

The Global and the National

If we are currently in a globalized world, has the nation-state become obsolete? Or is the nation-state instead accentuated, because its existence is needed for things and people to be "global"? That is, does the global rely on the existence of the national? What is problematic about continuing to use the notion of the national? What is problematic about celebrating "globalization"? What is the relationship between the notion of the global—as in "global competence" or "global citizens"—and race and class? Can anybody, regardless of race or class, gain "global competence"? Do immigrants—documented or undocumented—have "global competence" in the same way study abroad alumni students do? Who decides? This chapter seeks answers to these questions.

The global is a key term in study abroad. For instance, study abroad is considered "uniquely suited to promoting an appreciation for cultural differences in today's interdependent global community" (Laubscher 1994: xiv). And the goal of study abroad is often cited as nurturing "global competence" in students, turning them into "global citizens." Here, as we will see, the notion of "global" relies on the existence of "cultural difference," which is then connected to the idea of the nation. Globalization is defined as crossing "national" borders and/or rendering them obsolete, as well as dismantling the ideology of the nation-state. In his influential work on globalization, Arjun Appadurai (1990) characterizes globalization in terms of deterritorialization—people moving out of the territory to which the *nation* was supposed to be linked—and disjunctive flows of people, technologies, finance, media images, and ideologies across *national* borders. He thus discusses the dismantlement of the ideology of the nation-state—one nation, one people, one culture, one language, one territory, as will be discussed in this chapter—as a sign of globalization.

Paradoxically, however, this formulation of globalization actually works to perpetuate the nation-state ideology because it focuses on the *national* border that demarcates people, culture, and language. Andreas Wimmer and Nina Glick Schiller (2002) call it "methodological nationalism," a type of nationalism that emphasizes the importance of the nation-state as a unit by privileging national border crossing over crossing borders on other scales, such as regional borders. For example, while many researchers investigate history, changes, and contours of migration across national borders, regional migration within the national border tends to receive less academic interest and scrutiny mainly because it is not considered "global" flow, even if such regional migration have significant effects locally. Thus, the global relies on the unit of the national as what is connected to or crossed, leaving the nation-state ideology intact (crossing borders also maintains them). This is also the case in study abroad, as this chapter will show.

It is thus important that discussions of the global in study abroad revisit the notion of the national, critically analyze its ideologies, and avoid perpetuating them when formulating guidance for study abroad students. In what follows, I will review the notion of the national as it is discussed in the fields of political science and cultural anthropology; introduce critiques of the ideologies of nation-states; describe theories of globalization in general, in education, and in study abroad; discuss their ideological aspects as globalism; and suggest ways to incorporate these critiques into our discussions and implementation of study abroad programs.

The National

Imagining the Nation

The political scientist Benedict Anderson (1991) argues that the nation is an "imagined community." It is imagined because a member has a sense of shared belonging with the other members, even though the member will never meet most of them. This sense of shared belonging was developed through several "technologies." The spread of print capitalism, manifested in newspapers, gave individuals access to news about what was happening in the rest of the national territory, aiding development of a sense of community as a nation. The map, with its bird's-eye view, offered a visual framework for thinking and imagining the borders of a national territory, thus the nation. Indeed, it acted as the model *for* the nation, bringing the nation to be felt as a natural entity. And the totalizing classificatory grid of the census, which regarded individuals as countable and serialized into replicable plurals, created a human landscape of perfect visibility. Through these technologies, the nation-state came to be imagined as constituted by homogeneous people who speak a homogeneous language and all reside within the territorial boundary of the nation-state: the ideology of one nation, one people, one culture, one language, and one territory.

Other researchers suggest different ways in which the notion of nation came to be prominent. For example, Ernest Gellner (1983) argues that a shared *learned* language is what begets the sense of belonging to a nation. An industrial society with a complex division of labor needs mobile individuals with generic training, including literacy in a certain language to enable them to follow occupational instructions. The rise of mass education in this context, Gellner suggests, helped create interchangeable individuals for the labor force. The boundary of interchangeability, based on the boundary of the education system, then became the boundary of the nation.

Some suggest that language acts as a metaphor for the nation's homogeneity. Etienne Balibar (1988) argues that a language can provide a group of people with a clear grasp of their continued existence. Shared language makes it possible for "people" to be represented as an autonomous unit. Here, language is what John Comaroff (1987) calls a significant medium of the totemic consciousness of social relationships.

In late eighteenth-century Germany, Johann Gottfried von Herder argued that each nation was set off by "natural" characteristics of language and the intangible quality of a specific *Volksgeist*. The touchstone of a people, or *Volk*—what is essential to its national identity and spirit—is its possession of its own distinctive language. Herder argued that a *Volk*, a nation, a culture, and a polity must be homogeneous, and that diversity is unnatural and destructive of the sentiment that holds a people together. In fact, however, Herder was contributing to the *creation* of the *Volk*, more than describing his contemporary situation. His idea became a model *for* the nation rather than a model *of* the nation, resulting in an ideology of a one-nation, one-language nation-state. Following Herder, Johann Gottlieb Fichte (1968) argued that speaking a common language is the essence of a social bond. Language creates, within the members of a nation, an "internal border" that separates nations (see also Balibar 1994).

Others further posit various means by which individuals developed the sense of belonging to this "imagined community" that is the nation. A family metaphor is used to foster individuals' intimate and sentimental belonging to the nation (Borneman 1992; for different family metaphors for nations, see Brading 1985; Haberly 1983). In the predominant European imagining of the nation, fathers pass on land (which is the land they defend with their weapons rather than the land they cultivate) and mothers pass on the national language or "mother tongue" (Calvet 1998). Doris Sommer (1991) considers foundational novels that, by depicting founding European fathers and indigenous mothers with their mestizo offspring, connected readers' identification with the protagonists to their national belonging. Involvement in war also generated a feeling of shared nationhood in various ways, not only through patriotism encouraged by the government and shared sacrifice but also from different nations fighting alongside each other. For example, the sense of national belonging heightened among New Zealanders during the Second Boer War in South Africa and World War I when they fought alongside Australians and Britons that made them realize their "uniqueness" in relation to them (Sinclair 1986). Religion can mobilize a sense of solidarity and belonging in individuals who become connected to nationalism, as in the case of Ireland and Northern Ireland. And the devotedness some show in religion sometimes is used as metaphor of one's nationalistic feelings, calling patriotism a civic religion (Hobsbawm 1990).

The specificity of the notion of the nation-state is evident in the new treatment of minority groups within a national boundary as a nation-state established itself. In premodern Japan, for example, the appearance and lifestyles of marginalized groups such as Ainu in the north and Ryukyu people in the south were seen as totally foreign and exotic. This attitude stemmed from the *ka-i* order worldview imported from China, in which the farther away people live geographically, the more foreign and exotic they become. Rather than fixing a clear boundary, this perspective envisioned gradual differences in space in the world seen as concentric circles. Later, though, as Japan sought to become a nation-state in the late nineteenth century, it incorporated the ideology of the nation-state into its stance toward these marginalized groups so as to homogenize everyone in the nation and separate it from other nations with a single, unequivocal line. Hence, these marginalized groups could no longer be viewed as different and instead came to be seen not as foreign exotics but as "Japanese" at an earlier stage of development in "becoming" Japanese. Their forced assimilation into Japan's dominant ways was justified as "bringing them up to date." That is, in the new way of viewing their difference, they were no longer synchronically different ("foreign") but now diachronically different ("backward") (Morris-Suzuki 1998). This logic of nation-state and the corresponding assimilationist policies were seen all over the world: diversity within the nation, if recognized, was supposed to disappear through assimilation policies.

Challenges to the National

Challenges to the ideology of the nation-state arose in the 1960s. A first challenge took the form of resurgences of minority groups within nation-states. Frustrated by discrimination against them despite their successful assimilation, minority groups changed their strategies to encourage recognition of their cultural difference. Having to learn the dominant group's linguistic variant as the "standard" language came to symbolize oppression in some cases, such as the Occitan movement in France. Viewing assimilationist policies as internal colonization, ethnic movements challenged the façade of the one-nation, one-culture ideology of the nation-state: it never was homogeneous, assimilation policies to create homogeneity were oppressive, and minority ethnic groups' difference should be recognized and respected (Comaroff and Comaroff 2004; Kymlicka 1995; Omi and Winant 1994; C. Taylor 1994).

The reconfiguration of world alliances after the Cold War as various new nation-states emerged also pushed governments to allow minority groups' expression of their difference rather than to risk their political secession by forcing assimilation on them (Appadurai 1990; Kymlicka 1995). This shifted the scale of discussion of cultural difference to the level of "ethnic groups." Meanwhile, the emergent "globalization" of the 1990s came to be theorized as a challenge to the notion of the nation-state. As mentioned earlier, that same theorization retained the nation as the unit of cultural difference, which I further discuss in the next sections.

The Global

Researches into "Globalization" Processes

The changing contours of international relations that have increasingly been known and analyzed as "globalization" since the 1990s are discussed from various angles. One early influential theorization (though it does not use the term globalization) by the geographer David Harvey (1990) describes the post-Fordist development of time-space compression: as air travel and communication technologies developed and became available to many, the space across the globe became more accessible to more people, shortening the distance to people in these places.

Another influential theorization of the phenomena of globalization by the aforementioned cultural anthropologist Appadurai (1990) argues that globalization occurred with the breakdown of the ideology of the nation-state that unites a single territory, nation, people, and culture. This involves deterritorialization marked by global flows in five disjunctive landscapes: (1) the ethnoscape, in which people move across the globe; (2) the technoscape, in which technologies of communication and other domains are shared around the world; (3) the finanscape of financial systems that are increasingly connected globally; (4) the mediascape, in which TV and film from other countries—mainly the United States, but also India and other areas—are bought and broadcast worldwide; and (5) the ideoscape, in which ideologies such as "freedom," "human rights," and "democracy" spread around the globe. The flows in these five distinct landscapes are disjunctive: they do not necessarily go in the same directions.

While Appadurai's framework suggests uninterrupted global flows that go anywhere freely, others emphasize that these flows are channeled along certain paths as a result of individuals' and groups' active pursuit of linkages to globality (Broad and Orlove 2007) and that they may furthermore be interrupted or resisted, causing friction (Tsing 2005). For example, people's movement is unevenly restricted through differential access to visas in their countries of origin. Tariffs and trade regulations channel the flow of material goods as well.

Some researchers focus their analyses on the sensibility of individuals by examining the development of the global connectivity that allows individuals to feel that distant places are routinely accessible (Tomlinson 1999) through travel, the internet, commodities originating elsewhere, and so on. Others incorporate macro-level analyses to discuss the development of global governmentality via the spread of commodities (Bayart 2007).

While earlier discussions of globalization focused on the debate on whether globalization means homogenization of the world through the spread of "Western" things such as McDonald's and Coca-Cola, more researchers came to agree that such globally spread commodities are indigenized differently to particular locales' tastes and needs (Howes 1996). Susan Philips (2004) contends, in terms of the flow of ideas, that whereas some ideologies that enter into a particular configuration in a society may become incorporated in the local ideologies, others may not. Philips calls this an "ecology of ideas" akin to a locale where only certain plants take root.

Analyzing globalization from another angle, some researchers have examined various phenomena and events around the world in terms of how they are influenced by the global distribution of capital and technological expertise, regulated by national and local political and ideological institutions, and "territorialized in *assemblages*—they define new material, collective, and discursive relationships" (Collier and Ong 2005: 4). For example, particular research institutions may hire researchers from various countries and local technicians, receive funding from developed countries and research designs from yet other sets of countries, and disseminate their results in a particular pattern.

While many discuss three levels—the global, the national, and the local—and examine their interconnections, Richard Wilk (1995) highlights the emergence of "global structures of common difference" that organize diversity and allow us to communicate our differences to each other in ways that are widely intelligible. For example, cultural difference is expressed how cuisine or artworks differ among cultures. Here, areas of activities—cuisine, art—serve as shared frames to measure that difference. We can "measure" difference between Ghana, China, and Brazil by comparing their food and art, somewhat standardizing how they differ by reducing diverse contours of difference into these set criteria. Now that all cultural differences are defined by universal categories and standards, Wilk observes, people are becoming different in very uniform ways all around the world (see also C. Taylor 1994). Wilk's viewpoint is distinct from those of other researchers with similar ideas in that he regards the local not as in opposition to the global but as constitutive of a shared global system that organizes diversity. For Wilk, the prevalence of global structures of common difference *is* a form of global hegemony.

Globalization and Education

While the above researchers focus on analysis of globalization processes, educationists start with the understanding that globalization is already occurring. Therefore, they examine the effects of and responses to globalization in the areas of economics (e.g., changing job markets and the need for new skills), politics (e.g., international constraints on state policy making, citizenship education), and "culture" (e.g., global mass media, reactionary patriotism) (Burbules and Torres 2000a). Some critically analyze such effects of globalization as the spread of an Anglo-centered model of "effective communication skills"—such as speaking directly and positively, negotiating, and sharing feelings—as the norm (Cameron 2002). Others call for preparing students for the globalizing world, suggesting new pedagogies and institutional settings that nurture "global consciousness" (Mansilla and Gardner 2007: 56) and skills for working with people of different cultural backgrounds (Suarez-Orozco and Qin-Hillard 2004).

Higher education's engagement with "globalization" involves several overlapping notions: global education, intercultural education, global perspectives in education, and world studies. One name can mean different things, depending on national trends. British and Canadian definitions focus on everyone's interdependence in global systems and on social issues of poverty, power, inequality, and conflict, whereas American definitions focus on learning about and comparing the arts, cuisine, and fashion of various peoples around the world, emphasizing harmony (Pike 2000). There is no consensus on the definition of "global learning," either. An example I introduce for convenience is from the Global Learning VALUE Rubric, developed as part of the Association of American Colleges and Universities (AAC&U) initiative on learning (Hovland 2014):

> a critical analysis of and an engagement with complex, interdependent global systems and legacies (such as natural, physical, social, cultural, economic, and political) and their implications for people's lives and the earth's sustainability. Through global learning, students should (1) become informed, open-minded, and responsible people who are attentive to diversity across the spectrum of differences, (2) seek to understand how their actions affect both local and global communities, and (3) address the world's most pressing and enduring issues collaboratively and equitably.

Though higher education institutions continue to search for a common, clear, concrete definition of global education to ensure that students' education meets a particular "standard," (Reimer and McLean 2009), some suggest it may not be necessary (Pike 2000; Reimer and McLean 2009). Pierre Bourdieu (1989) argues that contestation of a term's definition is a political struggle to impose one's vision of the world and merits investigation as such, rather than a designation of one definition as neutral and objective. Following this view, what is clear, notwithstanding this diversity, is that these notions have been buzzwords in higher education since the late twentieth century (Gore 2009; Plater 2011).

In the US context, for example, institutions of higher education are urged to produce "globally competent" students, as a 2004 report by the task force of the National Association of State Universities and Land-Grant Colleges suggests (cited in Brustein 2009: 249). Other examples include the 2001 AAC&U initiative "Shared Futures: Global

Learning and Social Responsibility," aimed at engaging colleges to help students understand issues of diversity, citizenship, interconnection, and responsible action in the global world (Hovland et al. 2009), and the activities of the American Council on Education's Center for Internationalization and Global Engagement (Bringle and Hatcher 2011). Some have critiqued this trend as a neocolonialist imposition of West-centric views (Pashby 2012).

Besides curriculum changes, a main focus in the globalization of higher education has been to increase the number of students studying abroad by making study abroad programs accessible to diverse students (Cushner 2009), including students in nursing and other science-related fields, as well as minority and first-generation college students. It is worth noting here that problematically some experiences are overlooked as global learning and often discussed merely as nurturing multicultural competence (Fishman 2001). These include learning a nonmainstream heritage language, immigrants' learning to adapt to life in a new land, and learning by crossing racial, economic, and cultural borders within one's own country (Doerr 2012a, 2018).

Study Abroad and the Global

The notion of the global in the field of study abroad remains vague (Woolf 2010; Zemach-Bersin 2009), and the meanings of global competence and global citizenship are much debated. Bill Hunter, George White, and Galen Godbey (2006) nonetheless list common attributes of "globally competent" people: (1) various types of international knowledge on such topics as world history and events, (2) skills like awareness of and adaptability to diverse cultures, (3) beliefs and attitudes such as openness to difference, and (4) competences within specific disciplines such as the ability to collaborate across cultures. Richard Lambert's (1994) definition is often quoted; it similarly identifies five interrelated yet distinct components of global competence: (1) knowledge of globally cross-cutting issues like environment, energy, food, and human rights, or area-specific deep knowledge; (2) empathy, "the ability of an individual to psychologically put her or himself into another person's shoes" (1994: 15), which entails a progression from ethnocentric to "ethnorelativistic" (1994: 16) standpoints via the stages of acceptance, adaptation, and integration; (3) approval or favoring of things abroad; (4) foreign language competency; and (5) task performance in international arenas.

Definitions of "global citizen," a concept related to that of global competence, value similar attributes. Darla Deardorff (2009: 348) identifies common threads throughout the notion of "global citizen-ship": "(1) global knowledge; (2) understanding the interconnected-ness of the world in which we live; (3) intercultural competence, or the ability to relate successfully with those from other cultures; and (4) engagement on the local and global level around issues that impact humanity." Ross Lewin and Greg Van Kirk (2009) suggest that the com-petence described by Martha Nussbaum's notion of "world citizen-ship" is key to the goals of study abroad, though it differs somewhat from the understanding above: (1) "capacity for critical examination of oneself and one's traditions"; (2) "an ability to see themselves not simply as citizens of some local region or group but also . . . as human beings bound to all other human beings" and (3) "the ability to think what it might be like to be in the shoes of a person different from one-self." Other scholars further associate the notion of global citizenship with foreign language skills, "global imagination" that allows one to envision a plurality of the imagined world, and tolerance for ambi-guity (Brockington and Wiedenhoeft 2009; Rizvi 2000; Skelly 2009; Streitwieser 2009).

Once it is accepted that we know what global competence is, however, the discussions' focus shifts to how to effectively nurture and measure it. Arguing that study abroad does not automatically reinforce global competence, other researchers suggest a need for specifically designed activities to nurture "global competence," such as well-planned pre-departure experiences (Bennett 1998; Brustein 2009), enhancement of immersion experience via ethnographic projects (Goldoni 2013; Ogden 2006; Roberts et al. 2001), reflective writing (Chen 2002), and volunteer work, internships, and co-op programs that provide direct opportuni-ties to engage with the host community (Bringle and Hatcher 2011; Lewin and Van Kirk 2009; Plater et al. 2009).

These discussions, especially those regarding how study abroad enhances global competence and creates global citizens, are not with-out critics in the field of study abroad. Michael Woolf (2010) argues that study abroad programs' and researchers' claim to transform students into global citizens is an unachievable hyperbole that masks and dis-torts the tangible benefits of study abroad and supports the idea of global citizens as a new privileged class. Talya Zemach-Bersin (2009: 317) argues that many students consider the notion of global citizenship as something they gain by "purchasing" the study abroad experience. Promoted in conjunction with themes of personal advancement and consumerism, global citizenship appears as "a commodity with the pri-mary function of allowing Americans to succeed economically, socially, and politically in the globalized world." In order to change this, she suggests changing advertisements and creating rigorous predeparture courses that foster global responsibility, civic engagement, compassion, advocacy, and understanding through critique of students' own values and attitudes.

Globalism

While researchers on the globalization processes reviewed above assume that globalization is really happening, Anna Tsing (2000) argues that the existing debates on globalization are globalism, an ideology. Globalism valorizes global connections as breaking down barriers, she argues. That is, what is currently considered globalization and discussed as such is not a new phenomenon; what is new is the argument that treats it as new. For example, the cultural anthropologist Jonathan Friedman (2003: 744) argues that current globalization is "a phase of decentralization of accumulation, one that is accompanied by enormous dislocations and migrations, by class polarization and cultural fragmentation, and by the rise of new powerful regions." Friedman views world history as a cycle shifting between two poles—political and economic centralization on a global scale that forces cultural and linguistic "homogeny" on the world, and decentralization, which stresses cultural and linguistic diversity across the globe.

Thomas Hylland Eriksen (2003: 3) further argues that the literature on globalization merely reframes the social evolutionism and diffusionism of the late nineteenth and early twentieth centuries, which are about "the dissemination and recontextualisation of, and resistance to, modernity." That is, it views globalization as the "advanced West" spreading its ideas and commodities to the rest of the world while regarding the "non-West," their passive receptacle, as "evolving" from a lower to a higher stage by accepting these advanced "Western" ideas and commodities.

In this light, then, calling the newness of the present situation "globalization" is not a neutral description of current phenomena but an imposition of an ideological position that encourages global flow. Tsing further points out three intersecting problems of this globalism. First, it constitutes a kind of scaling practice, suggesting "the units of culture and political economy through which we make sense of events and social processes" (2000: 347). As mentioned earlier, globalist discourses spotlight the scale of the national with their focus on the crossing of national borders, reflecting methodological nationalism (Wimmer and Glick Schiller 2002)—and paradoxically perpetuating the ideology of the nation-state.

Second, the association of global flows with progress renders areas and people that appear to have escaped globalization backward. This is reflected in promotional materials for study abroad that depict not studying abroad as a deficiency in the process of encouraging minority students and other students to study abroad (see Doerr 2018), even though minority students, especially those with immigrant backgrounds, already have what is considered "global competence," as mentioned earlier. People in the host society, whom the discourse of immersion defines as immobile, are also often considered parochial (Doerr 2013b).

Third, globalism prevents critical analysis of the conditions that allow or hinder certain "global flows." People do not flow like water but rather are placed under "regimes of mobility" (Glick Schiller and Salazar 2013: 189) that work differently for different people: the mobility of the rich is encouraged as cosmopolitan, whereas that of the poor is often seen as illicit, if not forbidden as it is for "illegal" immigrants (see also Sheller and Urry 2006). An important effect of this regime of mobility is the aforementioned neglect and devaluation of the border-crossing experience of minority immigrant students who visit relatives in their ancestral homeland or attend colleges dominated by white, middle-class norms and students they find alien (Doerr 2018). David Conradson and Alan Latham (2005: 229) argue that study abroad is one of the "'middling' forms of transnationalism" that differ from the movements of both elites and "developing-world migrants." Thus, while study abroad students' experience is valued as global competence, minority immigrant students' travel experience (i.e., mobility), along with what they learn from it, is devalued in this hierarchy of regimes of mobility (see also Barnick 2010; Doerr 2012a, 2017c, 2018; Murphy-Lejeune 2002). In this context, then, to continue privileging study abroad as the main source of global competence is to reproduce these regimes of mobility.

It is worth noting here that the actual crossing of borders, paradoxically, also does not weaken but instead reinforces those borders. Just as Fredrik Barth (1969) argues in his seminal work on ethnic boundary maintenance that interethnic interaction perpetuates the boundary, international interaction among people flowing across the national border also perpetuates the importance of the nation as a relevant unit of loyalty. "Long-distance nationalists" have emerged as migrants across the globe romanticize and maintain connections with their homeland and engage deeply in its politics by taking advantage of the global spread of technologies (Anderson 1994). I elaborate this aspect of globalism further in the next section.

Study Abroad and the National in the Global

In the field of study abroad, the notion of the global continues to rely on the unit of cultural difference/nation-state. The common threads in the definition of "global competence" mentioned above include (2) skills such as awareness and adaptability to *diverse cultures*, (3) attitudes and beliefs such as open attitudes towards *difference*, and (4) competence specific to disciplines such as ability to collaborate *across cultures* (Hunter et al. 2006; emphasis added). Deardorff's summary of the common threads in the notion of "global citizenship" includes "(3) *intercultural* competence, or the ability to relate successfully with those from *other cultures*" (2009: 348; emphasis added).

These definitions show that the concepts of "global competence" and "global citizens" rely on the existence of "cultural differences"—often depicted as overlapping national borders with homogeneous insides (Doerr 2013b, 2014)—in two ways. First, the existence of "cultural difference" based on national borders works as a resource for gaining "global competence" and becoming a "global citizen." By studying *abroad*—that is, by crossing national borders—one supposedly experiences a "different culture" firsthand, which allows one to gain global competence and become a global citizen (Deardorff 2009). Without such difference, global competence cannot be gained. What undergirds this understanding that students gain global competence and become global citizens *only* by crossing national borders is the view that a nation-state is internally homogeneous culturally; thus, its citizens cannot learn "cultural difference" within it. And acknowledging diversity within the nation with a notion such as "study away" actually emphasizes the reliance on cultural difference to create global competence: as long as there is cultural difference, domestic experience can be considered a worthwhile nurturing of global competence.

Second, the existence of "cultural difference" based on the national border operates as a justification for studying abroad. The suggested logic goes as follows: cultural difference exists across national borders, so students need to gain global competence and become global citizens in order to survive this new globalizing world. Without this recognition of difference between national cultures, the need for global competence cannot be justified. The discourse of immersion, one of the most prominent features of study abroad, also enforces this overlap between the border of the nation-state and that of "culture" (Goldoni 2013; Hovey and Weinberg 2009; Loflin 2007; Oxford 2005) by emphasizing the fundamental difference between study abroad students' home and host countries at the scale of the nation-state (Doerr 2013b, 2014), as will be discussed in more detail in chapter 4.

In sum, study abroad discourses are paradoxically revitalizing the ideology of the nation-state with the notion of the global. Next, I suggest some ways in which practices of study abroad can avoid perpetuating this ideology of one nation, one people, one culture, one territory, which has been challenged in the field of political science and cultural anthropology.

Beyond the Global: New Goals for Study Abroad

Given the negative effects of globalism in study abroad discourses—reinforcement of the nation-state ideologies that construct "national culture" as a bounded unit with homogeneous "culture," marginalization of those who do not travel, and devaluation of particular types of global experiences, especially those of immigrants—I suggest three different ways to discuss the goal of global education and especially study abroad.

First, we can emphasize the mutuality of the shaping of policies and sociocultural conditions in each nation-state. Students need to be aware of historical and current international engagements in the realms of political, economic, and social relations that have mutually influenced those realms in each nation-state. For example, what we currently see in Japan has much to do with policies of the United States, which occupied Japan from 1945 to 1953 and designed Japan's post–World War II restructuring, including the current Japanese constitution that was drafted by the US government. Discouraging portrayals of nation-states as separate entities that people move through only by travel would reduce the impact of the nation-state ideology discussed above.

Second, study abroad promotional materials and campus events can highlight diversity within nations. At the wider institutional level, we need to position study abroad as not the best way but one of many ways to work toward "global education." We can acknowledge and appreciate the experiences, knowledge, and skills of students who, though they may not have traveled, have acquired what is considered global competence through other experiences, such as students with minority backgrounds who move back and forth between home and mainstream lifestyles. Experiences of minority students tend to be discussed in the context of multiculturalism, which is often separated from global education (Doerr 2017c, 2018). Here, I suggest combining these separated realms. For example, students with diverse backgrounds could be included in campus events focused on globalization—World Expo, Global Education Week, Global Competence Workshop, and so forth. I will later describe an example activity for the Global Competence Workshop—"global competence face-off"—that compares "global competence" of study abroad students and students with bicultural background due to their or their parents' immigration experience in order to put them in equal footings by highlighting oft-ignored latter' "global competence." This would not only discourage the perpetuation of the nation-state ideology but also reduce the marginalization of those who do not travel and promote the value of global competence gained in diverse ways.

Third, we can make students critically aware of the word "global" by introducing the concept of globalism in terms of its reliance on the existence of the national units or "cultural difference." Because "global" is ubiquitous and valorized as a buzzword in education, it is difficult to join in various conversations without seeing or using the term. Discussions in search of alternative phrasings are certainly welcome, but we may have to keep using the term in the meantime (see this discussion by Hall 1996 in the introduction). It is thus all the more important to alert students to the ideological nature of the term global, and to its connection to the "nation" and "cultural difference," so as to make them aware of the effects of its use, even as they use it.

Example Questions

To put in practice what I have discussed above, I suggest some example questions that should be modified and developed to fit each context. Eight sets of questions are offered as starting points.

Regimes of Mobility

First, the idea of regimes of mobility can be introduced before, during, or after a study abroad stay by asking students questions such as the following: Do you think business people in multinational corporation, study abroad alumni, and recent immigrants all have similar skills to navigate in diverse settings with people of diverse background? If not, how are they different? If yes, do we view them as the same skills or call them differently? Why? More example questions are listed at the end of the chapter (question series 1-A).

I also suggest an activity that I call "global competence face-off," mentioned earlier. There, two groups of students become contestants and answer several questions by narrating their own experience. Audiences are given flags resembling what people use in an auction to show which group they felt won for each question, and the winners can earn some small prizes. The questions are given to contestants ahead of time so that they can think of interesting and entertaining responses before engaging with the audience while still suggesting an important point: to highlight the regimes of mobility and how people in the different categories that correspond to these regimes—study abroad alumni and students with minority immigrant backgrounds who have never studied abroad—can compete for their "global competence." Because the discourse of global competence often suggests it is only gained through the study abroad experience as mentioned (see also Doerr 2012a, 2017c, forthcoming), showing the global competence of those who have not studied abroad but have bi/multicultural experience through their upbringing would make clear the double standard of the regimes of mobility.

The questions to be asked of both groups can be:

(a) What is the strangest dinnertime protocols you have ever experienced or food you had to eat? How did you deal with it? What past experience of yours helped deal with it?
(b) What is the worst stereotype about your group (race, class, gender, etc.) that you encountered? What did you do about it?
(c) What was the moment that made you feel that you are American? Also, if you or your parents immigrated to the United States, what in the past took you back from being American to that with your country of origin? If you studied abroad, what made you feel that you became part of that new place?
(d) What was the worst case in which you couldn't understand what the other person was saying? How did you solve it?
(e) What is the weirdest situation you found yourself in, and how did you handle it? What past experience helped you handle it?
(f) What was the most embarrassing experience in which you should have known something but you didn't? How did you handle it?
(g) What is a challenging task/chore you had to do, and how did you handle it? What past experience helped you handle it?

The idea of this activity is also to show how one deals with difference—not just "cultural" difference but all kinds of difference, including someone with prejudice, someone who is willing to commit criminal acts, and so on—and how skills to deal with difference can come from diverse sources: studying abroad, past experiences with diverse people, and border-crossing experiences of many minority and/or immigrant individuals who have to deal with mainstream lifestyles and values that they may not be familiar with (see Doerr 2018). This activity was designed as part of the Global Competence Workshop I organized in April 2018 at Ramapo College of New Jersey. I recruited several students—Jon Hernandez, Eddie Aditya Anand, Jarett Carlington, and Melanie Rose Intal—to work on this workshop, and we came up with this activity through brainstorming together. We also designed another activity, Daorb Yduts, discussed in chapter 4.

Global Flows

Second, regarding globalism—the valorization of global movement and devaluing of immobility—we can ask: Do you think the global flow of people is a good thing? Why? Is there anything bad about it? What do you think encourages/hinders such flows? The end of the chapter has further example questions (question series 1-B).

The Host Society

Third, students can discuss the portrayal of the study abroad host society in terms of its diversity as well as its perceived homogeneity. We can ask: Do you think the host society is homogeneous? What gave you that impression? Do you think the host society is diverse? What gave you that impression? Other example questions are at the end of the chapter (question series 1-C).

The Home Society

Fourth, study abroad students can similarly be involved in discussing the portrayal of their home society as homogeneous. It is important for students to be aware of their own social complexity—the diverse reality and the image of homogeneity that masks diversity—so that they can apply that understanding to other societies, including the host society during their time abroad.

Again, it is important to ask questions about the subject positions of people involved, power relations, and how to change them, as discussed in detail in the introduction (for the example questions to asked with the questions suggested in this subsection, see the end of the introduction). We can ask: Do you think your home society is homogeneous? If yes, what made you/others think that your home society is homogeneous? Were the discourses or promotional materials of study abroad involved? More example questions are found at the end of the chapter (question series 1-D).

Study Away

Fifth, regarding the notion of the home society's homogeneity, we can encourage students to think about the concept of study away: they need not go abroad to learn about other cultural practices and experience cognitive dissonance. To engage students in thinking about this point, we can ask questions that compare study abroad and study away as introduced at the end of the chapter (question series 1-E).

The Discourse of Immersion

Sixth, we can ask students about the discourse of immersion and its role in depicting the host and home societies as internally homogeneous (for further discussion, see chapter 4). We can ask questions like those introduced at the end of the chapter (question series 1-F) regarding its effectiveness, as well as why it is encouraged so much in study abroad.

Perceiving Difference

Seventh, we can engage students in revisiting the perception that study abroad students' host and home societies are fundamentally different, instead alerting them to the mutually constitutive relationships between different societies and the fact that "difference" is not spawned in isolation. The end of the chapter shows the questions (question series 1-G) tailored to discussion before departure or during/after the stay (see also the set of questions labeled "Z" in the introduction).

Questioning the Global

Eighth, we can engage students in questioning the concept of the global seen in the notions of global competence and global citizen and its reliance on the existence of national difference, as seen in at the end of the chapter (question series 1-H).

* * *

The notion of the global that is so prevalent in study abroad functions to encourage, justify, and sometimes even glorify study abroad. Uncritical acceptance of the notion of the global is problematic, but we can remedy this by involving students in critically thinking about the concept and its effects. That is, the very prevalence of the notion of global in study abroad provides educators with abundant opportunities to engage students in thinking about the notion and related concepts like the nation-state. Asking these questions can alert students to issues they may not have thought about and urge them to start thinking about them, hopefully triggering their own further questioning of various related concepts based on their experience.

The next chapter discusses the notion of culture, which is deeply related to nation-state ideology and its interconnection with "the national culture." However, it has its own genealogy and effects in the study abroad context that need to be examined carefully.

Recommended Readings

Anderson, Benedict. 1991. *Imagined Communities*. London: Verso.
  This influential work on nationalism views the nation as something that is imagined as a community.
Appadurai, Arjun. 1990. "Disjuncture and Difference in the Global Cultural Economy." *Public Culture* 2 (2): 1–24.
  An early analysis of globalization focused on disjunctive flows of people, media images, technology, finance, and ideologies.
Eriksen, Thomas Hylland. 2003. "Introduction." In *Globalization: Studies in Anthropology*, ed. Thomas Hylland Eriksen, 1–17. London: Pluto Press.
  An interpretation of globalization as a reframed modernist, diffusionist discourse that imposes "Western" ideas outside the West.
Glick Schiller, Nina, and Noel B. Salazar. 2013. "Regimes of Mobility Across the Globe." *Journal of Ethnic and Migration Studies* 39 (2): 183–200.
  Addresses the double standard of celebrating movements of white upper-middle class individuals as "globalization" while marginalizing movements of nonwhite individuals with lower socioeconomic status.
Harvey, David. 1990. *The Condition of Postmodernity*. Cambridge, MA: Blackwell.
  An influential work on globalization that discusses time-space compression in late capitalist society (Harvey does not use the notion of globalization).
Kymlicka, Will. 1995. *Multicultural Citizenship: A Liberal Theory of Minority Rights*. Oxford: Clarendon Press.
  A systematic examination of ethnic groups and nations.
Tsing, Anna. 2000. "The Global Situation." *Cultural Anthropology* 15 (3): 327–360.
  A critical analysis of globalization as "globalism."
Wilk, Richard. 1995. "Learning to Be Local in Belize: Global Systems of Common Difference." In *Worlds Apart: Modernity through Prism of the Local*, ed. Daniel Miller, 110–133. London: Routledge.
  An analysis of globalization as the spread of a common framework for arranging differences that connects the global, national, and local.

Wimmer, Andreas, and Nina Glick Schiller. 2002. "Methodological Nationalism and Beyond: Nation-State Building, Migration and the Social Sciences." *Global Networks* 2 (4): 301–334.
An analysis indicating that research on globalization actually accentuates national borders.

Zemach-Bersin, Talya. 2009. "Selling the World: Study Abroad Marketing and the Privatization of Global Citizenship." In *The Handbook of Practice and Research in Study Abroad: Higher Education and the Quest for Global Citizenship,* ed. Ross Lewin, 303–320. New York: Routledge.
A critique of "global citizenship" in study abroad discourses.

◖◗ Sample Questions

1-A: On Regimes of Mobility

1-A1: Who do you think has global competence?

1-A2: Do you think businesspeople working in multinational corporations have global competence? Are they global citizens? Why (not)?

1-A3: Do you think study abroad alumni have global competence? Are they global citizens? Why (not)?

1-A4: Do you think immigrants have global competence? Are they global citizens? Why (not)?

1-A5: Do you think children of immigrants who grew up surrounded by immigrants have global competence? Are they global citizens? Why (not)?

1-A6: Why do you think some people are *not* considered to have global competence or be global citizens?

1-A7: What does that tell us about the concepts of global competence and global citizenship?

1-A8: How do you think study abroad promotional materials encourage the notions of global competence and global citizenship? What can be changed?

1-A9: How do you think we should use the terms "global competence" and "global citizen"?

1-A10: How do you think you might interpret this [particular event or incident the student experienced] if you were an immigrant, an undocumented immigrant, or a businessperson?

1-B: On Globalism

1-B1: Do you think the global flow of commodities and other material goods is a good thing? Why (not)? Is there anything bad about it? What do you think encourages/hinders such flows?

1-B2: Do you think the global connection of financial systems is a good thing? Why (not)? Is there anything bad about it? What do you think encourages/hinders such flows?

1-B3: Do you think the global flow of ideas like "democracy" and "freedom" is a good thing? Why (not)? Is there anything bad about it? What do you think encourages/hinders such flows?

1-B4: Do you think the global flow of media images—TV shows, films, online videos, and so on—is a good thing? Why (not)? Is there anything bad about it? What do you think encourages/hinders such flows?

1-B5: During your study abroad experience, on what occasions did you feel that global flows are encouraged as a good thing?

1-B6: Do you think study abroad promotional materials encourage you to view global flows as a good thing or a bad thing?

1-B7: Outside your study abroad experience, on what occasions did you feel global flows were encouraged as a good thing? How about as a bad thing?

1-B8: Is staying in one's own birthplace instead of moving around a bad thing? Why (not)?

1-B9: When did you start thinking as you do? Who encouraged such a view?

1-B10: What are the effects of thinking that global flows are a good thing?

1-B11: What are the effects of thinking that global flows are a bad thing?

1-C: On the Host Society

1-C1: Do you think your study abroad destination is homogeneous? What made you think so? Study abroad promotional materials? Tourism commercials? People in the host society, say, a host family? Just in general? Why do you think such images are created?

1-C2: Have you experienced diversity in a host society? When?

1-C3: If these societies are not really homogeneous, why do we consider them homogeneous?

1-C4: What difference does *not* thinking of host societies as homogeneous make for our perceptions and practices during study abroad?

1-C5: Do you think everyone in the host country—including minority and dominant students—feels that the country is homogeneous? Why (not)?

Alternatively, you could ask questions that are more concrete:

1-CC1: List five things that represent the study abroad destination.

1-CC2: Why did you pick these items? What shaped your idea about the destination?

1-CC3: Do you yourself practice all the items you mentioned above while studying abroad?

1-CC4: Can you think of someone who does not practice things you mentioned above? Why do you think they do not? Is it related to their race, class, region, age, gender, sexual orientation, personal preferences, and so on?

Still other types of concrete questions could be starting points for discussion:

1-CCC1: How would you describe the ethnic composition of the host society?

1-CCC2: If you go to a supermarket in the host society, what kind of food do you think you will see?

1-CCC3: Were your expectations borne out? If not, how different were they from what you actually experienced? Why do you think this was so? Were there different expectations about the destination?

1-CCC4: In the park (or any typically public place), what kinds of people are there? Where are they from? What language do they speak? Did you include yourself in your answer? Did you include the students who are your compatriots? Why (not)?

1-CCC5: Did your expectation of ethnic composition differ from what you saw? If so, why do you think this is? What made you expect the host society to have a certain ethnic composition? Study abroad promotional materials? Media images? Books?

1-D: On the Home Society

1-D1: When have you experienced diversity in your home country?

1-D2: Did you notice similarity among people in your home country? When?

1-D3: If societies are not really homogeneous, why do we consider them homogeneous?

1-D4: How does refraining from thinking of societies as homogeneous affect our perceptions and practices before, during, and after study abroad?

Alternatively, questions that are more concrete can get to the same point:

1-DD1: List five things that represent your "culture."

1-DD2: Why did you pick these items? What shaped your ideas?

1-DD3: Do you yourself practice all the items you mentioned above?

1-DD4: Can you think of someone who does not practice things you mentioned above? Why do you think they do not? Is it related to their race, class, region, age, gender, sexual orientation, personal preference, and so on?

1-DD5: If there are people, including yourself, who do not practice what you mentioned, why do you think you feel that they represent the "culture" of your society? What made you think that? Media? Textbook? Peers?

Alternatively, the following questions can be asked:

1-DDD1: How would you describe the ethnic composition of the high school(s) you attended?
1-DDD2: In your high school(s), how many students spoke languages other than English? What was the percentage of such students? What languages did they speak?
1-DDD3: If you go to a supermarket in your neighborhood, what kinds of foods do you see?

We can also ask students about the heterogeneity of other students from their home country in terms of learning from them (1-D1) and in relation to people in the host society (1-D2):

1-D1-1: Spending time with other students from your home country while studying abroad is often discouraged. How did you feel about that? How did it shape your experience there?
1-D1-2: Have you learned anything new by interacting with other students from your home country? When? What?
1-D2-1: Have you noticed other students from your home country experiencing the host society differently from you? What do you think made the difference?
1-D2-2: Did you feel that people in the host society treated you and other students from your home country as if you were all the same?
1-D2-3: Did people in the host society treat you differently from the way they treated other students? What do you think made the difference?
1-D2-4: What does that tell you about the assumptions about your home country held by the people with whom you interacted in the host society?
1-D2-5: Do you think people in the study abroad program or study abroad promotional materials portrayed all students from your home society as homogeneous? How?

1-E: On Study Away
1-E1: Why do you think people tend to study abroad instead of study away?
1-E2: What makes study abroad different from the study away experience?
1-E3: What is the effect of valuing study abroad more than study away experience?
1-E4: Does the notion of study away—based on the understanding that the home society is also diverse—imply that in order to gain

global competence, one must be in a culturally different environment? That is, does global competence rely on the existence of cultural difference?

1-F: On the Discourse of Immersion
1-F1: Do you learn through immersion in your home country? Why (not)?
1-F2: If the lifestyle of the host society is similar to yours, do you still learn from immersion in the host society?
1-F3: What does immersion mean, then?
1-F4: Do you learn from immersion no matter what?
1-F5: Why do you think immersion is encouraged so much?

1-G: On Perceiving Difference
Predeparture (The numbers G1, G2, etc. indicate that these questions are of a similar topic, which is followed by the number that individualizes each question within the series)*:*
1-G1-1: Historically and now, what kinds of relationships have your country and your study abroad destination had politically, economically, socially, militarily, environmentally, and religiously? How have these relationships shaped the host society? How about your home society?
1-G2-1: How do you think your country's policies have affected the current political economic conditions, lifestyles, worldviews, and practices in the host society? Historically? Currently? How about the host society affecting your home society?
1-G3-1: How do you think the practices of your country's citizens affect your study abroad destination? As consumers? As voters? How about vice versa?
1-G4-1: What do study abroad promotional materials suggest about the relationship between studying abroad and studying in the home country?

During/after the stay:
1-G1-2: Did you learn anything new about the kinds of relationships your country has had, historically and now, with your study abroad destination, politically, economically, socially, militarily, environmentally, or religiously? When did you learn this?
1-G1-3: How do people in the host society view the kinds of relationships your country has had, historically and now, with your study abroad destination, politically, economically, socially, militarily, environmentally, or religiously? How did you learn this?

1-G2-2: Did you learn anything new about how policies of your country have affected current political economic conditions, lifestyles, world-views, and practices in the host society, historically and currently? When did you learn this? How about the host society affecting your home society?

1-G2-3: How do people in the host society view the effects of your country's policies on political-economic conditions, lifestyles, worldviews, and practices in the host society, historically and currently? How did you learn this? How about the host society affecting your home society?

1-G3-2: Did you learn anything new about how your fellow citizens' practices affect your study abroad destination? As consumers? As voters? How about vice versa?

1-G3-3: What views do people in the host society hold about practices of your fellow citizens that affect your study abroad destination? As consumers? As voters? How did you learn this? How about vice versa?

1-G5: How does awareness of the relationships between your home and host countries help deepen your understanding of what you have experienced in the host society?

1-H: On Questioning the Global

1-H1: What does "global competence" mean?

1-H2: What kinds of experience nurture global competence?

1-H3: If global competence involves bridging differences, what is the unit of difference?

1-H4: Within that unit, is there any diversity?

1-H5: If there is diversity within that unit, do we recognize it? If not, why not?

2

CULTURE

Is It a Homogeneous, Static Unit of Difference?

"Culture" in Study Abroad

When we imagine study abroad, do we imagine an encounter of one "culture" with another, where students from one "culture" jump into a pool of another "culture" to immerse themselves? When we encourage students to study abroad, do we imagine the world as a jigsaw puzzle of nation-states, each piece painted one color to represent a homogeneous "culture" within the bounds of the nation-state borderline? When we talk about "inter-cultural competence" and "cultural sensitivity," do we imagine "culture" as a preexisting, bounded, internally homogeneous unit? Do we imagine that we can "know" a "culture" fully? Do we imagine "culture" to consist of primordial aspects of life passed down through generations unchanging? Or is it an effect of various institutions, government policies, and the wider socioeconomic environment? Is "culture" the most important way to categorize people, or are there other, more important ways? Does "culture" develop in isolation or in relation to other "cultures"? If we imagine "culture" in these ways, whose perspectives are we privileging? Whose perspectives are erased? Do these views prevent students from understanding how difference is constructed in relations of power, dynamically, in changing contexts? How can we involve students in thinking about these questions? This chapter tackles these questions.

Study abroad relies on the existence of "cultural difference," envisioned as overlapping the boundaries of nation-states, as both a resource and a justification, as discussed in chapter 1. It is a resource that helps students learn particular skills—"global competence"—that are believed to be gained through dealing with "cultural difference" firsthand. It also justifies the study abroad endeavor: because there are "cultural differences" in the world, students need to gain global competence (see Doerr 2013b).

Study abroad is a rare educational field in that it makes "cultural difference" the main focus of learning, especially in the US context with short-term study abroad programs but also in many long-term programs. By incorporating daily life too as a realm of learning, it allows students to learn from various angles, a valuable practice. However, as seen in my own second study abroad experience in Aotearoa/New Zealand, the theoretical framework of "culture" that informs students' interpretations of their learning can be revisited to encourage students' engagement in more critical learning experiences. This chapter aims to do just that by reviewing how study abroad literature treats "culture," introducing various understandings of "culture" in cultural anthropology and educational studies, and suggesting ways to incorporate the cutting-edge understanding of the notion of "culture" in study abroad practices.

Two Types of "Culture"

Two types of "culture" are involved in study abroad: the "high culture" of European countries and the "exotic culture" of non-European countries. Study abroad traces its origin to the "Grand Tour" starting in seventeenth-century England, where aristocratic young men were sent to European capitals to complete their classical education. Its legacy lives on today, as most US students abroad are in Europe, studying European art, language, and literature—"high culture" (Lewin 2009).

The recent expansion of study abroad to "nontraditional" locations outside Europe also involves learning "culture," which in this case is framed as exotic. This resonates with the tradition of eighteenth-century colonial travels, in which Europeans wrote about non-European places to instill in European readers a sense of ownership, entitlement, curiosity, adventure, and moral fervor regarding their colonies (Pratt [1992] 2008: 4). Debbie Lisle (2006) argues that today's travel writing furthers this legacy with two intertwining visions: colonial visions that resuscitate the hierarchy where the "Western" writer judges the "less civilized" and cosmopolitan visions that celebrate "cultural difference" yet impose a universal standard by which to judge others. Students abroad in the "non-West" tend to mix these two visions, approaching such destinations with voyeurism and often a quasi-missionary zeal to engage with poverty (Woolf 2006).

Whether inside or outside Europe, these views of "cultural difference" posit "culture" as a unit of comparison reliant on the pre-existence of "cultural difference," and regard "cultures" as bounded, homogenous units. This view is perpetuated by the notion of immersion, whose effects I will discuss in more detail in chapter 4. In the next section, I discuss immersion's relation to the notion of "culture."

"Culture" as a Pool to Be Immersed In

"Immersion" is understood through an aquatic metaphor for the destination: it happens best when students are submerged in a pool of "culture" where they are "oriented to understand and respect local customs . . . become part of the culture by staying with local families and giving back to local communities . . . attend classes and participate in activities with local students and are taught by local staff who are paid fair wages and offer an inside view of the culture" (Hovey and Weinberg 2009: 37). Immersion is contrasted to the kind of program in which "students make minimal effort to learn local languages or customs, travel in large groups, and are taught in American-only classrooms. They live and go to bars with other Americans, often drinking too much and getting into trouble" (36).

This contrasts with an argument (see Benedict [1946] 1989) that one can understand how "culture" works by getting out of it: a fish does not see water unless it is out of it. In this line of argument, immersion in water prevents one from seeing the water. Getting out of your own environment (and studying abroad) allows you to understand your own society better, according to this argument. However, the notion of immersion in study abroad is used in the opposite way: immersing (in study abroad destination) allows one to understand the society you are immersed in.

In general, immersion is promoted by contrasting "good" immersion experiences with "bad" ones of insufficient length and intensity of interaction with the local. The discourse of immersion encourages the out-of-class component over classroom learning (Chen 2002; Laubscher 1994; Peterson 2002), staying with a host family over staying in a hostel or dormitory with fellow American students (Chieffo and Griffiths 2004; Gutel 2007, Hovey and Weinberg 2009), long-term over short-term stays (Currier et al. 2009; Deardorff 2009), direct enrollment over island-type programs (for a critique, see Woolf 2007), and spending time with the locals over fellow American students (Deardorff 2009; Hovey and Weinberg 2009).

This notion of immersion is not without its critics. Some argue that interactions that are more intensive are not necessarily optimal. For example, Michael Woolf argues that learning side by side with local students through immersion in college life in the destination is not the best way to learn, because (1) learning with fellow American students is preferable as comparisons are best made by those who have experienced both (or all) the "cultures" in question, (2) curricula developed for local students do not offer opportunities to comparatively analyze the relevant differing social codes, and (3) separate, innovative curricula catering specifically to study abroad students can be designed to allow study abroad students to depart from the local norm. He thus recommends "a modified immersion, in which the student is empowered by some separation from the host culture to observe and analyze" (2007: 499).

The critic of cultural anthropology James Clifford (1988: 41–42) offers an argument that can also serve to review the assumptions behind the notion of immersion. Clifford asserts that what anthropologists describe through participant observation is not "the experience and interpretation of a circumscribed 'other' reality, but rather . . . a constructive negotiation involving at least two, and usually more, conscious, politically significant subjects [ethnographers and people in the field]. . . . There is no neutral standpoint in the power-laden field of discursive positionings, in a shifting matrix of relationships." The same is true in study abroad: there is no circumscribed "other" reality or "culture" of the host society for students to be immersed in; what happens during study abroad is constructive negotiation between two politically positioned subjects with diverse backgrounds, as will be discussed in detail in chapter 5 when I focus on the space of the host family.

In a philosophical discussion of our relationships to "culture," Andrew Law and Susan Mennicke (2007) critique the assumption behind study abroad advocates' and researchers' understanding of immersion that we can *know* other peoples and societies and their attitudes in search of certitude, which creates promises of fulfillment; rather, they argue, we should encourage negotiating ambiguity and engaging with complexity.

The view of "culture" as a preexisting, bounded homogenous unit that is either high or exotic—and as something you can immerse yourself in, understand as a separate "reality," and can know fully—is not only inaccurate but also simplifies study abroad students' encounters, preventing them from developing a sound understanding of how difference becomes constructed in relations of power, dynamically, in changing contexts. This chapter builds on the aforementioned critiques of this view of "culture" by introducing further detailed theoretical discussions on the notion of "culture" in cultural anthropology and education.

Situating Theories of "Culture"

Theoretical concepts are "takes" on various phenomena in the world, as mentioned. Such takes allow us to think about situations and phenomena in certain ways. Anthropologists thought about human variation in terms of "race" in the nineteenth century and "culture" in the twentieth century (Wolf 1994). The most cited definition of "culture" is Edward Tylor's ([1871] 2016: 1) comprehensive one: "that complex whole which includes knowledge, beliefs, arts, morals, law, customs, and any other capabilities and habits acquired by [a human] as a member of society." For the purposes of this chapter, however, I will pass over earlier discussions about the concept of "culture" to focus on ones that relate to current understandings of and discussions on "culture."

One big shift in the anthropological framework of analysis was to view "culture" as a problem, not a given. This perspective emerged when research on ethnicity in the 1960s gave rise to a new way to stake claims to precedence and power—by upholding their right to a way of life rooted in the particular place—and "cultural" particularity has been a major ideological weapon in political struggles ever since (Wolf 1994). Anthropologists began investigating the objectification of "culture" in such a process, in which aspects of a social world are interpreted as typifying that world and represented as detached, object-like "traits" that the bearer of the "culture" is thought to possess (Handler 1985). Once objectified and named, people take a variety of stances, seeking an understanding about themselves and taking charge of their subsequent behavior (Holland et al. 1998). Anthropological works on objectification of "culture" emerged in the context of discussing nationalist movements' use of "culture"—sometimes in words like "tradition" or *kastom*, derived from the English "custom." Here, however, the notion of "culture" in the US educational arena may be useful, as the rise of "multicultural" education popularized the similar notions of "culture" in daily life. In the next sections, I trace five frameworks for viewing "culture" in the United States by following Joe Kincheloe and Shirley Steinberg's (1997) categorization of five types of multiculturalism, specifically in the context of education but also relevant to understanding "culture" in general.

"Culture" as Problem: "Normal" versus "Deficient"

Of the five types of multiculturalism that Kincheloe and Steinberg (1997) discuss, the first is called "conservative multiculturalism." Although Kincheloe and Steinberg call it multiculturalism, it is actually monoculturalism based on the belief in the superiority of "Western" patriarchy, viewing nonwhite children with low socioeconomic status as deprived. This conservative multiculturalism supports a monocultural curriculum centered on the white middle class norms, which it views as objective and politically neutral. Ignoring structural and institutional racism, conservative multiculturalism views critical multiculturalism that will be introduced later as divisive and racist against white and male individuals.

Based on this view, conservative multiculturalism pushes everyone to assimilate to white, middle-class norms, which is considered the universal norm for everyone to aspire to. For example, considering language as part of "culture," if a child speaks a nonstandard form of language learned in the home or neighborhood, their linguistic knowledge is considered deficient, so teachers try to teach them the standard variety as a replacement for the linguistic variety the child brought from home. This approach ignores the fact that a standard language is merely the linguistic variety spoken by the dominant group, here, the white middle class: there is no superiority to any variety, linguistically speaking (Milroy and Milroy [1985] 1991), which will be discussed more in chapter 3. Mastery of the standard language is important because it gives the child access to wider future career options, but it needs not involve replacing the home variety or denigrating it as deficient (Delpit 1995).

In short, conservative multiculturalism is based on an ethnocentric value system that celebrates the white middle class norms and considers everyone else deficient. "Cultural difference" is converted into hierarchy of desirability and development. In the study abroad context, this becomes manifest when going to developing countries to carry out service work. In these cases, what is considered desirable in a student's society often becomes imposed on the host society as something universally desirable—as the "normal" condition—that the host society should strive toward (e.g., that childhood should be full of play and fun activities instead of working to help parents) (Gray and Campbell 2007; Munt 1994; Sinervo 2011). That is, as will be discussed more in chapter 6, such service work is premised on what is a desirable state of being informed by "Western" standard, rendering the conditions in the community such students work in as deficient.

"Culture" as Division to be Ignored: Color Blindness

The second type of multiculturalism is what Kincheloe and Steinberg (1997) call "liberal multiculturalism," which emphasizes the commonality of individuals of different races and classes and promotes what some call "color blindness." Not noticing race and class differences here implies not having negative stereotypes about them and not acting with discriminatory intent. However, it still enforces white, middle-class ways of thinking and doing things as the "culturally invisible" norm because it ignores the ways in which race and class mediate and structure experiences for both the privileged and the oppressed. For example, children who did not learn the standard language at home because of their ethnic background are disadvantaged at school, as they must learn a new linguistic variety, the standard one, on top of what they know already. It is therefore important to recognize racial and class differences without portraying them as deficiencies (see Labov 1970).

Critiques of both conservative and liberal multiculturalisms also underline the beneficial use of the concept of "culture" to appreciate different ways of thinking and doing things without creating hierarchy. Reframing what is considered "normal" and "regular" as something that is based on the "culture" of the dominant group can help curb tendencies to see those who have other norms as deficient by instead presenting them as from a different "culture." This is the main argument of the whiteness studies popularized in the 1990s. Following the lead of authors like James Baldwin (1984, 1985) and bell hooks (1989, 1992), scholars of whiteness studies seek to reveal the meaning of being invisible or unmarked ethnically. They consider the dominant group to have the unmarked status of "normal" or "regular" because those in the dominant position define what is "normal" and "regular," perpetuating their dominance, since whatever they do is considered the norm. That is, their "culture's" invisibility is both the source and effect of its dominance. Whiteness studies expose whites' invisibility as an effect of privilege and seek to examine and challenge relations of dominance that construct and further support such invisibility (Baldwin 1984; Frankenberg 1993; Roediger 1991).

David Roediger (1994), for example, advocates for rejection of "being white" in the old way and calls instead for identifying the whiteness in order to mark one's experience as socially constructed in a position of privilege, rather than viewing it as the universal "norm" (see also Baldwin 1984, 1985; Frankenberg 1997; Ignatief and Garvey 1996). In

Aotearoa/New Zealand, this was done by using a Māori term for white New Zealanders, who otherwise consider themselves "regular" New Zealanders. Some researchers contend that the Māori label Pākehā should be used to mark white New Zealanders as an ethnic group with its own specific "culture" (King 1985; Spoonley 1991). Recently, this line of argument has been taken up in studies about class privilege (Nenga 2011).

In study abroad, this invisibility due to privilege is less common—especially when American students study abroad in Europe—because what students are familiar with and what they encounter in the host society are often viewed as having a relation of equality; thus, the encounter is viewed as "cross-cultural" or "intercultural" rather than one where "regular" people go into the host society to "educate them," as often seen when American students go to countries outside Europe to study abroad and especially when they do community service work as part of the experience, as mentioned regarding the conservative multiculturalism.

"Culture" as Safe Difference

The third type of multiculturalism that Kincheloe and Steinberg (1997) discuss, "pluralist multiculturalism," views diversity as intrinsically valuable and promotes tolerance of different "cultures" while keeping white, middle-class values as the norm. It touches on cultural relativism—the belief that all "cultures" are equal and that events/items/beliefs must be understood in their context rather than according to your own standard informed by your perspectives. This withholding of judgments based on your viewpoint is important. However, a problem lies in what is viewed as "culture." Pluralist multiculturalists celebrate "culture" by objectifying it into a safe diversity of cuisine, art, and fashion. Such "cultural difference" is seen as something anybody can try to appreciate without feeling threatened or being made to think about social oppression based on difference. Thus, "cultural difference" is depoliticized and decontextualized from the unequal socioeconomic conditions in which different groups operate.

As mentioned in chapter 1, Richard Wilk (1995) describes this situation on a global scale as an emergence of "global structures of common difference" that organize diversity and allow us to communicate our differences to each other in ways that are widely intelligible: "cultural difference" expressed in dissimilarity in cuisine or artworks. Wilk suggests that the tendency to use universal categories and standards to define all differences as "cultural difference" on a superficial level that objectifies "culture" has led to people becoming different in very uniform ways all around the world, via a shared global structure that organizes diversity. The difference is tamed into the "safe zone" of expressive "culture" (see also C. Taylor 1994).

This same understanding of "culture" is commonly used in study abroad at the level of advertisement, including at study abroad fairs, which often feature food, costumes, and music to represent the "culture" of the destinations. Once a student is in the host society, however, the understanding of "cultural difference" goes a little deeper into behavior patterns and beliefs. This may reflect the understanding of "culture" promoted by the ideology of the nation-state, which acknowledges language, lifestyle, and behavioral patterns but still views them as homogeneous, static, and bounded, as discussed in detail in chapter 1.

"Culture" as Political Resource

The fourth type of multiculturalism from Kincheloe and Steinberg (1997), "left-essentialist multiculturalism," focuses on self-assertions made by subordinated people based on their essentialized identities and "cultures." For example, some social movements by indigenous peoples have essentialized their claims as being based on an unchanging "culture" or "tradition" (see Mann 2006). Kincheloe and Steinberg (1997) critique this type of multiculturalism as failing to recognize the fluid, multiple natures of identification practices. Terence Turner (1994) criticizes this type of multiculturalism (calling it "difference multiculturalism") for not reflecting how cultural constructs mediate the social processes and political struggles.

This kind of cultural objectification for political ends has been much studied by anthropologists (see theme issues in *Mankind*, 1982; *Oceania*, 1992; and *Anthropological Forum*, 1993). For example, Allan Hanson (1989) argues that the diverse oral history of Māori migration to Aotearoa/New Zealand was put together and streamlined in the early twentieth century in order to present Māori as a unique distinct entity, different from Pākehā (white) New Zealanders. In the context of the world-level initiative in the 1990s to elevate indigenous people's positions and support their right to preserve and develop their "culture" and "identity" (Henze and Davis 1999; Kymlicka 1995; May 2001), the existence of *distinct* indigenous "cultures" and peoples, to be respectively revived and empowered, became a basis for correcting the past injustice of assimilation. In the process, features that help contrast indigenous beliefs with those of the settler descendants—environmentally sustainable practices and collective social practices, for example— came to be emphasized. This also forced indigenous peoples to shape their political claims and present their "cultures" in accordance with the criteria upheld by the courts—often involving objectification of "culture" by reducing it to practicing particular rituals and eating particular food—in order to be heard (Clifford 1988; Levine 1991; Povinelli 2002; Warner 1999; Whiteley 2003).

Such criteria often differed from the view of indigenous peoples themselves. For example, indigenous people felt they could be simultaneously "authentically indigenous" and "modern," whereas the courts often saw these qualities as mutually exclusive (Levine 1991; Povinelli 2002). In the United States, adopting a globally circulating structure of difference limited the ways in which Hopi language could be revitalized, because the idea of property rights behind the global discourse of language revitalization conflicted with Hopi linguistic philosophy (Whiteley 2003). Furthermore, the courts' criteria included ethnocentric moral judgment. For example, Elizabeth Povinelli (1998) shows the limits of tolerance in Australian multiculturalism, which at the time served as monoculturalism: there was but a single criterion by which to judge and (de)certify the difference of minority groups as "cultural." The Australian state delegitimized genital mutilation as repulsive, prohibiting it and refusing to consider the practice a "cultural difference."

Researchers' interest in examining objectification of difference as "culture," however, became problematic in the discussion of the "invention of tradition"—objectification of the past for present political purposes (Hobsbawm and Ranger 1992; see also Hanson 1989; Keesing 1989). The controversy is over how research about the invention of "tradition" by oppressed peoples risks undercutting these peoples' cultural authority by calling their authenticity into question (Levine 1991; Linnekin 1991). An underlying issue is who gets to define whom, and what these peoples are (Trask 1991).

Study abroad discourses share the view that a particular group is linked to a certain "culture." Yet study abroad discourses rarely take this view of "culture" as a strategy for group-specific right politics; rather, if anything, they use the notion of "culture" for commercial purposes—to promote study abroad as "adventure" (Zemach-Bersin 2009). This leads to an understanding of "culture" as a primordial, static given, as seen in my second study abroad experience (described in the introduction).

"Culture" as Constructed Difference

The fifth type is what Kincheloe and Steinberg (1997) call "critical multiculturalism," which views "cultural difference" not as a given but as constructed in relations of power. It connects cultural representations to their material effects, such as how resources are allocated, and challenges the normalization of the dominant group's ways of doing things. The construction of "cultural differences" also intersects with various axes of difference. This is currently a widely accepted viewpoint in the fields of cultural anthropology, political science, and history, as well as in other social theory.

In the next section, because this is the currently accepted approach, I introduce in more detail three different theoretical frameworks connecting the construction of "cultural difference" in relations of power in order to illustrate diverse ways this issue can be conceptualized.

Theories on the Construction of "Cultural Difference"

The first way the construction of difference can be thought of is to see difference not as a given but as something we are made to notice, out of many differences among ourselves, by our sociocultural environment. Ray McDermott and Hervé Varenne (1995) illustrate this with an example of the "difference" of deaf people. If the whole society used sign language, being deaf would not be a disability or even a "difference" that people would notice. Thus, their "disability" is caused not by the physical makeup of their ears but by the social arrangement in which people do not routinely use sign language. This social arrangement marks deafness as meaningful difference and *disables* deaf people. In this approach, "cultural difference" is not a given but something that particular sociocultural environments mark as meaningful difference, thereby privileging some and disadvantaging others.

The second way the difference is constructed in relations of power becomes apparent when there are competing ways to categorize people: contestations over whose view will prevail is a political struggle, as mentioned briefly in chapter 1. Pierre Bourdieu (1989) suggests that to impose one's division of the world (i.e., categorization of people into race, class, etc.) is to impose one's vision of the world. That is what is at stake in political struggle, he argues. Politicians, researchers, governments, and others compete for their views to prevail regarding what division should be treated as meaningful when discussing allocation of resources and so on (e.g., if a dialect is considered as a language, helping its speaker adjust to the standard language can be supported with funding for bilingual education). What counts as an important difference among people and which systems of difference we accept as legitimate, then, are political matters. The debates against fitting everyone into a binary notion of gender aptly show the political nature of acknowledging particular difference as legitimate.

The third framework to see the construction of difference in terms of relation of power concerns how individuals become involved in this game of construction of difference, a question analyzed by Louis Althusser (1971), who argues that ideology manifests itself as categories of people. Individuals are interpellated into these categories, and their practices, shaped by their subject positions, materialize ideology. This understanding that systems of categories are themselves an ideology spawned in relations of power is shared by many researchers, who theorize it using different terms: the structure of difference (Wilk 1995), chain of signification (Hall 1986), schemata of classification (Bourdieu 1989), matrices of difference (Butler 1993), schemata of co-figuration (Sakai 1997), and regimes of difference (Doerr 2009b).

An important aspect of this understanding is that each category is defined in relation to another that it is not. For example, a tall person is defined in relation to someone who is not tall. Therefore, we need to scrutinize the system of difference itself, not just the categorized items. In short, a category or "culture" is constructed in relation to other "cultures," with which it is contrasted. This is evident in the ways in which indigenous "cultures" are defined in relation to settler descendants' "cultures," as discussed earlier.

Building on Althusser's framework, Judith Butler (1993) further theorizes the role of individuals in the production of differences, arguing that individuals' performative act of *citing* a particular matrix of difference as a meaningful way to categorize people reinforces that matrix of difference's survival. However, there is some room for individuals to cite alternative matrices of difference, thus creating changes. We do this daily, every time we use a particular category. However, the citing practices of researchers or administrators in study abroad have more weight than our everyday citing, because those people are considered "experts" in the field.

Researchers also investigate the ways in which various systems of representation—race, class, gender—intersect to inform and shape meanings of categories in each system (Crenshaw 1992; Frankenberg 1993; hooks 1989, 1992; Lott 1995; McClintock 1995; Roediger 1991, 1994; Stoler 1995; Wiegman 1995). For example, Stuart Hall (1986) argues that each system of representation of race/ethnicity, class, and gender, with its own history and its own mode of operation for dividing the world in different ways, connotes or summons up each other when articulating differences. Being of a certain race, for instance, connotes being of a certain class. The concept of "culture," often linked to race, is then constructed in this intersection, incorporating the hierarchical view of these groups.

These intersections are important because they connect categorizations of race, "culture," and gender to class, which involves economic structures. This view links capitalistic organization of societies, as well as government policies, to discussions of "culture," suggesting not only "culture's" changing nature but also the possibility of further action to change the current situation. One example of such an intersection is the redlining done as a federal policy in the middle of twentieth century, and its persisting legacy. The Home Owners' Loan Corporation was created in the 1930s "to provide emergency relief to homeowners by refinancing or purchasing defaulted mortgages" (Aalbers 2014: 534). By creating maps with a neighborhood rating system (by way of five colors, with red being the lowest rated) for more than two hundred cities, it institutionalized existing practices in real estate and mortgage markets of not investing in socioeconomically disadvantaged areas by giving lenders an excuse not to grant mortgages in certain areas. The main problem with this rating system was its connection to race: when an African American person moved onto a block, its rating turned to red, as the race of black residents was perceived as driving down the value of property in a neighborhood (Tibaldo-Bongiorno 2007).

Created to insure private mortgage loans, the Federal Housing Administration (FHA) also implemented redlining practices. Since FHA insurance was meant as a public backup to ensure the provision of mortgage loans—"A borrower pays a loan premium for an FHA-insured residential mortgage loan; the premiums are used as reserves and would flow to the lender in case an insured borrower defaulted" (Aalbers 2014: 537)—FHA redlining contributed to disinvestment and abandonment, and thus neighborhood decline, in urban areas. In short, federal government policies, which formally existed until 1968 and continues informally to this day, contributed to "inner-city decay." To understand how people live in the "inner city," often marked racially as African American, we need to look at these public policies and their effects on socioeconomic conditions of the affected people.

This intertwined construction of difference in racial, cultural, and economic domains can also be seen at the global level, as discussed in chapter 1. One society's situation, which may be considered its "culture," are shaped by the practices, regulations, and other dynamics in other countries, which are increasingly connected with each other. That is, global links among countries are conduits of influence on each other's sociocultural, economic, and political landscapes. For example, as mentioned in the introduction, life in Guatemala now cannot be understood without recalling that the United States intervened through helping its military coup in the 1950s. This intervention has since factored into Guatemalan history, including its violent civil wars. Current trade relations and other political engagements between countries also affect ways of life in each society. What is perceived as "culture" does not exist in vacuum but is constructed and situated in diverse networks or systems of difference, regulations, and practices.

In short, "cultural difference" is not a given but something constructed in particular sociocultural environments that make us attach meaning to certain differences but not others, according to those whose view prevails. For this reason, researchers, especially cultural anthropologists, no longer use the notion of "culture" as an analytical term; rather, it is treated as a folk term by which individuals position themselves based on their multiple positionalities situated in relations of power.

Toward New Approaches to Study Abroad Encounters

In sum, I introduced above five frameworks of "culture" in the context of multicultural education. Although these are the notions of "culture" used in the domestic context in discussions of social justice in education, it is helpful to use these models and their critiques to analyze the notions of "culture" used in study abroad contexts.

Culture-as-problem and culture-as-division-to-be-ignored frameworks, the first two types of multiculturalism, are the only ones that would benefit from the use of the notion of "culture" because the notion denies the existence of hierarchy between different groups' ways of thinking and doing. The concept of "culture" challenges their privileging of the dominant viewpoint as "normal" and "regular" and critiques their devaluing marginalized viewpoints as "deficient." As mentioned, study abroad discourses tend to use these frameworks for non-European destinations, especially when service work is involved.

The culture-as-safe-difference framework, the third type of multiculturalism, decontextualizes, depoliticizes, and domesticates difference into safe, expressive cultural differences in cuisine, art, and fashion. Study abroad focuses more on behavior and belief systems, but it tends to use this framework, viewing a culture as bounded unit. The culture-as-political-resource framework, the fourth type of multiculturalism, views objectified "culture" as useful for political purposes and often involves strategic essentialism—use of preconceived notions of the link between "culture" and a group. Study abroad discourses often use the notion of "culture" not for political purposes but for commercial purposes. Culture-as-constructed-difference framework, the fifth and the last type of multiculturalism, views "cultural difference"—the unit of difference itself—as constructed and contested in relations of power. This is currently a widely accepted position in various disciplines, but study abroad rarely uses this framework to view "culture," tending instead to view "cultural difference" as preexisting.

Next, I suggest four ways in which we can engage students in thinking about their study abroad encounters using the culture-as-constructed-difference framework and thus nurturing critical awareness about "culture" and power.

Challenge the Notion that "Culture" Is a Homogeneous, Bounded Unit of Difference

First, we can alert students that "culture" as a homogeneous, bounded unit of difference is a constructed notion and that by continuing to use it, we are *citing* that unit as a meaningful way to categorize people, as Butler (1993) suggested. We can do this by asking two of the series of questions introduced in chapter 1 (see question series 1-C on the diversity of host society and 1-D on the diversity within the student's home society).

I encourage including questions about (W) subject positions, (X) power relations, (Y) how our world has been changing and how we can further change it, and (Z) mutual construction of difference between various societies, including study abroad students' home and host societies, as detailed in the introduction under question series W, X, Y, and Z (for the topics W and X, sets of questions that combine the issue of "culture" specifically are listed at the end of this chapter as question series 2-W and 2-X).

Acknowledge that the Complexity of Society Defies the Homogeneous Culture Concept

Second, to challenge the common view of culture as homogeneous and bounded unit, I also suggest getting students to realize the complexity within their own societies—the places they know the most about—before departure so that they can understand other societies, including the study abroad destination, as having same kind of complexity and sophistication.

To this end, I suggest prompting student to think of one thing that they have noticed as different from what they know in their home society and to connect this act of noticing to the wider contexts that constructed that difference. Here, students need to have a basic understanding of how capitalist economic systems and government policies shape our lives and how they are often articulated through "cultural difference" and other types of difference. To engage students in this way of thinking, we can describe some concrete examples like redlining and ask questions as introduced at the end of this chapter in example question series 2-A, "The Complexity within their Home Societies." In the context of study abroad, it is important to alert students to the relations between countries, especially their home and host countries, as listed in series 2-B, "The Relationships between Host and Home Countries."

It is also important to link a case to wider issues, treating it as an effect of capitalist systems and public policies that have touched the lives of the multiple people encountered while studying abroad. For example, the notion of the "testimonial" takes the example of one individual as a representation of larger issues for a group of people—such as a particular racial group or socioeconomic class—thereby urging students to cultivate a sense of solidarity and fight for these groups' causes (Menard-Warwick and Palmer 2012; see chapter 7). To do this, we can ask questions in question series 2-C.

Seeing "Culture" as Just One Way of Dividing People Up

Third, we can view study abroad students' perceptions of difference as effects of particular sociocultural environments that push them to notice it, as McDermott and Varenne (1995) suggest. We can push further and ask students how the noticing of certain differences, and not others, is situated in relations of power, privileging some people and marginalizing others. We can ask the questions detailed in chapter 6 (questions 6-A4, A5, A6).

Viewing "Culture" as Interconnected with Other "Cultures" Constructed in Global Relations

Fourth, we need to view "culture" not as separate entities. Rather, we need to view "cultural differences" as constructed in relation to each other and often positioned in relations of power. Therefore, people in the host society should be viewed not as having a separate, distinct "culture" developing on its own but as individuals whose lives have been impacted by historical and current relations between the host and home societies. Questions we can ask are the same ones listed in detail at the end of the chapter 1 in series 1-G, "On Perceiving Difference," which are on the mutual construction of home and host societies' images.

Also, in order to highlight institutional arrangements that shape different experiences in home and host societies, I have created, with Monica Cuello, a "Study Abroad Checklist" for the students. It is designed for the students to compare their experience and the experience of the people in their study abroad destination in concrete terms in order to show the students how macro-level settings, not mere "cultural difference," create differing experiences. Using the checklist, students ask themselves a set of questions—such as "What do you need to do to visit your country of destination?" or "What would your degree be worth in your country of destination in terms of available career, income, and social status?"—before they study abroad. Then, they ask the same questions to people in the study abroad destination. The students compare the results among themselves or with people in the destination and discuss the reasons and effects of the difference. It can be done during their study abroad experience (especially if involving people in the destination) or afterward. See the end of the chapter for the checklist.

* * *

While study abroad is a valuable field of education that pushes students to learn from daily practices in the name of learning another "culture," the prevailing notion of "culture" in the field tends to depoliticize it, viewing it as static and given. This chapter has sought to challenge that view by introducing current discussions about the notion in fields such as cultural anthropology and educational studies. It has also suggested four ways to incorporate this understanding into study abroad practices, encouraging students to use these new theoretical frameworks on "culture" to think critically about their experiences.

Recommended Readings

Clifford, James. 1988. The *Predicament of Culture: Twentieth-Century Ethnography, Literature, and Art*. Cambridge, MA: Harvard University Press.
   Discussion of how anthropologists have been "describing culture" and its critiques.

Frankenberg, Ruth. 1997. "Introduction: Local Whiteness, Localizing Whiteness." In *Displacing Whiteness: Essays in Social and Cultural Criticism*, ed. Ruth Frankenberg, 1–34. Durham, NC: Duke University Press.
About social norms being "invisible" — an introduction to whiteness studies.

Handler, Richard. 1985. "On Having a Culture: Nationalism and the Preservation of Quebec's *Patrimoine*." In *Objects and Others: Essays on Museums and Material Culture*, ed. George W. Stocking Jr., 192–217. Madison: University of Wisconsin Press.
Discussion of how culture is objectified for political purposes.

Hobsbawm, Eric J., and Terence Ranger. 1992. *Invention of Tradition*. Cambridge: Cambridge University Press.
Discussion of how "tradition" was invented.

Keesing, Roger. 1989. "Creating the Past: Custom and Identity in the Contemporary Pacific." *Contemporary Pacific* 1 (1–2): 19–42.
Discussion on the objectification of "culture."

Kincheloe, Joe L., and Shirley R. Steinberg. 1997. *Changing Multiculturalism*. London: Open University Press.
Examination of different approaches to "culture" in the context of multicultural education.

Kubota, Ryuko. 2003. "Critical Teaching of Japanese Culture." *Japanese Language and Literature* 37 (1): 67–87.
Suggestions for approaching the concept of "culture."

McDermott, Ray, and Hervé Varenne. 1995. "Culture as Disability." *Anthropology and Education Quarterly* 26 (3): 324–348.
Discussion of how we come to notice only particular differences as meaningful.

Wilk, Richard. 1995. "Learning to Be Local in Belize: Global Systems of Common Difference." In *Worlds Apart: Modernity through Prism of the Local*, ed. Daniel Miller, 110–113. London: Routledge.
Discussion of how "culture" is framed in a set way that is becoming common all over the world.

Wolf, Eric R. 1994. "Perilous Ideas: Race, Culture, People." *Current Anthropology* 35 (1): 1–7.
Examination of concepts of race, culture, and ethnicity positioned in the historical contexts of their emergence.

◖◖ Sample Questions

2-W: On Subject Positions
2-W1: How do you think people in your study abroad destination would feel if what you considered the host society's "culture" did not include their practices?
2-W1: If there are people whose practices do not include what you mentioned as the "culture" of the host society, why do you think you felt that was their culture? What shaped your view? Media? Textbooks? Peers? Study abroad promotional materials?

2-X: Power Relations
2-X1: In general, in talk about the "culture" of a country, whose practices do you think are referred to?
2-X2: Do you feel that the process of labeling certain people's practices as the "culture of a society" privileges some people and marginalizes others?
2-X3: Which views do you think are more publicized and given voice? Why?
2-X4: Do you feel your own use of the term "culture" helps perpetuate it as a meaningful category to divide people? What alternative practice would you prefer?

2-A: The Complexity within Their Home Societies
2-A1: How might government policies create disparity in wealth? Have you heard of redlining? [If "no," explain redlining and use that as an example case for the following questions; provide any other examples.]
2-A2: Do you know what institutional racism is? Can you give an example of it?
2-A3: How do you think the structure of past inequality can be passed on to the present?
2-A4: Do you know of a case of a government policy that created wealth disparity? How did it do so? How did you learn of it?
2-A5: Have you seen any examples of institutional racism in the host society? What were they? How did you learn about them?
2-A6: Have you seen any cases where the structure of inequality in the past has been passed on? What are they? How did you learn about them?
2-A7: Do you feel that the questions and vocabulary above changed the way you think about things and act? Some people say vocabularies and

frameworks shape how you view and experience the world. Do you feel that this shaping leads you to think in certain ways?

2-B: The Relationships between Host and Home Countries

2-B1: What made you think your host and home societies were different? Promotional materials of study abroad? People you encountered? Events you experienced?

2-B2: Do you disagree with any portrayals of difference between your host and home societies? Have you talked about it with your compatriot friends? How? Have you talked about it with people in the host society? How?

2-B3: In light of the questions above, how do you think your home country's policies and practices have affected what you viewed as difference in the host society, including current political-economic conditions, lifestyles, worldviews, and practices in the host society? How about vice versa?

2-C: Effects of Structural Settings

2-C1: Have you sensed similarity in the host society? What made you do so?

2-C2 (similar to 2-B3): How do you think your home country's policies and practices have affected what you viewed as similar/different in the host society, including current political-economic conditions, lifestyles, worldviews, and practices in the host society? How about vice versa?

2-C3: Do you think you would have acted differently if you had been told the destination's people would be very similar to people in the home society?

Activity: Study Abroad Checklist (designed with Monica Cuello)

This is an exercise to enhance your experience of crossing national borders.

(1) Answer the following questions about yourself.
(2) Ask someone from your country of destination to answer the same questions.
(3) Compare the difference in answers and discuss the reasons, implications, and effects of the difference in order to deepen your understanding of the relationship between your home country and your country of destination.
(4) Think about ways you are involved in sustaining or changing these differences—as a (voting) citizen, a consumer, an individual with means to express your view (via social media, marching, etc.), and so on.

Career:

- What are your career goals?
- What qualification (e.g., degrees, licenses, experience) do you need for it in your country?
- How much would your career earn in your own country?
- What qualification would you need to perform your career if you want to work in your country of destination?
- How much would your career earn in your country of destination?

Education:

- What would your degree be worth in your country in terms of available career, income, and social status?
- What would your degree be worth in your country of destination in terms of available career, income, and social status?
- Describe the admissions process to your university in your own country. How much does it cost to attend? If you cannot afford it, what ways are available to fund it?
- Describe the admissions process to your study abroad program in your country of destination. How much does it cost to attend? If you cannot afford it, what ways are available to fund it?

Living:
- What is the average cost of living for a middle-class family in your country?
- What is the life expectancy in your country?

Expressions:
- What constitutes "freedom of speech" in your country?
- How would your political beliefs be perceived in your country?

Travel:
- Describe what you need to do to visit your country of destination.
- Describe what you need to do to migrate to your country of destination.

3

"NATIVE SPEAKERS"
Do They Really Exist, and Should Students Aim to Speak Like Them?

The "Native Speaker"?

Studying abroad means constantly interacting with "native speakers" of the language spoken there, as this is the fastest way to improve your language proficiency—or so goes a common statement about learning language by studying abroad. But is this really the case? Is the notion of the "native speaker"—someone who innately knows everything about the language—accurate? If the notion is inaccurate, why do we use it? What would be wrong with continuing to use it? Does the notion of "native speakers," coupled with the aim of becoming like them by interacting with them, help students learn their language? Does the use of the notion of "native speakers" have any social effects? Does it rely on and further perpetuate problematic premises, giving some an advantage and marginalizing others? Should we use this notion at all? How does it relate to our understanding of language and linguistic competence?

A quick answer based on discussions among many linguists is that the notion of the "native speaker" is inaccurate and based on inaccurate premises. However, as in the notions of "nation," "globalization," and "culture," what is important is not just to forbear use the concept but also to guide students to understand why it is inaccurate, why it is used nonetheless, what effects its use has, and what other kind of notion exists elsewhere (thus, they can sharpen critical investigating eyes on various things). This chapter aims to explain how and why the notion is inaccurate and to suggest ways to guide students to learn through critically analyzing this notion of "native speaker."

The Concept of "Native Speaker" in Study Abroad Literature

Study abroad is often viewed as an ideal occasion to learn a foreign language (though an increasing number of programs do not require students to learn the language of their destination) because interacting with "native speakers" in daily life is seen to provide the best opportunity to learn a language through "immersion" in a "real" and "authentic" environment with its various communicative settings. Language educators tend to claim that knowledge learned in classroom back home supposedly "becomes immediately relevant and intimately connected to lived experience" and "tend to greet study abroad with unqualified enthusiasm, as if it were intrinsically superior to classroom learning" (Kinginger 2008: 1). Guidebooks encourage students to make friends with "native speakers," because "learning the language is much quicker and easier when you are with native speaking friends" (Oxford 2005: 117). A host family is another source of "native speakers" to "practice the language" with (Williamson 2004: 235). At the policy level, study abroad is encouraged as a way of "producing foreign language speakers and enhancing foreign language learning," as a report by the Commission on the Abraham Lincoln Study Abroad Fellowship (2005: vi) suggests.

However, researchers are skeptical of assumptions that the link between study abroad and increased proficiency in the language of the destination is automatic. Barbara Freed (1995) reports that marked gains compared with those who have not studied abroad are limited to students who had low fluency before studying abroad. Various other factors also merit consideration. Freed questions the notion of fluency by showing that multiple factors that are not quite linguistic—speed, presence of silent pauses, length of sentences, tone of voice, comfort and confidence in one's ability to converse—are used as indicators of "fluency" in the students who studied abroad. Other researchers point out that the specifics of particular activities and of students' race, gender, and other backgrounds need to be examined, because they have significant effects on linguistic achievement (see the summary in Kinginger 2008). Stephen Ryan and Sarah Mercer (2011) argue that learners' belief in what helps increase language proficiency—for example, immersion over classroom learning—influences the efforts they make and their consequent acquisition, as well as their perception of it. However, the notion of immersion—that being in the country where the language is spoken, often meaning interaction with "native speakers," is sufficient to acquire the language—makes the student a passive learner.

In this chapter, I shift attention away from the assumed automatic link between studying abroad and gaining proficiency in the language of the destination. Instead, I focus on the key concept in that understanding—the "native speaker"—and introduce theories that dispute its status as a model for language learners to emulate. I will review the concept of the "native speaker" in terms of three ideological assumptions—its link to the ideology of the nation-state, the notion that language is homogeneous, and belief in the innate competence of "native speakers"—and the treatment the notion of "native speaker" has received in linguistics, especially in the Second Language Acquisition (SLA) theories and its critiques thereof (for details, see Doerr 2009a). The chapter ends with suggestions for overcoming this notion in the study abroad context.

The "Native Speaker" Concept

The "native speaker" is usually viewed as an ideal person with "a complete and possibly innate competence in the language" (Pennycook 1994: 175). Recent works challenging its empirical accuracy and theoretical utility (Canagarajah 1999; V. Cook 1999; Firth and Wagner 2007a; House 2003; Jenkins 2006; Pennycook 1994; Phillipson 1992) will be reviewed in this chapter. Still, the notion of "native speaker" continues to be used widely, not only in "second," "foreign," and "heritage" language education but also in daily life (Amin 1999; Braine 1999a; Canagarajah 1999; Firth and Wagner 2007b; Liu 1999).

In fact, "native speaker" is a folk concept premised on the three aforementioned interrelated ideologies of the connection between language and nation-state, language as a homogeneous system, and "native speakers'" innate competence in their "native language." In the following three sections, I will review discussions about these ideologies.

The "Native Speaker" and the National Language

The first ideological premise of the concept of the "native speaker," that being a citizen of a nation-state makes one a "native speaker" of its national language, is closely related to the way in which language is linked to nation-states. As described in chapter 1, in the modern world made up of a jigsaw puzzle of nation-states, a nation is imagined as a homogeneous unit that is defined in relation to other nations (Anderson 1991).

Language played an important role in the imagining of the nation as homogeneous, as discussed in chapter 1: the "natural" characteristics of a language helped mark a distinct *Volk*, which should match a nation, a "culture," and a polity, creating a model *for* the nation in the ideology of nation-state (Fichte 1968; see also Balibar 1994). Diversity within the nation, if recognized, was supposed to disappear through assimilation or standardization processes. Language is linked to the nation through a metaphor of family: in Europe, mothers are said to pass on the national language as the "mother tongue" (Calvet 1998).

However, the definition of mother tongue is complicated by the multilingual reality in most places around the world. According to Tove Skutnabb-Kangas and Robert Phillipson (1989), there are four possible definitions of mother tongue: (1) the language(s) one learns first; (2) the language(s) one knows best; (3) the language(s) one uses most; and (4) the language(s) one identifies with. That is, one person may have different languages as one's mother tongues depending on the definition used, and one's mother tongue may not be one's national language. In the study abroad context, though it is often assumed that all "local" people whom the student encounters are "native speakers" of the official (if not prevalent) language as mentioned, these "local" people's "mother tongue" situations can be more complex given these varying definitions as above.

It is worth noting here, however, that, as globalization became the predominant way to perceive the contemporary conditions, as discussed in chapter 1 (Appadurai 1990; Kymlicka 1995), English came to be considered a "global language" (Phillipson 1992). This made the language-nation link for English speakers somewhat ambiguous: "[English] is only international [global] to the extent that it is not their [native speakers'] language. It is not a possession which they lease to others, while still retaining the freehold. Other people actually own it" (Widdowson 1994: 385).

Though study abroad's destinations include countries that share the same language as the students', its discourses are mainly based on the premise that the host nation equals the community of "native speakers" of the national language that differs from that of the study abroad students. Thus, students studying abroad are expected to learn the language of the destination—the national language—through interaction with the locals. Allowing students to question this premise pushes them to think about language politics discussed below in both the destination and their own home society.

Language as a Homogeneous System

The second ideological premise of the "native speaker" concept is that language is a homogeneous system spoken by a homogeneous speech community. This premise is rooted in the original "one nation, one language" model of modern nation-states discussed in chapter 1, as well as earlier linguistic theories that developed against this backdrop (Pennycook 1994). Philosophers such as Johann Gottfried Herder viewed language as a homogeneous entity shared by the members of a homogeneous nation (although they saw that not all its members developed their capacity to its full extent) (Bauman and Briggs 2000).

Even before the birth of nation-states, the history of language is the history of people seeking to manage multilingualism and variations in language, Louis-Jean Calvet (1998) argues. By converting differences into subordination and considering the language of others inferior, human beings laid down the premises of a war of languages right from the beginning. For example, political authorities' tendency to be suspicious of multilingualism stems from a view of multiple languages as multiple loyalties and thus a temperamental flaw, a lack of trustworthiness (see also Irvine and Gal 2000).

One noteworthy language ideology concerns the standardization of language that became prevalent with the rise of nation-states, though it existed before their birth. James and Lesley Milroy ([1985] 1991: 22–23) summarize what is involved in standardization:

> Standardisation [is] a historical process which . . . is always in progress in those languages that undergo it. Standardisation is motivated in the first place by various social, political and commercial needs and is promoted in various ways, including the use of the writing system, which is relatively easily standardised; but absolute standardisation of a spoken language is never achieved (the only fully standardised language is a dead language). Therefore it seems appropriate to speak more abstractly of standardisation as an *ideology*, and a standard language as an idea in the mind rather than a reality. . . . Standardisation aims to ensure fixed values for the counters in a system. In language, this means preventing variability in spelling and pronunciation by selecting fixed conventions uniquely regarded as "correct," establishing "correct" meanings of words . . . uniquely acceptable word-forms . . . and fixed conventions of sentence structure.

This ideology is implemented in overlapping, interconnected stages: selection of the standard and its acceptance by influential people; accordance of prestige to the linguistic variety and its diffusion to the public;

and maintenance by means of codification and prescription (Milroy and Milroy 1991; see also Crowley 1989).

Standardization has always been a tool of governance. For example, a standardized language based on the vernacular of the dominant group emerged in fifteenth-century Spain as a way of governance. Elio Antonio de Nebrija set down a grammar of Castilian and presented it to Queen Isabella for the purposes of colonizing the speech of the subjects of her empire, famously stating: "Language has always been the consort of empire, and forever shall remain its mate." It was the first time a grammar was established not to teach "classical" language to a select few but to teach the dominator's language to everyone in her domain (Illich 1981: 35; see also Train 2009).

Pierre Bourdieu ([1977] 1991) argues that hierarchy emerges among linguistic varieties when the state imposes an official language on its citizens as the only legitimate one. This establishes a "linguistic community" in which the legitimacy of the standard is (mis)recognized even if access to it remains uneven. The standard language gains symbolic capital from a unified education system that teaches it as the only legitimate language, from a unified labor market that employs a labor force differentiated by the education system, and from a perceived connection between the standard language and social qualities like moral rectitude, civilization, and education (see also Bauman and Briggs 2000; Romaine 1997).

In nineteenth-century Britain, for example, its standard pronunciation, Received Pronunciation, was based not on common pronunciation but on that of well-educated individuals, whom the linguists considered "civilized" and thus to be emulated (Crowley 1989; Milroy 1999). Revitalization of minority languages can also involve standardization insofar as it relies on the maintenance of normative forms of language, marginalizing those who are culturally invested in that language yet lack proficiency in it because of past assimilation policies (Frekko 2009; Makihara 2009).

Standardization simultaneously homogenizes and differentiates people. It homogenizes people by creating a shared criterion by which to measure the difference in language uses (Foucault 1977). Ideologies of language standardization are likewise aimed at homogenizing linguistic communities, though this never actually materializes. Nonetheless, the ideology seeks to homogenize by claiming that speakers of a language need mutual intelligibility (see Quirk 1985). Researchers contend that such a justification supports and disguises social, cultural, and linguistic domination both "at home" and abroad (Doerr 2015b; Romaine 1997). Larry Smith (1992) argues that one needs only to be intelligible to those with whom one needs to communicate, usually, though not necessarily, those who live in the same area and share the same "accent" (see also Kachru [1982] 1992a, [1982] 1992c).

Standardization processes also differentiate speakers in order to measure gaps and determine levels of assimilation (Foucault 1977). By using the same criteria of assessment, standardization allows certain differences but not others to be objectified as markers of a speech group. It also differentiates by privileging one form of language over others and allowing for differential access to the privileged form (Pennycook 1994). The "deficit" approach to linguistic difference and educational achievement analyzes this aspect of standardization processes without viewing it as an ideological process: categorizing the code of working-class children's speech as "a restricted code" (of simple grammar and many assumptions) that is thus deficient, compared with middle-class children's "elaborated" (grammatically accurate, logical, and descriptive) code, disadvantages the former in the matter of success in school (Bernstein 2003), for example. In contrast, the "difference approach" regards the differential outcomes of dominant and marginalized groups' success in school as arising from discontinuity between school and home/neighborhood cultures/languages, and urges that school culture/language be made more compatible with that of marginalized groups. The deficit approach supports the standardization process by highlighting the hierarchy, whereas the difference approach challenges it.

The field of linguistics developed in relation to this political landscape. Against a backdrop of assimilation policies in the late nineteenth and early twentieth centuries, the structural linguistics of Ferdinand de Saussure ([1916] 1959) viewed language as a fixed code shared by a homogeneous speech community. Since the early twentieth century, however, this static view of language has been challenged. The Bakhtin Circle, a group of scholars including Mikhail Bakhtin in early twentieth-century Russia, compared the meaning of an utterance to the light in a light bulb: the meaning can only be seen when the light switch is turned on; it cannot be set like a definition in a dictionary (Volosinov 1973). That is, they saw language as heterogeneous, fluid, and constantly emerging.

More recent research in linguistics has shown that language is not a homogeneous system. Rather, language consists of continuous variations whose linguistic statuses are all equal:

> There is no such thing as a single language used at all times by all speakers. There is no such thing as a single English language; rather, there are many English languages (dialects and idiolects) depending on who is using the language and what the context of use is ... variation in

language is so pervasive that each language is actually a continuum of languages from speaker to speaker, and from group to group, and no absolute lines can be drawn between different forms of a language. (Akmajian et al. 1995: 261–264)

Arguing for "an anti-foundationalist view of language as an emergent property of social interaction and not a prior system tied to ethnicity, territory, birth, or nation," Alastair Pennycook urges us to view language as "a sedimentation of acts repeated over time within regulated contexts" (2004: 7, 15). Similarly, the notion of "languaging" suggests viewing language as constantly constructed through interactions in a given context. Despite this understanding, some linguists continue to use the notion of "a language," as if it were a single, monolithic entity, by drawing on the criterion of "mutual intelligibility," that is, similar "pronunciation, vocabulary, and grammar" (Akmajian et al. 1995: 262). Some linguistic analytical concepts also imply the existence of homogeneous, discrete languages. For example, concepts such as "code-switching," "code-mixing," "language borrowing," and "multi-lingualism" presuppose bounded and thus countable languages or codes (Pennycook 2004; Urciuoli 1995).

Other linguistic theories propel the standardization processes by offering concepts to frame linguistic differences in hierarchical ways, such as dichotomies of language/dialect, "native /non-native," and standard/nonstandard, as well as the notion of interlanguage (the variety spoken by "non-native" speakers), which is considered deficient compared with the "native speaker's" language. Both the dichotomies and the notions themselves are based on and naturalize the view that certain varieties of language are more "correct" and "desirable" than others—the less "correct" ones being often described as "broken" or "accented" and needing correction—justifying the imposition of the former on the latter (Bhatt 2001; Firth and Wagner 2007a; Romaine 1997; Urciuoli 1995). This has policy implications. For example, whether or not a language variety is considered a separate language or a dialect has implications for demands for "bilingual education," receipt of appropriate educational support, and claims of authenticity and legitimacy, as mentioned (Nero 2006).

The notion of language as a homogeneous system is also prevalent in study abroad discourses, along with the other notions implied by the ideologies of nation-state, as discussed in chapters 1 and 2. As study abroad highlights the difference between students' home and host societies, language difference is accentuated as two nonoverlapping systems. The experience of increasing number of "heritage" study

abroad students—who study in the country with family/ancestral connection, some of whom have some knowledge of the language spoken
in the destination—challenges this view of linguistic border crossing
through studying abroad. The in-between status of "heritage language
speakers" suggests that language is not a bounded system and that
there are people who have proficiency in diverse ways (for details, see
Doerr and Lee 2013).

"Native Speakers" as Completely Competent in Their Language

The third ideological premise of the "native speaker" concept is the
belief that they possess "complete and possibly innate competence,"
if not an automatic "high level of proficiency in all domains of the
language" (Pennycook 1994: 175, 176). Especially in SLA theories, as
the next section will demonstrate, researchers view "native speakers"
as having complete competence in their first languages (Amin 1999;
Braine 1999a; Quirk 1985), though some began challenging it (Doerr
2009c; Firth and Wagner 2007a, 2007b; Jenkins 2006).

In formal linguistics, ability in one's "native" language is taken for
granted. However, such ability is not necessarily "intrinsic." For example,
when Leonard Bloomfield ([1933] 1984: 43) states that "the first language
a human being learns to speak is his *native language*; he is a *native speaker*
of his language," he is making the point that language is not hereditary:
"The particular language he learns is entirely a matter of environment.
An infant that gets into a group as a foundling or by adoption, learns the
language of the group exactly as does a child of native parentage; as he
learns to speak, his language shows no trace of whatever language his
parents may have spoken." Referring to the difference between one's
first and second languages in the discussion of social semiotics—where
language is seen as facilitating certain kinds of interactions, representing ideas, and allowing individuals to create texts—Michael Halliday
(1978: 199–200) meanwhile claims, regarding the presumably intrinsic
superiority of "native speakers'" linguistic skills, that "no language ever
completely replaces the mother tongue. Certain kinds of ability seem to
be particularly difficult to acquire in a second language."

Noam Chomsky (1964: 24) brings in the concept of the intrinsic, but
not in the context of comparing "native" and "non-native" speakers:

> A grammar can be regarded as a theory of a language; it is *descriptively
> adequate* to the extent that it correctly describes the intrinsic competence
> of the idealized native speaker. The structural descriptions assigned
> to sentences by the grammar, the distinctions that it makes between
> well-formed and deviant, and so on, must, for descriptive adequacy,

correspond to the linguistic intuition of the native speaker (whether or not he may be immediately aware of this) in a substantial and significant class of crucial cases.

Although Chomsky does not discuss the "native speaker" as such in depth, his theoretical approach led to "native speakers" being privileged as authorities on their languages by suggesting that they have innate knowledge of them. This notion became influential in various branches of linguistics, including SLA theories (Canagarajah 1999; Firth and Wagner 2007a).

The premise that the "native speaker" has innate competence in their "native language" has been critiqued as assuming that a homogeneous linguistic system exists. I brought up this critique in an earlier section because such competence is judged against a set of "correct" grammar rules established in the process of standardization based on the dominant group's use of the language. When this competence is measured in terms of ability to communicate—communicative competence—the evaluation is usually based on whether other "native speakers" understand the utterance and thus relies on and perpetuates the standardization processes that privilege certain speakers (Doerr and Kumagai 2009; Mashiko 2000, 2003; Smith 1982).

Study abroad discourses rely on the inherent competence of "native speakers." As chapter 5 will show, immersion in a host society and staying with a host family—"native speakers"—are considered good ways to acquire their language (Goldoni 2013; Jackson 2009; Raymond and Hall 2008). These views are based on assumptions that host families provide students with "authentic" language uses. Study abroad discourses also rely on the resultant hierarchical relationships between "native" and "non-native" speakers. Some researchers argue that this causes the conversation between student and host family to be framed as if they were in a classroom—the student is a student, being a "non-native speaker," and the host family members are teachers, as they are "native speakers" (Wilkinson 2002). Next, I will introduce the language acquisition theories that relate to this topic.

Learning a Second Language and the "Native Speaker"

There are diverse approaches to the "native speaker" concept within linguistics. At one pole are the branches of applied linguistics, especially SLA theories, that focus on practical teaching of the second/foreign language:

> Applied linguistics makes constant appeal to the concept of the native
> speaker. This appeal is necessary because of the need applied linguistics
> has for models, norms and goals, whether the concern is with teaching
> or testing a first, second or foreign language, with the treatment of a lan-
> guage pathology, with stylistic discourse and rhetorical analysis or with
> some other deliberate language use. But when we look for a definition
> of the native speaker which will act as an applied linguistic benchmark,
> the concept slips away and we wonder whether after all Lewis Carroll's
> snark is only a boojum. (Davies 2003: 1)

In official pronouncements in this area, the "native speaker" is often
regarded as a model speaker whose intuition in the language makes
them a natural judge. In "second" language education in the United
States, English-as-a-Second-Language (ESL) standards for students
before tertiary education in "TESOL's Vision of Effective Education for
All Students" includes the following statement: "Effective education
for TESOL [Teachers of English to Speakers of Other Languages] students includes *native-like* levels of proficiency in English" (TESOL 2005:
8, emphasis added; see also Doerr and Kumagai 2009).

The "native speaker" concept is also explicit in the guidelines for
foreign-language teaching in the United States. The American Council
on the Teaching of Foreign Language's speaking guidelines describe a
speaker at the "superior level" thusly: "[They] demonstrate no pattern
of error in the use of basic structures, although they may make sporadic
errors. . . . Such errors, if they do occur, *do not distract the native interlocutor* or interfere with communication" (ACTFL 2012: 5, emphasis added;
see also Doerr and Kumagai 2009). Similarly, the writing guidelines for
the "superior level" state: "writers demonstrate no pattern of error. . . .
When present, these errors do not interfere with comprehension, and
they *rarely distract the native reader*" (ACTFL 2012: 11, emphasis added).

Alan Firth and Johannes Wagner (2007a: 763–764) describe the
underlying assumptions (seen above) about "native speakers" and
"non-native speakers" in the SLA theory as follows:

> (A) the NS [native speaker] is a seemingly omniscient figure. . . . NS data
> are thus viewed as the warranted baseline from which NNS [non-native
> speaker] data can be compared, and the benchmark from which judgments
> of appropriateness, markedness, and so forth, can be made. (B) NNSs
> are unproblematically viewed as the NSs' subordinates, with regard to
> communicative competence. (C) The SLA researcher approaches NS and
> NNS interactions in an overwhelmingly a priori fashion, viewing them as
> inherently problematic encounters. (D) NS and NNS are blanket terms,
> implying homogeneity throughout each group, and clear-cut distinctions
> between them. So a NS is assumed unproblematically to be a person with
> a mother tongue, acquired from birth. . .(E) the identity categorizations

NS and NNS are applied exogenously and without regard for their emic relevance . . . a multitude of social identities . . . is . . . a nonissue in SLA [theory]. (F) monolingual orientation of SLA . . . fails to take account of the multilingual reality of communities and the reality of more transient, interacting groups. (G) a common practice within SLA is to compare observed features of interaction with "comparable" NS interactions (i.e., so-called "baseline" data).

In short, at one end of the linguistic spectrum, the notion of the "native speaker" continues to thrive as a model, norm, and goal in teaching "second," "foreign," or "heritage" languages as a basis for language and educational policies as well as a concept to make sense of linguistic interactions in diverse contexts (Amin 1999; Braine 1999a; Liu 1999). At the opposite end of the spectrum are sociolinguistics—which contend that no linguistic variation is better than another, thus rendering the hierarchical binary opposition between "native" and "non-native" speakers obsolete (V. Cook 1999)—and sociocultural and socio-interactional research (e.g., Kramsch 2002; Larsen-Freeman 1997, 2002), which question such linear models of language learning (Firth and Wagner 2007b; see also Block 2007; Canagarajah 2007; Zuengler and Miller 2006).

Firth and Wagner (2007a) suggest viewing what "non-native" speakers can do not as deficient but as resourceful and strategic deployments to accomplish social and interactional ends, such as displaying empathy or achieving mutual understanding. Also, the "non-native" status is used as a resource for sense making, as when "native speakers" take it into account in interpreting "non-native speakers'" utterances. This may be something that study abroad students learn through their experience of interacting with speakers of the language in the destination.

In the study of English-language teaching in particular, the debate centers on the hierarchical relationship between "native" and "non-native" speakers, with the former positioned as the model to which the latter should aspire. Braj Kachru (1992a) suggests recognition and legitimation of separate linguistic norms in places where people's use of English as their second language among themselves has local connotations, calling them "World Englishes" in the plural. Cases of "heritage" study abroad students may benefit from the basic tenet of this framework in understanding their experience because many reports being undermined for their linguistic variety if they come from the country where the nonstandard variety of the language of the destination is spoken. For example, students from Colombia and Guatemala reported negative experiences in Spain (Doerr 2018; Doerr and Suarez 2018). However, ultimately I would not suggest applying this framework similar to World Englishes because it would merely pluralize English based on a nationalist framework and exclude "any other possibilities that destabilize this notion of global English in more fundamental ways" (Pennycook 2007: 104; see also Canagarajah 1999; Sakai 1997).

Research on English-as-a-Lingua-Franca (ELF)—a language "developed independently [from "native speaker" English], with a great deal of variation but enough stability to be viable for lingua franca communication" (Seidlhofer 2001: 138) among "non-mother-tongue speakers" of English—seeks to render the notion of "native speaker" obsolete not by emulating "native speaker" speech but by aiming at communication (Jenkins 2006). The framework of ELF does not measure the deviation of ELF speakers' speech from that of "native speakers"; rather, it defies a single yardstick by which to measure proficiency: each ELF interaction ushers in its own unique dynamics. That is, ELF researchers view what conventional English as a Foreign Language (EFL) researchers consider linguistic deficits as viable communication strategies (Canagarajah 2007a; Seidlhofer 2001). If a yardstick is needed, it "should be an 'expert in ELF use' [rather than 'native speaker']" (House 2003: 573), though relations of hierarchy remain, to the extent that ELF speakers themselves view themselves as subordinate to "native speakers" (Doerr 2009a).

In light of these critiques, the next section suggests ways to involve study abroad students in critically examining both the notion of "native speakers" and the prevailing understanding of "learning the language of the destination" during study abroad.

Involving Students in Understanding the Political Nature of Language Homogeneity and Competence

How can we involve study abroad students in critically understanding the notion of language in terms of its diversity and political nature, along with the notion of linguistic competence that creates the hierarchy of "native" and "non-native" speakers? Doing so is important, not only because it informs how they situate their linguistic abilities as they relate to studying abroad but also because it gives them critical understanding of language politics in general, including what they experience in their own home society. In this section, I focus on three aspects— the notion of the "native speaker," the diversity of language, and the notion of competence—and make some suggestions.

The questions of how one's subject positions affect one's perceptions and actions (W), whose viewpoints are privileged and whose are marginalized (X), how things change (Y), and how the study abroad students' experience may be affected by the relationships between their home and host societies, as detailed in introduction, can also be asked.

The "Native Speaker" Notion

Ben Rampton (1995) suggests challenging the notion of the "native speaker" by differentiating the notion into "expertise" in and "allegiance" to the language. For example, some individuals who have expertise in a particular linguistic variety do not have the ethnic ties usually associated with that variety. Such a reconceptualization reveals the diversity within a nation and the language one speaks. We can incorporate this and other ways to encourage students to think about the notion of "native speaker" differently by asking questions regarding (1) the notion of the "native speaker," (2) what is involved in deciding who the "native speaker" is, (3) learning from "native speakers," and (4) the "native speaker's" proficiency. Series 3-A at the end of the chapter shows some questions divided into predeparture and during/after the stay occasions.

Diversity of Language

The discussion above showed that when it comes to diversity of language, what exists is not a homogeneous language but continuously different linguistic varieties. These varieties are positioned hierarchically—some as "language" as opposed to "dialects" and others as "broken" or "non-native" varieties—because of the political status of the speakers of particular varieties. The latter are pushed to approximate the "standard" as language is continued to be imagined as a bounded unit, a product of the ideology of the nation-state, as discussed. The "native speaker" is believed to speak their national language, its standard form.

Applying this understanding to the study abroad context, we can ask questions regarding how language is portrayed in study abroad promotional and other materials, as introduced in series 3-B at the end of this chapter. They can ask how diverse linguistic varieties that they encountered in the destination differ from what they have been familiarized with in classroom prior to studying abroad and how that difference informs them in terms of the notion of language as countable, hierarchy among linguistic varieties, and what the notion of "native speaker" implies. Regarding diversity within the host society and the student's home society in general to be connected to the diversity of language, we can ask the questions listed in chapter 1 under the respective labels 1-C and 1-D.

Notion of Competence

Earlier, I reviewed the discussion that shows the notion of linguistic competence to be constructed based on a set of grammar rules distilled from the speech of the dominant group, deemed the "standard." Linguistic competence also includes communicative ability; here, it is speakers of the "standard" variety or "native speakers" who are constructed as ideal speakers. Rejecting the view that "non-native speakers" are deficient language speakers, some researchers point out that, in fact, competence is often judged according to nonlinguistic factors, as mentioned (Freed 1995), and suggest alternative ways to judge the proficiency of language learners. It could, for example, be judged based on expertise in the form spoken as a lingua franca rather than on the degree of proximity to the "native speaker's" speech (House 2003). A lingua franca's focus on contextual communicability with a given interlocutor evades the use of set standard criteria for judging communicative competence.

Following this lead, we can get students to think about the notion of competence by asking questions regarding how competence is talked about, what assumptions become apparent through such talks, and what the effects of these assumptions are. Example questions on the topics of (1) what is considered correct and who decides, (2) communicability, and (3) standard language—as well as on W, X, Y, and Z mentioned in the introduction—that can be asked are introduced in series 3-C. By asking these questions, we can hope to engage students in thinking about both the political grounding and the implications of the judgments we make about "learning the language of the study abroad destination," thereby arriving at a more in-depth understanding of the notions of "native speaker," "language," "correctness," and "competence."

Students will most likely gain linguistic competency through studying abroad. With guidance such as the questions above, they can also stand to gain critical understanding of aforementioned notions and how they operate to shape their perceptions and actions. We can also start talking about how to change the circumstances to make them more egalitarian for speakers of all linguistic variations along the way.

Recommended Readings

Calvet, Louis-Jean. 1998. *Language Wars and Linguistic Politics.* Oxford: Oxford University Press.
  Historical examination of language politics and how it always involved power politics.
Firth, Alan, and Johannes Wagner. 2007a. "On Discourse, Communication, and (Some) Fundamental Concepts in SLA Research." [Republication from the *Modern Language Journal* 81 (1997): 285–300.] *Modern Language Journal* 91 (S1): 757–772.
  Discussion of false assumptions about the "native speaker."
Irvine, Judith T., and Susan Gal. 2000. *Language Ideology and Linguistic Differentiation in Regimes of Language: Ideologies, Polities, and Identities,* ed. Paul V. Kroskrity, 35–83. Santa Fe, NM: School of American Research Press.
  Description of language ideologies.
Kachru, Braj B. (1982) 1992a. "Models for Non-native Englishes." In *The Other Tongue: English Across Cultures,* ed. Braj B. Kachru, 48–74. Urbana: University of Illinois Press.
  Critique of standardization of English worldwide, and suggestions of alternative ways to frame it.
Milroy, Lesley. 1999. "Standard English and Language Ideology in Britain and the United States." In *Standard English: The Widening Debate,* ed. Tony Bex and Richard J. Watts, 173–206. London: Routledge.
  Description of language standardization processes.
Pennycook, Alastair. 1994. *The Cultural Politics of English as an International Language.* London: Longman.
  Discussion of the "native speaker" concept.
Phillipson, Robert. 1992. *Linguistic Imperialism.* Oxford: Oxford University Press.
  Critical description of the spread of English and its becoming an "international language" understood in terms of power politics.
Skutnabb-Kangas, Tove, and Robert Phillipson. 1989. "'Mother Tongue': The Theoretical and Sociopolitical Construction of a Concept." In *Status and Function of Languages and Language Varieties,* ed. Ulrich Ammon, 450–477. Berlin: Walter de Gruyter.
  Discussion of what a "mother tongue" is, providing insights for one's understanding of the notion of the native speaker.
Urciuoli, Bonnie. 1995. "Language and Borders." *Annual Review of Anthropology* 24: 525–546
  Discussion of the concept of language as a bounded unit.
Warner, Sam L. No'eau. 1999. "Kuleana: The Right, Responsibility, and Authority of Indigenous Peoples to Speak and Make Decisions for Themselves in Language and Cultural Revitalization." *Anthropology and Education Quarterly* 30 (1): 68–93
  Discussion of the notion of the native speaker from the viewpoint of indigenous peoples who are facing the loss of their language due to colonial assimilation policies.

◖◖◉ Sample Questions

3-A: The Notion of the "Native Speaker"
Predeparture:
3-A1-1: Have you heard the term "native speaker"? What is it?
3-A1-2: What language(s) are you a "native speaker" of? How did you learn these languages?
3-A1-3: Do you think someone can be a "native speaker" of more than one language?
3-A1-4: Do you think that, over time, you can become a "non-native speaker" of your "native" language?
3-A1-5: Do you think you and your parents can be "native speakers" of different languages?
3-A1-6: Do you think "non-native speakers" can become "native speakers"?
3-A2-1: Who decides who is or is not a "native speaker" of the language?
3-A2-2: Do you think being a "native speaker" of a language relates to one's ethnicity? For example, can you be French but not a "native speaker" of French?
3-A2-3: Do you think that everyone in a study abroad destination is a "native speaker" of the dominant language in that country? Why (not)?
3-A3-1: Do you think talking with "native speakers" will help you acquire proficiency in that language? Why (not)?
3-A3-2: Do you think talking with "non-native speakers" will increase your proficiency in that language? Why (not)?
3-A4-1: Can you imagine a scenario in which a "non-native speaker" could correct a "native speaker"? If yes, can you give an example? If no, why not?
3-A4-2: Do you think "native speakers" know everything about their language? Do you think "native speakers" never make mistakes in their language? If they do, what kind of mistakes are these?
3-A4-3: Do you think "native speakers" do not need to take classes in their own language? If they do, what kind of classes would these be, and what would they learn?

During/after the stay:
3-A2-1: Do you think everyone in the study abroad destination is a "native speaker" of the dominant language in that country? Why (not)?
3-A3-1: Do you think talking with "native speakers" has helped you gain proficiency in their language? If yes, how?

3-A3-2: Do you think talking with "non-native speakers" has helped you gain proficiency in that language? If yes, how? If no, why not?

3-A4-1: Have you seen a scenario in which a "non-native speaker" could correct native speakers? If yes, can you give an example? If no, why not?

3-A4-2: Judging from your study abroad experience, do you think "native speakers" know everything about their language? Do you think they never make mistakes in that language? If they do, what kinds of mistakes do they make?

3-B: Diversity of Language

3-B1: Do you think study abroad promotional materials portray people in the destination as all speaking the same way? Why do you think so? What are the effects of such a portrayal?

3-B2: Do you think that the teacher in the language class you took at home portrayed people in the destination as all speaking the same way? Why do you think so? What are the effects of that portrayal?

3-B3: Do you think people in the destination all speak the same way? If no, what do you think made the difference?

3-B4: Have you noticed any differences among people's way of speaking in the destination? If yes, what do you think made the difference?

3-B5: Have you noticed any mismatch between a person and the language/linguistic variety you expected them to speak? When? How?

3-B6: Why do you think a language is expected to match the people who speak it? What promotes this view?

3-B7: Do you think people in your home country speak differently from each other? What do you think makes the difference?

3-B8: Have you noticed any hierarchy between different linguistic varieties at home? If yes, how did you notice it?

3-B9: Where did you feel you were located in the hierarchy? Why? What made you think so?

3-B10: Who/what do you think decides which linguistic variety is better than others? Whose voice is privileged and whose voice is erased in such a process?

3-C: The Notion of Competence
Predeparture:

3-C1-1: Who decides what the "correct" form of the language is in the study abroad destination? In your home country?

3-C1-1-Y: Do you think the "correct" form of the language has changed? If so, what caused the change?

3-C1-1-X: Does such a change privilege some and marginalize others? If yes, how can we make it more egalitarian?

3-C2-1: In your home country, has your use of language ever been corrected? Who corrected you? How did you feel about it?

3-C2-1-X: Does correcting language privilege some and marginalize others? If yes, how can we make it more egalitarian?

3-C3-1: Have you ever challenged someone who corrected your language? When? How? Why?

3-C4-1: Have you ever corrected others' language? When? How? Why?

3-C4-1-X: Does that privilege some and marginalize others? How can we make it more egalitarian?

3-C4-1-W: Do you think the experience differs depending on a student's race, class, gender, and other background? If yes, how? Why?

During/after the stay:

3-C2-2: Has your language use ever been corrected while you were studying abroad? What was corrected? Who corrected you? How did you feel about it?

3-C3-2: Have you ever challenged someone who corrected your language? When? How? Why?

3-C3-2-W: Do you think that the experience differs depending on a student's race, class, gender, and other background? If yes, how? Why?

3-C2-3: In your home country, has your language use ever been corrected? Who corrected you? How did you feel about it?

3-C2-3-X: Does such a correction privilege some and marginalize others? How can we make it more egalitarian?

3-C4-2: Have you ever corrected another person's language? When? How? Why?

3-C4-2-X: Does that privilege some and marginalize others? How can we make it more egalitarian?

3-C4-2-W: Do you think that the experience differs depending on a student's race, class, gender, and other background? If yes, how? Why?

3-C5-1: Have you ever had the experience of being unable to understand your interlocutor? If yes, whose "fault" did you think this was? Did the interlocutor speak incorrectly? Or you did lack the proficiency needed to understand the interlocutor's utterance?

3-C5-2: What determines your answer to that? Does it change according to whether you are in the host society or in your home society? Why does that make a difference?

Additional post-stay questions

3-C6-1: Have you heard of "standard" language? [If not, the one who is asking this question explains what it means to the student.]

3-C6-2: Do you think "standard" language is the "correct" form of language?

3-C6-3: How do you think the "standard" language is chosen?

3-C6-4: How do you think the standardization process occurs in the study abroad destination? In your home country?

3-C6-4-X: Does that privilege some and marginalize others? How can we make it more egalitarian?

3-C6-5-Y: Do you think the standard language has been changing historically in the study abroad destination? In your home country?

3-C6-5-X: Does that privilege some and marginalize others? How can we make it more egalitarian?

3-C7-X1: Have you noticed whether any linguistic variety is considered better than others? More "correct" or "beautiful" than others? If yes, how did you notice this?

3-C7-X2: Who/what do you think decides which linguistic variety is better than others?

Whose voice is privileged and whose voice is erased in such a process?

4

IMMERSION

Is It Really about "Living Like a Local"?

"Living Like a Local"?

Immersion — "living like a local" — is a key concept setting study abroad experience apart from other types of learning. Immersion in the study abroad destination uniquely allows, it is claimed, students to gain "global competence" and become "global citizens" by understanding "another culture," being sympathetic to people of other cultural backgrounds, gaining proficiency in another language, and learning to navigate an unknown environment (Brockington and Wiedenhoeft 2009; Currier et al. 2009; Cushner 2009; Kinginger 2008). Researchers value study abroad as a holistic learning experience in a "living laboratory" that encourages intellectual, psychological, and emotional learning experiences (Laubscher 1994: xiv).

Seldom discussed, however, are the social effects of this discourse of immersion. What images of the host society, the home society, and relationships between students and other people does the label "immersion" create? Is any act of living like a local considered immersion? What if you are an immigrant trying to adjust to a new country — is that an act of immersion? If you are staying with your aunt who lives there, is it an act of immersion? Is staying with an immigrant family in the study abroad destination an act of immersion? Why? Why not? What determines whether it is? Who makes this determination? How do we decide who is "local"? What if there are many different local ways of doing things? If "immersion" does not describe all acts of living like a local, then what does calling an act "immersion" mean? What are the effects? These are questions asked in this chapter, which overall explores whether immersion is really a learning method, discusses effects of this discourse, and suggests ways to capitalize on its merit in a new way so as to highlight rarely explored potential for study abroad.

In what follows, I first review the notion of immersion in study abroad literature and examine the effects of the discourse of immersion in terms of how it creates imaginings of students' host and home societies and the relationships between them, as well as a hierarchy of learning experience. In the section that follows, I will also explore whether all acts of living like a local in another place are considered immersion. If not, it is not really a learning method but a way to label particular acts in a certain way. This chapter ends with two suggestions as to how we can reframe the notion of immersion to highlight unique contributions of study abroad in a new way—critical social analyses based on observation of daily activities—along with kinds of questions proffered to involve students in thinking critically about the discourse of immersion.

Immersion in Study Abroad

Study abroad guidebooks encourage "immersion," explained as "living your life as a native [local]" (Loflin 2007: 119). If students travel as tourists, they "miss much of their [the locals'] culture" (Williamson 2004: 254). Through immersion, students will have a good time in the host society: the most "exciting and interesting" experience comes from "interacting directly with the native citizens" because they know the good places to travel to and local hot spots to visit (Oxford 2005: 114).

The discourse of immersion suggests that students immerse themselves in the life of their study abroad destination in two ways: first, by leaving their "comfort zone," which, the discourse implies, takes various shapes. "Home," consisting of family members and friends back home, is regarded as one such comfort zone students are reminded to stay away from because it is accessible via phone and the internet. Staying in another type of comfort zone—the company of fellow students from the student's home country—is also discouraged by the discourse of immersion. The world of technology, encompassing the internet, phone, TV, and computers in general, is another comfort zone that the discourse of immersion warns students against (Hovey and Weinberg 2009; Loflin 2007; Oxford 2005; Williamson 2004). Such a view assumes that students are playing a zero-sum game in which the home (framed as "comfort zone") and host societies vie for students' time, interest, and commitment. Comfort zones, it suggests, consume time, drain mental energy, and interrupt language learning. Yet this perspective ignores the merits of such comfort zones, which can be a buffer for those who would otherwise feel anxious about leaving their home country. They can also be sites of meaningful learning experiences when two or more student compatriots compare and contrast the host and home societies, something that is difficult to do with people who do not know both, as mentioned in chapter 2 (Doerr 2013b; Woolf 2007).

Second, proactive engagement with people and activities in the host society is encouraged as a way to immerse oneself. As will be discussed in chapter 5, the immersion discourse views staying with a host family as the best way to immerse oneself in the host society because it provides students with opportunities to experience the daily life of the local (Cohen et al. 2005; Goldoni 2013; Jackson 2009; Raymond and Hall 2008); also, host family members help students understand what is happening in the host society by acting as students' "informal teachers" (Fobes 2005) or advocates (Lindenberg 2015)—although, as I argue in chapter 5, host family experience is not necessarily "authentic" local life. Making "native friends" is seen as a good way to immerse oneself in the destination, as they can introduce students to other locals. Talking with strangers is likewise considered "interaction with locals" (Loflin 2007: 134). Also recommended is floating around in the environment itself, as walking down the streets, looking in shops, dining in local cafés, and even getting lost are all considered "the authentic and *real* experience" (Williamson 2004: 253; see also Loflin 2007). In this context, less value is attached to classroom learning than is usually the case in the home country.

Some researchers, on the other hand, worry that mere immersion does not lead to learning experience unless it is supplemented by intentional activities that encourage students to both engage with local people and reflect intensively on their experiences. Such intentional activities include conscious proactive engagement (Vande Berg et al. 2009); spending much time with a host family (Vande Berg 2009); ethnographic projects (Goldoni 2013; Ogden 2006; Roberts et al. 2001); getting help from a well-trained "cultural mentor" to reflect on, hypothesize about, and actively test cultural concepts and skills (Vande Berg 2009: 23); using reflective writing (Chen 2002) to increase opportunities for reflection; and doing volunteer work to increase one's engagement with local people (Bringle and Hatcher 2011; Plater et al. 2009).

In this chapter, while acknowledging the importance of immersion for student learning, I suggest several unintended effects of the discourse of immersion in terms of its creating (1) images of the host and home societies and of relationships between them (effects of the immersion discourse), (2) a hierarchy of learning experience (effects of the discourse of immersion), and (3) images of the people with whom students interact and their relationships to each other (effects of labeling an act as immersion). After analyzing these effects critically based on my previous work (Doerr 2013b; Doerr and Suarez 2018), I will connect the notion of immersion to critical pedagogy and suggest how we might incorporate these understandings into the ways in which we encourage students to immerse themselves when studying abroad.

Effects of the Discourse of Immersion

The discourse of immersion creates particular effects for the imaginings of what the host society is like, what the students' home society is like, and how they relate to each other. Because immersion is regarded as better than other types of experience, the notion of immersion also creates a hierarchy of experience, which is not necessarily warranted. In this section, I will draw on my previous analyses of study abroad guidebooks (Doerr 2013b) and interviews of American study abroad students in France and Spain (Doerr 2015a, 2016) to discuss these points.

Imaginings of the Host Society

By suggesting that doing *anything* in the host society—including talking with *any* strangers and staying with *any* family as a host family—constitutes meaningful experience, the notion of immersion constructs people in the host society as homogeneous. By generalizing any experience or anyone occupying the local space as representative of the life of the entire host society, immersion discourse implies that such an experience or person shows what it is like to live in that society. In fact, though, such experience is just one kind that merely provides a sense of how one stranger on the street thinks and how one family lives when someone from another society is staying with them (for a detailed discussion on host family space, see chapter 5). If the discourse fails to acknowledge the specificity of such experiences, it risks ignoring the presence of diverse people, such as sojourners and other immigrants with diverse cultural backgrounds, as well as study abroad students, who themselves are part of the local scene (see also Doerr 2013b, 2016).

Chapter 5 will show that ignoring such diversity is a way to further valorize homogeneity. This is done by denouncing what I call "outsider space," which is seen to exist in pockets of the host society, as something to be avoided. The discourse of immersion discourages students from acting like tourists by gathering at museums or spending too much time with other compatriot students at the dorm or in groups at bars (Hovey and Weinberg 2009). Any warning to stay out of this out-sider space is itself an acknowledgment that such outsider space exists within the host society, rendering meaningless the claim that immersion can happen anywhere. When talking about their experience, study abroad students whom I interviewed in France and Spain (Doerr 2016) put this warning into practice by distancing themselves from outsider space, which allowed them to highlight their proactive involvement in local space. Here, outsider space works as an abject space (Butler 1993) that helps keep the supposedly homogeneous host society space intact. This is a contradiction: even though one's own presence as a visitor from elsewhere changes the configuration of the supposedly homoge-neous destination, one still seeks to see the destination as homogeneous exclusive of the visitor, framing study abroad as an encounter between two distinct "cultures." I urge students to challenge this contradiction in the discourse of immersion and instead view study abroad experi-ence as something constantly co-constructed by study abroad students and people in the host society along with other diverse peoples in the space of the host society (see Massey 2005).

Imaginings of the Study Abroad Students' Home Society

The discourse of immersion also renders the study abroad student's home society homogeneous by asserting that spending time with com-patriots is not meaningful. The suggestion that fellow nationals offer nothing new from which the student can learn implies homogeneity among them. However, student's experience diverges from the above assertion. Some students reported learning much about habits, per-ceptions, or even what to wear when going out from other students from different regions in the home society. For example, a student from New Jersey was shocked to see how students from Texas dress to go out. Other students also talked about being viewed stereotypically—as though being from New Jersey meant that they were like cast members from the reality TV show *Jersey Shore*—by other students from different regions of the home society (Doerr 2015a).

Susan Talburt and Melissa Stewart (1999) report on how students with different ethnic, class, or gender backgrounds experience the host society differently. In Spain, for example, African American students experienced what borders on sexual harassment, which they perceived as racialized; fewer Anglo-American students experienced them. Talburt and Stewart argue that it is important to acknowledge such difference and suggest that diverse experience can become a learn-ing resource for all students. It is worth mentioning, however, that this view of study abroad students' home societies as homogeneous is increasingly being challenged (see chapter 5), for example, by the emergence of notions like "study away" inside the home country and learning within one's own region from other groups, such as immigrants of different backgrounds (Jorge 2006; Hovland et al. 2009).

Imagined Relationships between Host and Home Societies

The discourse of immersion suggests two kinds of relationships between the host and home societies. First, it renders them fundamentally different from each other. By making daily life in the host society the object of learning for the student abroad, the discourse constructs the host people and how they live as fundamentally different, making learning about them worthwhile. After all, if the host people live as students do back home, the claim that exposure to their ways is a learning experience for the students loses validity. This is in line with the ideology of the nation-state discussed in chapter 1, which views the world's nation-states as having distinct "cultures" separated by clearly demarcated geographical boundaries. That is, the discourse of immersion is built on and perpetuates the ideology.

I have shown in chapters 1 and 2 that this view is inaccurate: in fact, people are connected around the world in various ways throughout the history. Not only do international trade agreements and shared regulations among countries shape each country's domestic policies and situations, but multinational corporations and international organizations change people's daily lives. Flows of people, media images, and commodities affect people's sensibilities (Appadurai 1990; Tomlinson 1999). What we observe in the life of someone in the study abroad destination is quite likely influenced by what is happening in students' home country and vice versa. So, what the student experiences is not a fundamentally different "culture" but a manifestation of things co-constructed or constructed in relation to each other by people in the student's home and host societies and elsewhere.

Second, the discourse of immersion constructs the students' home and host societies in hierarchical relations according to their degree of globalization. On the one hand, the discourse of immersion suggests that the students' home society is globalized when it advises them to stay away from the internet and other ways to connect with the home society: the home society is imagined as globally accessible. On the other hand, the discourse presents the host society as not globalized but parochial by implying that people in the host society are not connected globally through the internet—for otherwise, students who go online (e.g., connecting with people around the world via social media or watching videos from various countries) would still be "living like the local." Situated in the discourses of study abroad, where global connections are generally valued and celebrated, staying parochial suggests backwardness (see chapter 1). Thus, the discourse of immersion places the home and host societies of the study abroad students in a hierarchical relationship by rendering the former as globalized and the latter, not (Doerr 2013b).

Hierarchy of Experience

Viewing immersion as the ideal way to learn creates a hierarchy of experience as well, by contrasting one activity with others that are rendered less desirable, such as "touristic" activities, various "non-immersive" activities in the host country, classroom learning, and not studying abroad. By contrasting students who immerse themselves in the host society with tourists and claiming the former to be superior to the latter, the discourse of immersion creates a hierarchy of sojourning experience abroad. This is similar to anthropologists' quest to establish cultural anthropology as a "scientific" discipline in contrast to the activities of tourists, missionaries, and explorers, characterizing fieldwork the former is based on as consisting of "intensive, 'deep' interaction" and the latter, not, though the borderline between such activities is quite blurry (Clifford 1997). Considering that tourists can gain meaningful, deep understanding of the host society by learning about its history, art, and other things by visiting historical landmarks, museums, and so on, this hierarchy can be challenged, for example.

By suggesting that immersion is the most effective way to learn while studying abroad, the discourse of immersion creates a hierarchy of study abroad learning experience (see chapter 2): valuing time spent with locals over that spent with compatriots (Hovey and Weinberg 2009), out-of-class experience over classroom learning (Chen 2002), homestay over accommodation in a hostel with compatriot students (Chieffo and Griffiths 2014), a semester-long over a shorter stay (Deardorff 2009), and direct-enrollment over island-type programs led by American faculty (Hovey and Weinberg 2009). However, some researchers disagree with this valorization of immersion as the most effective learning method (see also the discussion of my own "fully immersed" study abroad experience in the introduction). Michael Vande Berg argues that, overall, research fails to support the view that the method of immersion—"throwing them into the deep end of the study-abroad pool" (2009: 19)—works, as results differ among students. In terms of gender, he suggests for instance, male students who studied abroad learned significantly more than male students at home, but female students who studied abroad made significantly greater gains than the male students who did. No significant link is established between experiential activities like internships and field experiences, and language or "intercultural" learning. Vered Amit (2010) notes that the perceived hierarchy of experience has not been examined empirically. Michael Woolf (2006) suggests that being with local people is not necessarily the best way to learn how home and host societies differ, as mentioned.

Furthermore, Sharon Wilkinson (2002) argues that immersion is not as much "outside the classroom" as researchers want to believe, because classroom interactional patterns are used outside the classroom between the "non-native" speaker who is thus a student and the "native" speaker in the host society who is thus a teacher, as both take their roles for granted (see chapter 3). The discourse of immersion even devalues classroom learning. This is stressed in language learning especially, where immersion is considered the most efficient method because of the variety of opportunities to use language with "native speakers" in "authentic" contexts. Yuri Kumagai (2017) summarizes major critiques of this common belief: it assumes learning processes are automatic and natural, rendering the learner passive and portraying classroom learning as inferior, and it ignores that individual differences in students' learning outcomes often depend on their proficiency in the language before the immersion experience.

By celebrating immersion's importance as the best way to learn another "culture" and gain "global competence," the discourse of immersion devalues learning about cultural others in the domestic context. Although researchers have found that meaningful learning occurs through interactions with immigrants or visiting international students (Jorge 2006; Hovland et al. 2009), and through the crossing of race, cultural, and economic lines without leaving the United States (Hovland et al. 2009; see also Plater et al. 2009), as mentioned earlier, the discourse of immersion applies predominantly to study abroad contexts, valorizing them as more important than such domestic experience. It is worth noting here, however, that Norris Palmer (2015) argues that immersion abroad is different from immersion in another ethnic group at home because in the former, students themselves become outsiders in terms of wider institutional and other norms, which pushes them to question their own assumptions, whereas this does not happen in the latter context.

These hierarchies influence students' perceptions. Some feel apologetic about spending time on schoolwork while studying abroad

(Doerr 2017c; Kumagai 2017) or staying in a dorm instead of a host family (Doerr 2015a). Students may also feel satisfied by simply being immersed in the destination, leaving room for more reflective thinking and discussions (Doerr 2015a). Thus, I suggest engaging students in thinking critically about the discourse of immersion itself.

The Effects of Labeling an Act as Immersion

A focus on labeling certain acts as "immersion" is an essential part of engaging students in thinking about that notion. I have discussed this elsewhere (Doerr and Suarez 2018) based on a collaborative case study of a study abroad student who stayed with his uncle before his study abroad stay in Spain and traveled alone afterward. In this section, I introduce the argument from that case study and supplement it with other research.

Not all acts of "living like a local" are considered immersion. Rather, immersion is a label put on particular activities (thus, it is not about the activity itself but about the *perception* of that activity) that reveals assumptions about the immersed person, the people among whom the person is immersed, and the relationships between the two. That is, what is or is not considered immersion tells us much about assumptions behind the notion of immersion. For this reason, it is important to engage students in reflecting on how we label certain acts immersion.

Assumptions about the Person Doing the Act

That an act is considered immersion says less about the act itself than about the labelers' perception of the purpose of the act and thus of the person doing it (in the case of labeling an act "volunteering," see Doerr 2015c). That is, an act—say, the act of using a pair of chopsticks—can be called immersion or not depending on the perception of who is doing it and for what purpose. There are four assumptions about a person who is immersed.

First, immersion is done as a luxury—an enrichment on top of a regular college education, like studying abroad. Newly arrived immigrants who "live like the local" in the new homeland are not considered immersed because the purpose of their "living like a local" is not luxury but survival. For example, the student in the case study did not think that his Colombian immigrant parents were "immersed" in the United States, whereas he was "immersing" himself in Spain as a study abroad student. It is similar to using a pair of chopsticks in Japan: it may be luxury enrichment practice for study abroad students but is an act of survival for an immigrant trying to fit in.

Second, immersion is an enrichment: learning about a new "culture" through immersion does not replace one's original "culture." In contrast, when it is done for survival, as in the case of immigrants, they are instead seen as "assimilating" and are expected to replace their original "culture" with that of their new home society, though it is often not what happens. The language education of immigrant children often reflects this starkly, where their "native language" has been seen as obstacle in learning the language of the new society despite its actual benefit (Cummins 2001), though it is changing. Immersion is an additive for enrichment; assimilation is replacement.

Third, immersion has an end on the horizon: if you end up settling in the destination, it is not immersion. Study abroad students who will return to their own homeland are immersed; immigrants settling in a new homeland are not, as the student under discussion compared his own experience in Spain and his parents' experience in the United States. This complicates experience like my own—coming to the United States for graduate school and ending up staying. At what point did my "living like a local" stop being immersion? After graduation? After deciding to stay in the United States? Or was it never immersion in the first place?

This relates to my fourth point: immersion is a willed activity of "learning culture." The students' immigrant parents did not come to the United States to "learn culture" but to "make a better life," which also necessitated them to "learn the US culture" in due course; so it was not "immersion," he said. My graduate study in the United States contrasts starkly with my second study abroad experience in Aotearoa/New Zealand, during which my aims included adjusting to and learning "the culture of Aotearoa/New Zealand." I came to the United States to do graduate study and become an anthropologist, not to "learn American culture," so from the very beginning of my stay I never really thought about "immersion." Immersion is about "learning culture" intentionally.

In sum, "immersion" is not just the ordinary activity of "living like a local" as it is usually regarded but rather an additive, done as a luxury with an end on the horizon and focused on "learning culture," and the people doing it tend to be study abroad students who want to learn the "culture" of the host society for enrichment, not immigrants who learn various ways of doing things to adjust in their new homeland for survival.

Assumptions about the People among Whom the Person Is Immersed

Designating an act as immersion also reflects the labeler's perception of the people among whom the act is done, especially regarding whether they are marginalized in the host society. In the case of the student in Spain (Doerr and Suarez 2018), he felt that staying with his uncle was not immersion because his uncle was "not quite Spanish" for several reasons: the uncle himself asserted that he was not Spanish but Colombian; he was there for economic reasons rather than to become Spanish socially and culturally; and he was *othered* by Spaniards who discriminated against him as an immigrant. The student felt that because he was staying with someone who was not quite Spanish, his experience was not immersion in Spain.

This raises the question of the discourse of immersion suggesting a particular image of "the local" that often reflects stereotypes of the people living there: usually the dominant ethnic group and its (upper) middle class. For example, advertisements for study abroad in Paris often show white French people in touristic settings such as the Eiffel Tower, Champs-Élysées, and the Louvre (e.g., CIEE 2018a; StudyAbroad.com 2018). The images rarely feature Roma or other nonwhite people who also live in Paris. This perpetuates a stereotype of who "locals" are, ignoring the diversity of people in the host society and marginalizing others as "not quite local" or not "legitimate" locals. But as an educational endeavor, study abroad should be accurate and equitable in every aspect. As I discuss in greater detail in chapter 5, study abroad promotional materials' accurate portrayal of the study abroad destination, especially in light of its diversity, is important. Proactive inclusion of the diversity of the host society's people in promotional materials would go some way toward this end.

Though seldom discussed, inclusion of host families from nondominant backgrounds would be a significant step, not only toward students' accurate understanding of the study abroad destination but also toward the reduction of some people's marginalization in the host society. Immigrants who bring with them the lifestyles of their original homeland may live differently from nonimmigrants, but the experience of staying with an immigrant family itself should not be viewed as inferior to staying with a family of the dominant ethnic background. Closer attention to the fact of diversity among people in the destination in the discourse of immersion would also help reduce marginalization of minority populations.

Assumptions about the Relationship between Immerser and Immersed

Labeling an act as immersion also tells us about the social distance between the person doing the act and the people among whom the act is done. Another reason the student in the case study did not regard staying with his uncle as immersion was that the uncle was a family member. The student's prior trips to Colombia to visit relatives likewise were not immersion because he was visiting family even though he was "living like a local" there (he immigrated to the United States at the age of one, so Colombia is his ancestral homeland, but he has not lived there).

Staying with somebody whose lifestyle is similar to one's own is not immersion, either, the student said. Thus, staying with his uncle was not immersion because his lifestyle as a Colombian immigrant was similar to the student's lifestyle back home. This relates to the notion of border crossing as learning (see chapter 6): the experience was not quite crossing a border, so there was no "cognitive dissonance" or sense of "adventure." Here, the argument is not whether he crossed the border but whether he perceived it as crossing a border, which he expressed by using the label "immersion." In short, the act of labeling one's experience as immersion is more about asserting one's relationship (e.g., family) to the people you are interacting with than about describing the type of activities.

Effects of Labeling an Act as Immersion

What, then, are the effects of labeling an act "immersion"? Regarding the person doing the act of immersion, the label means that the doer is a sojourner doing the act for enrichment, and the trip a luxury with an end in sight, focused on "learning culture." This contrasts with how immigrants' activities are considered—not immersion because they migrated there with no leaving date in sight and learn their new homeland's "culture" for survival. As someone studying abroad is often part of the "regime of mobility" (Glick Schiller and Salazar 2013) that is valorized and immigrants, not, as discussed in chapter 1; here labeling of an act as immersion is linked to the immerser's social status as well.

Regarding the people among whom one is "immersed," to label an act "immersion" is to call these people legitimate members of the host society. Which people are considered a "legitimate" host family providing the quintessential "immersion space" reflects this assumption. I encourage consciously ensuring that host families reflect the diverse makeup of the host society.

As for the relationship between the person doing the immersion and the people among whom the act is done, labeling the act "immersion" suggests that the labeler perceives social distance between the former and the latter. That is, calling one's activity immersion is an act of othering oneself from the people in the society: "I'm not one of you." In short, no act is intrinsically an act of immersion. Calling an act immersion is a loaded, political act that we should analyze critically, involving students in the process.

A New Notion of Immersion and an Activity to Engage Students in It: Daorba Yduts

Given the potential risks demonstrated by the above critiques of the notion of immersion, I suggest a new direction that capitalizes on an aspect of the concept of immersion, as also mentioned in the introduction: detailed focus on our daily life. Study abroad, with its emphasis on immersion, can be an occasion to focus on daily activities and social interactions with others more than students would in a home society where immersion is usually not encouraged as a learning experience. The concept of immersion urges students to focus on daily experience as the source of knowledge and understanding. The people with whom they interact in daily life can be anybody because no two persons are the same. Students can interact with long-time residents, recent immigrants, and travelers they encounter in their study abroad destination, as they all make up the diverse host society. Examining any such encounters and interactions for deeper understanding of the destination would be worthwhile and can be extended to the daily life in the students' home society.

I suggest an activity that draws attention to daily life in the way in which study abroad does, which I call "Daorba Yduts." It is inspired by a classic work by Horace Miner (1956: 504) called "Body Rituals among the Nacirema." Miner describes a tribe called Nacirema and their daily activities:

> The Nacirema have an almost pathological horror of and fascination with the mouth, the condition of which is believed to have a supernatural influence on all social relationships. Were it not for the rituals of the mouth, they believe that their teeth would fall out, their gums bleed, their jaws shrink, their friends desert them, and their lovers reject them. . . . The daily body ritual performed by everyone includes a mouth-rite . . . This rite involves a practice which strikes the uninitiated stranger as revolting. It was reported to me that the ritual consists of inserting a small bundle of

hog hairs into the mouth, along with certain magical powders, and then moving the bundle in a highly formalized series of gestures. In addition to the private mouth-rite, the people seek out a holy-mouth-man once or twice a year.

As some may have noticed, Nacirema is "American" spelled backward. This is a parody of an ethnographic writing, especially how things are described. It shows how certain vocabulary, phrases, and tones of discussion turn what are mundane activities into exotic ones. That is, this is a powerful critique of anthropologists who made their object of study — cultural Others — into mythical and exotic people through their writing styles.

Inspired by this suggestion about the effect of language one uses to describe someone, we can do the same for the study abroad language, with keywords such as "explore," "life-changing," and "transformative." Hence, I suggest an activity that highlights how our daily activities are as important, exciting, and full of new experiences as study abroad immersion experience by using these study abroad keywords: I call it the Daorba Yduts activity, with "study abroad" spelled backward. Though there could be a variation, here is how it works (for convenience, the same instructions and questions are listed at the end of this chapter, so that study abroad practitioners can just look at these last pages when doing this activity):

(1) Prepare a list of study abroad keywords (see the end of the chapter for a sample list, which was created based on going through study abroad testimonials and study abroad promotional materials). Divide the keywords into three or four categories (e.g., noun, verb, adjective, phrases).

(2) Suggest a group of student (regardless of their study abroad experience) to think of something they did for the first time this past week (if the focus of the activity is to critique the study abroad narrative, which may be also relevant to the discussion in chapter 7, this length for students to look into can be twenty-four hours).

(3) Ask students to write a paragraph or so about that new experience using three keywords and phrases from each category. Give them about ten minutes to write it.

(4) Ask students to share what they wrote with the group. Discuss what that practice made them become aware of.

I had done a same activity in class once with something new they did within past twenty-four hours. Below are two examples of what students wrote (used here with their permission; keywords are marked in italics):

I made cold brew coffee for the first time. I was *motivated* to *try something new* and making the coffee *broadened my knowledge* on the various coffee types. It was an *experiential* process, and the result was better than I expected. It tasted great and was cheaper than purchasing it at Starbucks. The result could honestly *change lives*. It is stronger than regular coffee and kept me energetic longer than hot-brew coffee. This *transformative* process was made possible with coffee grounds, a mason jar, cold water, and a filter. The making of the coffee *helped me build valuable skills* that will *forever change my breakfast game*. I highly recommend *exploring the incredible* world of cold brew coffee. You won't be disappointed with this *rewarding experience*.

Last night, I *embarked* on a *life-changing journey* to Brady's for the first time. It *broadened my horizon* and *pushed me out of my comfort zone and sipped a cup of L.I.T.* It also *gave me new perspective* on the people I've had class with for three years. It was such a *rewarding* and *transformative* experience. It was an *exciting* and *meaningful border crossing* that *changes lives*.

After sharing these narratives, we had discussed what this activity made them realize. Students mentioned that this activity made them feel that the language in study abroad advertisement exaggerates the students' experience, although they were too used to them to realize until then. We also discussed how we do not focus on daily activities as much as when we study abroad. This is an exercise most fitted to the post-trip meetings for study abroad students to encourage them to use the same observational rigor to their daily life after their return, but it also can be useful in diverse classes if we add more analytical component to it, as will be discussed later.

Daily Othering Processes

The focus on social interactions via "immersion" can make study abroad an occasion to observe the daily construction of differences—othering processes—and connect it to wider sociocultural structures. As noted in chapter 2, sociocultural environments push us to notice particular kinds of difference over others (McDermott and Varenne 1995). Students can explore what made them notice certain things and people they encountered as "different" during their study abroad, and analyze both the sociocultural environments that pushed them to notice that difference—including the aforementioned study abroad keywords—and the effects that the perception of difference had on the students' behavior, expectations, and perceptions. Based on this, the notion of immersion can be understood in a new way, not as plunging into the cultural other's world but as focusing on the construction of difference among people.

Building on the activity suggested above, Daorba Yduts, we can add comparative exercise for the purpose of understanding and analyzing the specificity of study abroad context that highlight difference in comparison to daily life at "home." This helps urge students to understand how we end up "noticing" certain difference in general—because that is the common categories we talk about as "difference" (e.g., race, class, gender, sexual orientation, etc.), because some people are "made different" by the institution that does not serve them as much as it serves others (e.g., deaf people in the world where oral communication dominates), because we are told to "find difference" so that we can say we learned something from that encounter (e.g., study abroad discourses), because we are nudged to pay attention to that particular difference (e.g., reflective exercise questions after studying abroad; see chapter 7 for further discussion on "coaxers" of narratives), and so on.

For example, after the students write their paragraph(s) about new experience—here, I use the cold brew coffee example—questions such as the following can be asked for further discussions:

(a) Did you really feel as you described here about learning to make cold brew? Has your life really changed?

(b) Have you ever thought it could be a very exciting and meaningful learning experience?

(c) How different would it be if you learned how to make cold brew while you were studying abroad in Italy or France or Ghana or Korea? Would you have thought it is an exciting learning experience?

(d) If there is any difference between (b) and (c), what made the difference? What made you feel that new experience is not so meaningful when you did it at home (if that was the case)? What would make you notice and celebrate that new experience if you did it while studying abroad (if that was the case)?

(e) If that new experience were connected to the study abroad destination (e.g., coffee or cold brew and Italy, France or Ghana), would that new experience highlight the difference of that destination from your home country?

(f) In our daily life, what serves as something that pushes us to notice certain experience as meaningful or marking different lifestyles of different people? Stereotypes? Pressure to find something meaningful? Concrete effects the experience brings about? Anything else?

(g) What would push us to notice "new" and "different" experience in our daily life more?

We need to see what new experiences the student raise and modify questions, as some experiences are more tied to particular group of people (e.g., coffee and Italian). These questions would push students to think about the othering processes in which we notice certain newness and difference and ignore others. At the same time, it would allow them to relativize study abroad experience and help direct the students' eyes to our daily life of learning, difference, and "wonder" at home, which then can be directed to social analyses in general, as mentioned in introduction.

This noticing of our mundane encounters of difference is important because it moves us away from resorting to culturalist explanation—that all things are different because of different "cultures." Instead, we can see how institutional settings and structural arrangement may create difference or make us notice that difference, often in hierarchical ways. In order to push students' eyes further to this direction, we need to ask more questions, as introduced in the next section.

Not Just Cultural but Also Structural

This focus on daily experience can allow students to connect social structures of the society to their lived experience. As mentioned in the introduction, Paulo Freire ([1970] 1997) suggests valuing knowledge that students have derived from their own experience and viewing them as student-teachers learning together with the teacher-student. Learning by connecting their lived experiences to wider social forces that shape them, these student-teachers can become active citizens who effect social changes. Inspired by this pedagogy of the oppressed, proponents of critical pedagogy also encourage students to reflect on their lived experiences as manifestations of the workings of wider socioeconomic, political, and cultural forces that structure them. Critical pedagogy also encourages students to become active agents in changing oppressive social orders that privilege some and marginalize others (Giroux 2001; Giroux and McLaren 1989).

Building on the activity suggested above, Daorba Yduts, we can add this aspect of connecting mundane activities to wider social structures and institutions by asking the following:

(a) You said you have never made cold brew. Why do you think? What stopped you from making cold brew before?
(b) If it is a new thing in the United States, who brought it here? Why? What are the effects on different groups of people—coffee importers, coffee roasters, coffee shop owners, consumers? Who make more

money from this introduction? Who loses money from this introduction? If this creates inequality and inequity, how could we change it? As voting citizens, as consumers, and as community members?

(c) Can anybody make cold brew? Who can and who cannot? How are these differential accesses structured? Money? Leisure time? Accessibility to stores that would sell the tools? Accessibility to the information? How about around the world? People in what country would (not) be able to make cold brew?

(d) Is there any connotation attached to making cold brew? Can this then become a status symbol? A political statement?

In this way, study abroad with its focus on immersion can be redirected. Instead of viewing immersion merely as a way to "learn about another culture" or experience cognitive dissonance, we can capitalize on this attention to daily activities to guide students to connect daily practices to the wider social, economic, political, and cultural forces that shape them. That way, we can engage them in understanding how society works and how they can be part of change for the better (Giroux 2001; Giroux and McLaren 1989).

Study abroad can then be considered an important occasion for students to develop skills in attentiveness to their daily practices toward that end. Ways of observing, interpreting, and analyzing such social encounters can be used upon their return home, too. And this skill transcends assumptions of preexistence of "cultural difference" by equipping students to analyze the sociocultural dynamics through which some people are othered. Clear and critical understanding of such processes will further students' engagement in social processes at home and abroad.

Engaging Study Abroad Students in Critical Investigation of the Immersion Discourse

The notion of immersion is a useful conceptualization of a way of learning. However, as I described earlier, it has several pitfalls: it has the potential to evoke inaccurate and problematic imaginings of the host and home societies, as well as of their relationships, and to create a hierarchy of students' experience. Moreover, labeling certain acts as immersion can differentiate people and mark them hierarchically. In this section, I suggest ways to avoid such pitfalls, especially by engaging students in critical reflection on these pitfalls, as well as ways to capitalize on the benefits of learning through immersion during study abroad.

Again, for each question series we ask, I suggest including questions about (W) subject positions, (X) power relations, (Y) how society, "culture," and people have been changing and how we can change it, and (Z) the mutual construction of difference between various societies, including study abroad students' home and host societies (see the introduction question series W, X, Y, and Z).

Labeling Certain Acts as Immersion

With regard to the act of labeling certain acts as immersion, we should encourage students to think that the label is not an objective one to describe students as "living like a local" but a loaded label that tells us the labeler's perception about the person doing the immersion, the people among whom that person is immersed, and the relationships between them. Therefore, we should focus students' reflections on how they label certain acts as immersion. We can ask the students to identify acts they felt as "immersion" and the acts they did not feel as "immersion" and ask questions during their stay and/or after their study abroad experience regarding (1) the notion of immersion itself, (2) the perception of the person doing the immersion, (3) the perception of the people among whom a study abroad student immerses themself, (4) the perception of the relationships between the person doing the immersion and the people among whom the person is immersing, and (5) the act of labeling certain actions as immersion in general. Example questions are listed in the question series 4-A at the end of this chapter.

With these questions, we can hope to engage students in thinking critically about the effects of the immersion discourse and of the act of labeling something immersion. We can pick and choose the questions suggested above and come up with more locally specific, locally relevant questions.

Avoiding Imagining the Host Society as Homogeneous

The notion of immersion encourages the imagining of the host society as homogeneous. That homogeneous space is perceived as that of the "locals," which is then valorized in relation to "outsider space" occupied by study abroad students as well as other visitors like tourists. Avoiding the latter (i.e., "outsider space") allowed one to be part of the former, the imagined homogeneous host society, allegedly authentically immersing oneself (see chapter 5).

When encouraging students to immerse themselves in the host society, I instead suggest highlighting the diverse spaces of the host society, where "the locals," who are diverse themselves, mingle with visitors and sojourners. Instead of viewing the study abroad encounter as dropping a student with a particular cultural background into a homogeneous host society of a different "culture," we can think of the host society as a space where diverse participants co-construct the life there (see Massey 2005).

What is perceived as "difference" between the student's home and host societies is mutually constructed, an issue raised for students in chapter 1 in the question series 1-G. To explore the diversity within the host society, we can use questions I introduced in chapter 1 as series 1-C. For the diversity within the student's home society, we can use the question series 1-D in chapter 1. For the notion of immersion in particular, however, see questions introduced at the end of this chapter as the series 4-B for the effects of the discourse of immersion on the constructed view of the student's home and host societies.

Connecting Daily Activities to Structural Arrangements

In order to capitalize on the merit of the discourse of immersion—its close attention to daily activities—inspired by Freirean approach of the critical pedagogy, we can ask students questions regarding how various daily acts are effects of structural arrangements and how we can change them. For example, we can ask students during and after their studying abroad what they routinely did, for example, after waking up or before going to bed and choose one act and ask in-depth questions. For example, we can ask following questions regarding water use:

(a) How often have you showered/bathed while you were studying abroad? Was it more frequent than local people you knew (e.g., host family, local students)? How? Why?
(b) How long was your shower? Do you think others had showers of the same length? Were you told to have a shower within a certain length of time?
(c) Was there water in abundance or did you have to make sure to leave water for others?
(d) Did you have hot water? Did the hot water run out while showering? How do they heat water?
(e) Where does the water come from? Who pays for it?
(f) Do you think everyone in the community has the same access to (hot) water? How about in the country? If not, what makes the difference?

(g) What were the effects of the government regulations on water use? What were the effects of international agreements, regulations, etc. on it? What were the effects of (multinational) corporations on it?

(h) Do local people want the situation to be changed? How?

(i) What do you think you can do to change the situation? As a citizen of your own country? As a consumer? As a visitor to their country?

(j) How does this all compare to how you shower/bathe in your home country? (If there are differences) What do you think makes the difference?

We can then ask them the same questions about their home countries, which would allow them to develop comparative perspectives as well as the awareness that this way of thinking can be applied to any settings, including their own home society. For the effects of structural arrangements in constructing "differences" between students' home and host society, we can ask questions suggested at the end of chapter 1 as the series 1-G and in chapter 2 as the series 2-C. Questions listed at the end of chapter 2 as the series 2-A as well as at the end of chapter 7 as the series 7-Z can provide similar questions that can be used to address how our daily life is shaped by structural arrangements.

Answering these kinds of questions may require some research and interviewing. Therefore, these questions can be given to students as a kind of assignment for them to work on rather than questions to be answered on the spot. Various topics—clothes they wear, kinds of food they eat and how, kinds of transportation they use, and so on—can be used depending on the contexts and students' interest.

Despite its prominence as a notion in study abroad, the discourse of immersion has not been critically analyzed except to determine its effectiveness as a learning method. Neither the discourse's effects on imaginings of study abroad students' home and host societies and the relationships between them, nor its creation of a hierarchy of experience, nor the effects of labeling an act immersion have been much discussed. While urging students to be critical of these effects, this chapter, following what I started in the introduction, has suggested two new applications of the notion of immersion: its attention to daily activities can be harnessed to examine daily construction of difference and to analyze how students' daily lives are shaped by the wider social, economic, political, and cultural forces with an eye for changing them.

Recommended Readings

Doerr, Neriko. 2013. "Do 'Global Citizens' Need the Parochial Cultural Other? Discourses of Study Abroad and Learning by Doing." *Compare* 43 (2): 224–243.
Critical discussion of the discourse of immersion and its effects.

Doerr, Neriko. 2016. "Chronotopes of Study Abroad: The Cultural Other, Immersion, and Compartmentalized Space-Time." *Journal of Cultural Geography* 33(1): 80–99.
Critical discussion of the dual construction of the host society space by the notion of immersion.

Doerr, Neriko, and Richard Suarez. 2018. "Immersion, Immigration, Immutability: Regimes of Learning and Politics of Labeling in Study Abroad." *Educational Studies* 54 (2): 183–197.
Discussion of what it means to label certain acts as immersion.

Lave, Jean, and Etienne Wenger. 1991. *Situated Learning: Legitimate Peripheral Participation*. Cambridge: Cambridge University Press.
Discussion of learning through experience by participating in the community of practice.

Talburt, Susan, and Melissa A. Stewart. 1999. "What's the Subject of Study Abroad? Race, Gender and Living Culture." *Modern Language Journal* 82 (2): 163–175.
Discussion of the diverse immersion experience of study abroad students from different ethnic backgrounds.

◖◉ Activity: Daorba Yduts

Table 4.1 Keyword List

verb	noun	adjective	phrase
adventure	adventure	cross-cultural	add another level to my xxx
broaden	awareness	exciting	amaze myself
challenge	border crossing	experiential	better myself as a person
discover	comfort zone	fantastic	broaden my xxx
embark	connections	holistic	build valuable skills
engage	journey	incredible	change lives
enhance	leader	independent	change the world
explore	life knowledge	innovative	enable me to learn in a new way
immerse	memory	life-changing	expand my world
inspire	new perspectives	meaningful	gain new perspectives
motivate	new skills	stimulating	learn about myself
	opportunity	stronger	open my eyes to new xxx
	passion	transformative	open the door to
	personal growth	world-class	see the world
	positive impact		sipping a cup of xxx
	rewarding experience		stay with me for the rest of my life
	self-reliance		think and live differently
			xxx of lifetime

Instructions
(1) Prepare a list of study abroad keywords (see Table 4.1). Divide the keywords into three or four categories (noun, verb, adjective, phrases).
(2) Suggest a group of students (regardless of their study abroad experience) to think of something they did for the first time this past week (if the focus of the activity is the critique of study abroad narrative, which may be also relevant to the discussion in chapter 7, this length can be twenty-four hours).
(3) Ask students to write a paragraph or so about that new experience using three keywords and phrases from each category. Give them about ten minutes to write it.
(4) Ask students to share what they wrote with the group. Discuss what that practice made them become aware of.

Example answer (keywords in italics)
I made cold brew coffee for the first time. I was *motivated* to *try something new* and making the coffee *broadened my knowledge* on the various

coffee types. It was an *experiential* process, and the result was better than I expected. It tasted great and was cheaper than purchasing it at Starbucks. The result could honestly *change lives*. It is stronger than regular coffee and kept me energetic longer than hot brew coffee. This *transformative* process was made possible with coffee grounds, a mason jar, cold water, and a filter. The making of the coffee *helped me build valuable skills* that will *forever change my breakfast game*. I highly recommend *exploring* the *incredible* world of cold brew coffee. You won't be disappointed with this *rewarding experience*.

Questions for highlighting the othering processes in daily life (discussed in subsection *Daily Othering Processes*)
(a) Did you really feel as you described here about learning to make cold brew? Has your life really changed?
(b) Have you ever thought it could be a very exciting and meaningful learning experience?
(c) How different would it be if you learned how to make cold brew while you were studying abroad in Italy or France or Ghana or Korea? Would you have thought it is an exciting learning experience?
(d) If there is any difference between (b) and (c), what made the difference? What made you feel that new experience is not so meaningful when you did it at home (if that was the case)? What would make you notice and celebrate that new experience if you did it while studying abroad (if that was the case)?
(e) If that new experience were connected to the study abroad destination (e.g., coffee or cold brew and Italy, France, or Ghana), would that new experience highlight the difference of that destination from your home country?
(f) In our daily life, what serves as something that pushes us to notice certain experience as meaningful or marking different lifestyles of different people?
(g) What would push us to notice "new" and "different" experience in our daily life more?

Questions for highlighting how our daily practices are shaped by structural forces (discussed in subsection *Not Just Cultural but Also Structural*)
(a) You said you have never made cold brew. Why do you think that is? What stopped you from making cold brew before?
(b) If it is a new thing in the United States, who brought it there? Why? What are the effects on different groups of people—coffee importers, coffee roasters, coffee shop owners, consumers? Who makes

more money from this introduction? Who loses money from this introduction? If this creates inequality and inequity, how could we change it? As voting citizens, as consumers, and as community members?

(c) Can anybody make cold brew? Who can and who cannot? How are these differential accesses structured? Money? Leisure time? Accessibility to stores that would sell the tools? Accessibility to the information? How about around the world? People in what country would not be able to make cold brew?

(d) Is there any connotation attached to making cold brew? Can this then become a status symbol? Any political statement?

◖◖ Sample Questions

4-A1: The Notion of Immersion
4-A1-1: Do you think all acts of "living like the locals" constitute immersion? What acts do you think are more likely to be considered immersion than others? For you to use knives and forks [if they are commonly used in the destination]? For you to use chopsticks [if they are commonly used in the destination]? For you to watch local TV show there? For you to watch American TV show there? Why (not)? What has influenced your views?

4-A1-2: How were you told to immerse yourself? What kind of activities were encouraged in study abroad promotional materials and by people in the study abroad programs and offices?

4-A1-3: How did this advice shape your preparation for and experience of study abroad?

4-A1-4: Are you glad that you received this advice? In what way? Did you feel that some of the advice was not helpful? When?

4-A2: The Perception of the Person Doing the Immersion
4-A2-1: Do you think immigrants immerse themselves when they live like the people in the society? Do you call that immersion? Why (not)? What is the difference between that and immersion by study abroad students?

4-A2-2: Do you think that a businessperson sojourning in a particular society and learning to live like the people there is considered immersed? Do you call that immersion? Why (not)? What is the difference between that and immersion by study abroad students?

4-A2-3: Do you think students pursuing an academic degree are immersed? Do you call that immersion? Why (not)? What is the difference between that and immersion by study abroad students?

4-A2-4: What does that tell you about the concept of immersion?

4-A3: The Perception of the People among Whom a Study Abroad Student Immerses Themself
4-A3-1: Was there ever a time when you were learning to do things like the people you met there but did not think these acts were immersion? When? Why?

4-A3-2: Is there any host family with whom living would not be an immersion experience? Why?

4-A3-3: If your host family is of the dominant ethnic background, is staying with them immersion? Why (not)? What makes the difference?

Do you think people have different opinions about that? What makes the difference?

4-A3-4: If your host family is of a minority ethnic background, is staying with them immersion? Why (not)? What makes the difference? Do you think people have different opinions about that? What makes the difference?

4-A3-5: If your host family is of immigrant background, is staying with them immersion? Why (not)? What makes the difference? Do you think people have different opinions about that? What makes the difference?

4-A3-6: If your host family is in a higher socioeconomic class, is it immersion? Why (not)? What makes the difference? Do you think people have different opinions about that? What makes the difference?

4-A3-7: If your host family is in a lower socioeconomic class, is it immersion? Why (not)? What makes the difference? Do you think people have different opinions about that? What makes the difference?

4-A3-8: What does that tell you about the concept of immersion?

4-A4: The Perception of the Relationships between the Person Doing the Immersion and the People among Whom the Person Is Immersing

4-A4-1: If your host family's ethnic background is similar to yours, is it immersion? Why (not)? What makes the difference? Do you think people have different opinions about that? What makes the difference?

4-A4-2: If your host family's socioeconomic background is similar to yours, is it immersion? Why (not)? What makes the difference? Do you think people have different opinions about that? What makes the difference?

4-A4-3: If your host family are friends of your family, is it immersion? Why (not)? What makes the difference? Do you think people have different opinions about that? What makes the difference?

4-A4-4: If your host family consists of your relatives, is it immersion? Why (not)? What makes the difference? Do you think people have different opinions about that? What makes the difference?

4-A5: The Notion of Immersion and Students Accommodation

4-A5-1: It is often suggested that if the aim is immersion, staying with a host family is better than staying in a hostel. What did you think about that?

4-A5-2: How did that perception influence the way you acted when studying abroad?

4-A5-3: Based on your observations, how would you compare students who stayed with a host family to students who stayed in a hostel?

4-A5-4: It is often suggested that staying for a semester is more conducive to immersion experience than staying for several weeks. What did you think about that? Do you think it's true? Why (not)?

4-A5-5: How did that perception influence the way you acted when studying abroad?

4-A6: The Act of Labeling Certain Actions as Immersion
4-A6-1: What do the answers to the above questions tell you about the concept of immersion?

4-B: Constructed View of the Student's Home and Host Societies
4-B1: What did you think when you were told not to be on the internet all the time?

4-B2: Do you think people in the host society use the internet to access various things from around the world? Do they do this less than you do? Why?

4-B3: Do you feel that your home society is more globalized than the host society? How? What makes you feel that way?

4-B4: Do you feel that people in the host society lack global competence? What makes you (not) think that? What do you think is global competence?

4-B5: Do you feel that people in the host society are not global citizens? What makes you (not) think that? What do you think is global citizen?

4-B6: Did you do any "touristic" things during your study abroad stay? What were they? What did you learn from them?

4-B7: What do you think makes these activities touristic?

4-B8: Do you think people in the host society engage in these activities? If yes, why do you think they are considered touristic?

4-B9: What are the connotations of calling something touristic? Why do you think something is called touristic?

4-B9-X: What are the effects of calling certain acts touristic? Who gets privileged by that? Who gets marginalized?

4-B10: How do you think the concept of immersion influences that process? How can we change it? What does that tell you about the concept of immersion?

4-B11: It is sometimes suggested that people learn more outside the classroom than in it. What did you think about that? How did it influence the way you acted when studying abroad?

4-B12: Where do you think you learned more: in the classroom or outside it?

4-B13: What things did you tend to learn in the classroom?

4-B14: What things did you tend to learn outside the classroom?

4-B15: What advice would you give other students about balancing time spent learning inside and outside the classroom?

4-B16: Do you feel outside-classroom learning should be guided? How? Why?

4-B17: What do you think are the effects of the opinion that learning outside of class is better than classroom learning?

4-B18: Do you think that people in the host society regard learning outside the classroom as better than classroom learning? For study abroad students? For their own students? Why the difference (if answers differ)?

4-B19: Do you think there are diverse views about this? What makes the difference?

4-B19-X: Whose viewpoints are privileged? Whose viewpoints do you think are erased?

4-B20: Does learning outside the classroom during study abroad differ from learning outside the classroom in your home country?

4-B21: What does that tell us about the school systems (i.e., classroom learning) in the host society and your home society?

5

HOST SOCIETY AND HOST FAMILY
Who Are They, and Who Shapes Their Lives?

Imagine a street in Paris, a plaza in Tuscany, a side street in Shanghai, a market in Kinshasa, a train station in Wellington. What language do you hear spoken by passing people? What religion do they follow? Where were they born? Who are they? How would they identify themselves? What shapes their lives? And how do you think students would answer these questions before, during, and after their study abroad stay in that place?

The host society is a specific space that is imagined, arranged, and managed in particular ways in relation to the discourses of study abroad, especially that of immersion, discussed in chapter 4. The image of the host society is tied to the specific notion of time in study abroad—that is, a demarcated duration with a clear beginning and end. And a host family is often viewed as the ideal base in the host society during the study abroad trip. But is that really the case? Is staying with the host family the best way to learn about the host society? Is the host family's life typical of all people in the host society, and is it "authentic"? Is the host family always very different from student's own family? This chapter discusses discourses of the host society with a special focus on the host family. Below, I will point out assumptions about the host society and host family, introduce studies that challenge such assumptions, and suggest alternative ways to understand and talk about a host society and host family. At the end of the chapter, I suggest questions to ask students as well as host family members.

The Host Society

As was discussed in chapters 2 and 4, the discourse of "immersion" argues that students best learn about the host society by immersing themselves in daily life. Spending time with compatriot students—in the classroom, traveling, going out at night—is not considered immersion and is discouraged (Chieffo and Griffiths 2004; Deardorff 2009; Hovey and Weinberg 2009). By valorizing physical interaction with anyone present at the destination, the discourse of immersion suggests that the host society is homogeneous (as they all are seen to be different from the students and thus learning experience). And by devaluing time spent with fellow compatriot students, it suggests that the home society is likewise homogeneous, as its members can offer nothing new to each other. Situated in the ideology of nation-state, this discourse of immersion helps shape imaginings of the space-time of the host society. I have argued elsewhere (Doerr 2016) that two types of space-time are held in tension: the homogeneous space filled with the host society's people, and heterogeneous space where people of the host society and outsiders coexist. In the next subsections, I describe what they are and the relationships between them.

The Homogeneous Space-Time of Insiders

One view of the host society depicts it as a homogeneous space where every minute is full of learning through immersion (see chapter 4). Study abroad students I interviewed also portrayed the host society as being filled by the people of the host society. Perceiving all the people on the streets of Paris as "local," despite the city being one of the world's biggest tourist destinations, one student viewed them as models as well as judges of how much she was "fitting in": she not only copied their appearance and behavior as "the local style" but also measured her successes in passing as local from the reactions of people in that space.

In the homogeneous space of the host society, study abroad time is "full" time. Everything and everyone that students encounter there is considered "local"; therefore, experiencing them is considered learning that is meaningful and hence "full." Regarding everything around her as Spanish, another student considered everything she did in Spain—including getting lost—a learning experience about Spain. It was impossible to waste time because everything was learning experience. Everything one does in the host society is viewed as "authentic" experience.

The Heterogeneous Space-Time of Insider and Outsider Space

The second type of space-time in the host society is a heterogeneous space where the space of locals (people of the host society) and that of outsiders (students and tourists from abroad) coexist, though they are positioned hierarchically. Study abroad students stressed that they tried to avoid the latter "space of outsiders." Students I interviewed talked about avoiding fellow American students who hung out among themselves wearing stereotypically American clothes and talking loudly (which is considered very "American"), or the space of dorms or bars where American students hung out, partying on their own.

Students viewed the time spent in such "outsider space" (what I call "wasted time") negatively in a zero-sum game of apportioning the limited, demarcated time of study abroad. The discourse of immersion views outsider space as a comfort zone (along with "home," to which students connect via technologies like the phone and internet) to which students can escape (see chapter 4). The narrative about avoiding outsider space-time implies that they exist everywhere around study abroad students, who thus need to make conscious efforts to avoid it. One student perceived two types of fellow American students: those who learn (in the "local space") and those who party (in the "outsider space"). Being critical of the latter relieved the former of any suspicion that they might not be "good study abroad students."

Their conscious positioning of themselves as engaging in local space-time by narrating how they avoided outsider space-time suggests that being in the host society itself does not automatically constitute having "authentic" experience and thus learning experience, in contradiction to the first image that the host society is nothing but local space-time. That is, here, the existence of outsider space-time allows students to highlight their proactive involvement in local space-time.

Productive Tension between Two Images of Host-Society Space-Time

The first and second images of the host society's space-time coexist in a productive tension. The first evokes an ideal state, the existence of the nothing-but-local. While depending on the existence of this ideal space, in the second image, the coexistence of local and outsider space-times allows students to differentiate and hierarchize themselves as either active participants in local space-time or nonpartici-pants, and to identify themselves with whichever group they want. This tension is inherent in the worldview that considers each space to be occupied by a particular homogeneous group—an outlook that informs the discourses of nation-state, immersion, and travel writing (see chapters 1, 2, and 4). Moving through such space is necessarily contradictory: even as one's presence as a visitor changes the configu-ration of the supposedly homogeneous destination, one still seeks to see the destination as homogeneous, exclusive of the visitor (oneself).

Anthropologists too have struggled with this contradiction. The concept of participant observation was first developed as a unique ethnographic method of anthropology—the anthropologist engages with the community and learns "natives' point of view" (as a "participant") while retaining "outsider's" viewpoint, comparing what they see with cases from other places and in relation to abstract theories (as an "observer"). While the notion of "participant" also indicated that the presence of an anthropologist transforms what they are observing (e.g., people may become self-conscious of their actions, try to present themselves to look in certain ways, etc.), anthropologists tended to see societies as independent realities to be observed and an ethnography as an objective description of them. This began to change in the 1980s, as the critic of anthropology James Clifford (1986) pointed out the need to see societies portrayed in an ethnography as a result of co-construction by both the observer and the observed (see chapter 2). Similarly, I suggest encouraging students to examine and recognize study abroad not as an encounter between two distinct "cultures" in which the study abroad student immerses themself in the host society but rather as diverse individuals joining in the ongoing production of heterogeneous life in the host society, as will be detailed at the end of this chapter.

The Host Family

Anthropologists analyze interactions between the host and the guests/tourists as marked by "strangerhood" (Nash 1989: 45), the host's "emotional labor" to cater to the guests (Hochschild 1983), the immobility of the host and the mobility of the guest (Clifford 2007), and often the economic hierarchy between the host and the guest (Nash 1989). In cultural tourism specifically, the host is expected to embody cultural otherness through self-commodification: "any type of product performance that requires the individual to adjust [their] values, emotions, or both, to achieve an economic goal" (Bunten 2008: 381). Hosts who create self-commodified persona—for example, tour guides who embody the "culture" they are presenting—however, often have agency in controlling how to respond to the tourist gaze, acting as cultural brokers (Bunten 2008).

Positioned as "education," the study abroad context nonetheless differs from cultural tourism and thus this host-guest relation. First, the host is positioned as teachers of the "culture" of the destination, which students are to copy and adjust to, as opposed to becoming voyeurs that is common in cultural tourism, especially in "traditional" study abroad destinations. Second, while tour guides can compartmentalize their performance as the cultural Other, a host family's performance, if there is any, is usually nonstop. Third, while interactions between the host and the guest are usually dictated by "strangerhood" (Nash 1989: 45) in tourism, host family and study abroad students seek to act as family members.

In study abroad, the host family is often portrayed as the quintessential representation of the host society, especially in the discourse of immersion (see chapter 4). Study abroad guidebooks rave about staying with a host family. It is "a great way to acclimate to the culture" by getting "to eat what the locals eat, sleep like locals sleep, and interact with the locals on a daily basis, from the time you wake up to the time you pass out in utter exhaustion" (Williamson 2004: 195, 235). You can also practice the language: indeed, "you can't have a more authentic experience than with a host family. There is absolutely no better way to learn a culture and language than to live with a family and experience their day-to-day life" (235). Researchers agree (Goldoni 2013; Jackson 2009; Raymond and Hall 2008).

Students often also consider staying with a host family an ideal type of immersion experience: "Those students who did participate in a home stay tended to be more vocal about the rewards of their experience abroad than those who lived in dorms. They believed their immersion in the culture was beneficial" (Loflin 2007: 14). There is value in staying with a host family as an entry point to the host society, as an occasion to meet and get to know some people in the host society, and as experience of living with some people in the host society. Relationships developed with host family members can endure and flourish throughout one's lifetime. A homestay experience highlights some benefits of study abroad experience.

Blanket valorization of host family experience, however, can lead to problematic understandings of the host society. In the following subsections, I introduce existing research in study abroad, much of it focused on language acquisition though applicable in other areas, that identifies and challenges four problematic assumptions behind discourses that idealize host family experience: (1) staying with a host family is the best way to learn, (2) the host family represents the entire host society, (3) the host family provides students with "authentic" experience of the host society, and (4) the study abroad student and the host family are different. Seeing some value in staying with a host family, I will also offer suggestions about how to turn away from these assumptions and move toward alternative discourses.

Assumption 1: Staying with a Host Family Is the Best Way to Learn

Many researchers suggest that staying with host families is one of the best ways to learn while studying abroad (Deardorff 2009; Hovey and Weinberg 2009). Host families can provide valuable learning experience about the host society and language (Goldoni 2013; Jackson 2009; Raymond and Hall 2008). Some report that members of the host family act as "informal teachers" (Fobes 2005: 184) who help their students with homework and with shopping and bargaining at markets, and encourage them in their language practice. Host families also act as advocates and surrogate parents for study abroad students, providing them with much-needed support (Lindenberg 2015). Andrew Cohen and colleagues (2005) suggest that host family members serve as guides while students adjust to the host society, noting that pre-trip orientation and guidebooks affected adjustment levels only for students who did not stay in a host family.

However, staying with a host family does not necessarily guarantee "the best" learning experience. Three major factors contribute to differences in learning outcomes of staying with a host family. The first is the amount of engagement and time spent with that family (Vande Berg et al. 2009). However, the amount of interaction with locals affects students' learning outcomes in complex ways. Homestay students gained more oral linguistic proficiency than students who did not study abroad *only* when they spent abundant time with the host family (Vande Berg 2009). Some students who spent a lot of time with the local population were overwhelmed and ended up becoming more ethnocentric (Vande Berg et al. 2009).

The second factor is the student's attitude. "Colonial students" is the term Anthony Ogden (2007, 2008) uses to describe critically those who take an interest in the host society but remain reluctant to leave their comfort zone and give up their amenities. The degree of a student's outgoingness or shyness mattered as well: shy students found it harder to learn by staying with the host family (Kinginger 2008; Taguchi 2008; Yashima et al. 2004). Students' attachment to their own ethnicity mattered too, as it could result in reluctance to adopt new ways of acting from people in the host society (Wilkinson 1998).

The third factor is the host family's attitude, including their willingness to develop a good rapport with the student (Popadiuk 2009; Yashima et al. 2004) and spend time with them. For example, one host family may choose to spend much time discussing prevalent practices in the host society and explaining them to students, whereas another might leave the student alone most of the time, ignore them by mostly watching TV, and provide only instant food (Kinginger 2008). It is worth noting here that if this happens to be how the hosts usually live, then the student is really experiencing an "authentic" local daily life. This may also raise the question of a good or bad match between the student and the host family: some students appreciate being left alone with their own free time (Mendelson 2004). In short, staying with a host family does not automatically guarantee the most effective learning experience.

Assumption 2: The Host Family Represents the Entire Host Society

One of the most prevalent assumptions about a host family is that it represents the entire host society. This view stems from the idea that individuals are human vessels that reflect and express the group's gestalt, which likewise assumes homogeneity within the group (Iino 2006). Actually, however, the host family members are a specific type of people. As noted earlier, the "ideal" host family needs to have extra time to spend with students and extra space for them to stay in. If the host family is uncompensated, they need extra cash to support the expense of the student's food and transportation. A host family must also live in a safe neighborhood, a factor that often reflects their income level (Doerr and Suarez 2018). This all leads to a tendency for host families to be middle class. Further, the "ideal" host family is often, though not always, imagined as a heterosexual nuclear family. A single-parent household, for example, often is not considered an "ideal" situation (Doerr 2009b).

Moreover, a host family is likely to exhibit specific tendencies such as openness to strangers, different lifestyles, and novel perceptions (Doerr and Suarez 2018). Not everyone in the host society lets strangers into their home and/or is interested in interacting with people from different cultural backgrounds. Host families who express racist views—for example, by requesting only white students—are usually rejected by the study abroad program (Doerr 2016). Though I would condone limiting host families to those that are open-minded and unprejudiced, it is important to acknowledge that such a filtering process restricts host families to those who pass the test and therefore represent an "ideal" part of the society. Comparing the homestay situation to an ethnographer's experience during fieldwork, Federica Goldoni (2013: 371) further suggests that local people who befriend study abroad students are "those who are culturally marginalized within their own society," as people in the host society usually already have their own circle of friends and thus do not seek out study abroad students to befriend. In this way also, a host family is not representative of the host society.

Given the specificities of host family people as members of the middle class and often of the dominant ethnic group as well, saying a host family is representative of the host society actually erases the legitimacy, if not the very existence, of other members of the host society. Here, as I suggested in chapter 4, it is important to encourage families of nondominant backgrounds to become host families. Not only would this help students understand the diversity of their study abroad destination, but it would also produce images of the host society that are more accurate, and foster equitable relations by including marginalized groups in national imaginings.

I would thus call for creating an alternative discourse depicting host families as specific individuals with spare time and space who are willing to engage with study abroad students, rather than as representatives of the entire society. What students experience in that society is interaction with this specific type of people. As one can never interact with everyone in the society, it is fine to acknowledge this; it becomes problematic only if we ignore this aspect of experience and assume that the host family is representative of the entire host society.

Assumption 3: Host Families Provide Students with "Authentic" Host Society Experience

Another prevalent assumption is that host families provide students with "authentic" experience of the host society (Iino 2006; see also Mendelson 2004). This assumption prevails in many studies (Jackson 2009; for the "voluntourism" context, see Raymond and Hall 2008). Here, I use the term "authentic" to mean that family members did not change their behavior because of the student's presence. The term is actually problematic because it assumes that all members of the society share something unchanging, whereas in fact everything changes and the host society is diverse. Also, most problematic is the process of authentication itself: who has the right and power to claim what is authentic and what is not. Still, I use the term "authentic" for the sake of convenience here, turning the focus to whether host family members modified their behavior because of the student's presence, following the implication when it is used in the context involved.

"Authenticity" has been critiqued because a host family usually modifies their daily routines when a student is staying with them. Researchers report that some host families made extra effort to spend generous quality time with students or otherwise "went out of their way to ensure that the students staying with them felt comfortable and had a rich and memorable experience" (Goldoni 2013: 370; see also Doerr 2013a; Iino 2006). If the student is treated as a guest, hosts serve more expensive food rather than junk food or leftovers, and the home tends to be tidier and cleaner than usual (Iino 2006). A host family may also seek to accommodate the student's needs, for example, by serving food they feel students would prefer. Sometimes they intentionally serve food seen as closer to the students' home society (e.g., hamburgers for American students or rice for Thai students). A vegetarian student must be served vegetarian food, even if it is a considerable departure from the hosts' daily diet (Doerr 2013a; Knight and Schmidt-Rinehart 2002).

The language a host family uses in the presence of the student often differs in various ways from their usual talk. They may speak slowly and clearly to students who are learning the language, or intentionally use "textbook expressions," rather than colloquial terms, to make it easier for the student to understand (Doerr 2013a). Furthermore, the language variety that hosts use when speaking to students often differs from the local linguistic variety the family usually uses. In the case of Japanese host families in Kyoto, Masakazu Iino (2006) reports that even though many of them wrote in a questionnaire that they believed the Tokyo variety on which standard Japanese is based was the appropriate speech variety to use with the student, they tended to use neither the Kyoto nor the Tokyo variety but rather "foreigner talk" with simplified sentence structures, easier words, and more foreign loan words that differed from both. Similarly, conversation patterns between host family members and the student differ from common patterns among "native speakers": classroom conversational patterns remain in host family–student conversation because the student (a "non-native speaker") talks with the host family ("native speakers") as if the latter were teachers, as mentioned, and expects and accepts the host family to correct their speech if they made some mistakes (Wilkinson 2002).

The relationship between student and host family is also governed by particular, often unspoken rules that keep the host family experience from being "authentic." For example, one understanding is that the student, as someone who is being cared for, should be grateful to the host family as the care provider and therefore should avoid confrontation with the family (Iino 2006). Such an unwritten rule has a positive effect. Tomoko Yashima and colleagues (2004) argue that the relationships a student develops with a host family affect their gains throughout the study abroad experience. It is important that students are confident and thus comfortable spending a lot of time engaged with the host family. Students' confidence and comfort—including willingness to engage with the host family, openness to sharing their feelings with others, and lack of anxiety about their linguistic proficiency—derive not only from their own personalities but also from the host family's willingness to spend time engaging with the student, it is argued (for how shyness affects the quality and quantity of interaction, see Taguchi 2008).

Life with a host family is also governed by roles assigned to the student and the family members. Hosts are expected to follow family member roles—host father/mother, host son/daughter, host brother/sister. Students, for their part, are sometimes expected to play the role not only of a family member but also of a "foreigner," acting and talking like a foreigner. Fluent speech in the language of the destination can even be considered inappropriate because it defies the expectations of the role (Iino 2006). Some people in the host society may regard a student who talks with "native-like" fluency in the host society's language as perplexing, rude, and uncomfortable to talk to (Wilkinson 2002). Though assuming the first role, that of family member, would make the student's experience more "authentic," the role of "foreigner" would not.

Lastly, it is crucial to note that every homestay ends after a couple of weeks or several months or so, which renders tolerable things that would, in a long-term relationship, be intolerable (Iino 2006). In this regard, interactions between the student and the host family differ from what "local" family members would do. All this goes to show that what study abroad students experience is not how a host family usually lives but rather how it lives with a guest in the home. I thus suggest viewing the host family space as a hybrid space where residents accommodate each other in ad hoc ways according to how they perceive each other's "cultural background" and needs. In this perspective, living with a host family is not "living *like* a local" but "living *with* locals" who modify their daily routine to cater to their student guest.

As a framework, then, a view of study abroad experience as "living like a local" risks perceiving the study abroad student as being dropped into a host society's unchanging, static life, rather than as participating in the ongoing dynamics of life in the host society. At the micro level, meanwhile, housing a student changes the host family's daily routine. It is vital to alert students to this fact in order to discourage them from seeing the host society as static when instead they can view that society as changing constantly, and themselves as involved in those changes (see chapter 4).

Assumption 4: The Study Abroad Student and the Host Family Are Different

The study abroad student and the host family are typically assumed to be different (Iino 2006), based on the understanding that student's home society is fundamentally different from their study abroad host society, in line with the nation-state ideology of unique, internally homogeneous nations (see chapter 1). The assumption of difference between the student and the host family makes staying with the host family meaningful as a sustained interaction with difference. If the host family lives just like your own family, you will not learn much; therefore, there is little point in living with them. This assumption links to the discourse of immersion, which discourages students from staying at a hostel with their student compatriots (Hovey and Weinberg 2009). Because much learning is supposed to occur through "immersion" outside the classroom in study abroad, learning and recognition of difference are intrinsically connected: the moment of learning is often identified as the moment of encountering difference. Recognition of a different way of behaving (e.g., forbearing smiling at strangers in France lest it be taken as flirting) is considered a moment of learning (Doerr 2017b), as will be discussed in chapter 6.

Any distinct "cultural difference" and "sameness" between the student and the host family is neither given nor static—rather, it is constructed by being sanctioned in the host family space, as I have argued elsewhere (Doerr 2013a). This is paradoxically linked to how the host family does or does not tolerate certain behaviors of the student. On the one hand, behavior that is perceived to be rooted in cultural or linguistic difference is tolerated, and host parents change their behavior to accommodate the student's needs in this regard. For example, host mothers in Aotearoa/New Zealand reported trying to speak English slowly and clearly, sometimes even writing things down or using "textbook" expressions to non-Anglophone study abroad students. One host mother served rice to Thai students every day, and another brought meals to a Japanese student's room in the middle of the night, perceiving these acts as accommodations of "cultural difference."

On the other hand, host parents did not tolerate behavior that they did not feel was based on "cultural difference." For example, host mothers of students in Aotearoa/New Zealand cited such difficulties as a Japanese student hiding pornography in his room, a Korean student behaving aggressively and rudely by kicking a hole in the wall when told she could not go to a party she wanted to attend and by never saying "please," and a male Iranian student treating female teachers, students, and host family members as inferiors and engaging in what was considered sexual harassment. In all these cases, the student ultimately had to move out of the host family's home. Responding to some lesser "problems," host mothers asked students to change their behavior, for example by taking shorter showers. These mothers saw these not as culturally based behaviors but as behaviors that could also be seen among teenagers in Aotearoa/New Zealand. That is, while host parents hoped study abroad students would accept "our way of life," they discouraged some sameness (Doerr 2013a).

In short, the host family's household is a space where "cultural difference" is negotiated and managed, and where what is different and what is the same—or what behavior is "culturally" inspired and what is not—are negotiated by being sanctioned differently. For example, it is unclear whether the Korean student's nonuse of "please" was "culturally/linguistically" inspired. The Korean language does not have a stand-alone equivalent to the word "please." Politeness is instead conveyed by using a verbal ending (e.g., *hae juseyo*). There is an adverb, *chebal*, that is translated as "please," but it is inappropriate to use in ordinary situations because it is specifically reserved for situations of pleading, such as when your life is threatened. Thus, the Korean student's not saying "please" may have been because of how Korean language is structured. Nonetheless, the host parents did not consider this a "culturally" inspired difference and assumed that the student shared their own code of behavior and was merely being rude (Doerr 2013a).

This understanding of the constructedness of "cultural difference" between the student and the host family goes squarely against the assumption that students are immersing themselves in the host society with a different "culture."

Engaging Students in Critical Examination of Their Life with a Host Family

It is important that we reflect on our assumptions about what a host society is like and what it means to stay with a host family, and teach students to be equally reflective. In this section, following the points made above, I suggest urging students to think about these notions critically by considering two sets of questions about the host society and four sets of questions about the host family (see the end of the chapter for example questions). For each topic, as described in the introduction, questions about (W) subject positions, (X) power relations, (Y) how society has been changing and we can change it, and (Z) mutual construction of difference between various societies, including study abroad students' home and host societies, can also be asked.

The Host Society: Constantly Changing and Being Co-Constructed by Diverse People

To deal with the image of the host society, I suggest perceiving it anew: not as a static homogeneous society but as a society that changes constantly via co-construction by diverse people occupying and moving through the space.

I suggest advancing this understanding, first, by encouraging students to examine prevalent perceptions and reflect on how their study abroad experience was shaped by specific setups and various discourses in relations of power. Study abroad providers can ask further questions, customized to their own students and their study abroad destinations, about how the students' perceptions affect the ways they spend time in local/outsider space-times, how other students and local people view them, how these views reflect what is perceived as learning and how we legitimize studying abroad, how these views relate to the discourse of immersion, how relations of power are involved in the process, and so forth. Questions in series 1-C and 1-D (see chapter 1) can alert students to ways in which representations of the host society and home society, respectively, suggest that these societies are internally homogeneous, when in fact they are heterogeneous inside.

Second, we can urge students to perceive the study abroad experience not as an encounter between two bounded "cultures," as implied by the discourse of immersion, but as diverse study abroad students joining in the ongoing production of life and meanings in the host society's space, which is heterogeneous (see chapter 4). Instead of seeing the host society's space as a static, homogeneous space of the cultural Other, we can view it as heterogeneous space, and students abroad as participants in its ongoing co-production. And instead of freezing time and viewing people met during study abroad time as forever doing what they were seen doing then, we can view a study abroad sojourn not as moving across space-as-surface but as crossing paths with people in their ongoing life, and participating in the continuing production of the space as travelers, who alter the space (Massey 2005). We can ask questions regarding these issues in series 5-A listed at the end of this chapter.

As for assumptions about host families, we can encourage students to think about them by asking various questions listed below in four categories, following the points discussed in the previous sections.

Challenging the Assumption That Staying with the Host Family Is the Best Way to Learn

The first assumption about homestays abroad was that staying with host families is the best way to learn. In fact, various factors contribute to the learning outcome—the amount and quality of student engagement with the host family, the student's attitude, and the host family's attitude. Regarding the quantity and quality of students' engagement with the host family, it is important not to adhere to the discourse of immersion, which automatically assumes a host family is better than a dorm with compatriot students, and instead to determine what is the best match for the student at hand. Though many students felt that staying with a host family was beneficial, some appreciated the dorm for its relaxed atmosphere: the choice was about preferences and goals of each student (Mendelson 2004). Therefore, we can ask students what they want most from their study abroad experience and what kind of lifestyle suits them best (see question series 5-B).

In terms of students' attitude, it is hard to say that one particular attitude is the best. But for the sake of investigation, and to encourage students to shed "colonial student" attitudes (Ogden 2007, 2008), we can ask students questions that might motivate them to rethink their potential ethnocentric viewpoints, as introduced as question series 5-C. Answers to such questions need to be followed up appropriately and flexibly depending on what they are in order to discourage ethnocentrism (a belief that one's own culture is the best and practice to judge others according to one's own cultural criteria without putting others' practices in their own cultural context). Questions on difference being effects of wider structural causes, covered in the question series 1-G introduced in chapter 1, can be asked as well.

Iino (2006) argues that there are two types of host family–student relationships. The first type sees difference as "cultural deficiency" and could lead to the student being treated as helpless and deficient, like a baby, doll, or pet. In seeking to protect students, host families can risk being condescending to them. In such a case, the host family could be asked questions introduced as question series 5-D, intended to remind them that not knowing about the host society or the language prevalent in the host society does not make a visiting student deficient.

Iino (2006) calls the second type of host family–student relationship the two-way enrichment approach, in which assumptions about the host society, the student's home society, and other things too are challenged and modified through interaction between host family members and the student. A host family may give credence to some folk beliefs and stereotypes. For example, Florencia Riegelhaupt and Roberto Luis Carrasco (2000) report that host families in Mexico tend to view students who speak Chicano Spanish as "uneducated" because they lack proficiency in academic Spanish, despite appearing to be "native speakers." Students can correct such misperceptions and stereotypes. Haruko Minegishi Cook (2006) reports that conversations between the host family and the student can present opportunities for the student to challenge host family members' stereotypes and cultural assumptions by providing counterexamples and offering alternative viewpoints—or, vice versa, the student can be the one whose assumptions are challenged. Following this argument, we can encourage students to question their hosts' assumptions (5-E).

Also, to dispel the assumption that staying with a host family while studying abroad is the best way to learn about the host society, we can also suggest a different arrangement: staying with a host family in the students' home country. Ethel Jorge (2006) proposes a model in which students studying at their home institutions would spend time with "host" families of local immigrants for a semester or more, visiting them for several hours every week and talking with them about various topics, just as they would with a host family abroad. The families would receive some monetary compensation for playing this role.

This practice would serve several functions. If the families had a linguistic/cultural background similar to that in the student's study abroad destination, this experience could serve to prepare students for what they will encounter when studying abroad. Upon their return from studying abroad, continuing to interact with their local "hosts" would help them with their reentry process as they reflect on their study abroad experience and come to realize that it is not an isolated event but is connected to their life at home. Additionally, for those who cannot afford to study abroad, this experience of another linguistic and cultural environment can substitute for it. It can also improve any student's understanding of how immigrants live in their home country. From the college's point of view, such an arrangement could also be a way to foster community engagement; it could also be modified to include English tutoring for immigrants' children, or guidance for college entrance preparation, or any other guidance regarding institutional settings that may differ from their home country, if such things are helpful for them.

Challenging the Assumption that the Host Family Represents the Entire Host Society

When it comes to perceptions of a host family, we need first to recall that host family life does not represent the quintessential life of the host society but is rather an experience of a unique, individual family in the host society that is modifying its routine to accommodate the student. This is important because host families tend to come from the society's dominant group, that is, middle- or upper-middle-class people of the ethnic backgrounds that constitute mainstream society. Taking them as representative of the host society ignores or can even delegitimize the lives of marginalized groups in the host society. That is, to acknowledge that a student's host family is merely one example of a family in the society is to acknowledge the diversity of the host society.

Meanwhile, host families' attentiveness to the students they host varies in degree, as does students' commitment to spending time with their host families. The experience of staying with a host family is something unique to each case and should be treated as such, rather than viewed automatically as an ideal experience. This perspective encourages students to consciously work hard to make the most of it. To raise awareness of this issue among students, we can ask the questions in series 1-C (chapter 1) on diversity of the host society. Additional questions we can ask students about a specific host family are introduced in series 5-F.

Challenging the View that the Host Family Provides Students with "Authentic" Host Society Experience

We need to cultivate students' awareness that when living with a host family, they experience what it is like to "live *with* locals" who are accommodating students, not what it is like to "live *like* a local," as mentioned. Host families change their routines to accommodate the needs of the students they are hosting, so what the students experience is not necessarily, and often not at all, what the host family members do in their daily life when they have no guests. Even though students are likely to notice that their host families are making accommodations for them, they still tend to view their experience as "living like a local." Therefore, it is important to ensure that they understand the ways in which that is not the case.

They need not only to acknowledge the efforts that host families make for them by altering their practices, but they also need to understand their relationship to the host society as something dynamic whose construction they participate in. That is, a student who understands how their presence influences the host family's daily routine also understands themself as part of the host society's changing dynamics. This contrasts with the view of a student being dropped into the life of a host family and perceiving it to be the way it always is, no matter who joins in. Such a view denies both the changing nature of life in the host society and the role that study abroad students play, suggesting a static view of life in the host society (for similar observations about travelers' experience, see Massey 2005). The aforementioned series of questions, 5-A, for understanding students' co-constructing the host society, can also be asked for this purpose.

This also means that students need to be aware of their own individuality and how it influences their experience living with the host family—that is, to know that one's experience is not what anybody would have but is uniquely created through the interaction of individuals with various subject positions. For this issue, we can also ask the question in series W mentioned in the introduction chapter.

Challenging the View that the Study Abroad Student and the Host Family Are Different

Students need to be aware that the similarities and differences discussed here are not objective facts but perceptions that are subjectively constructed by both students and host families. As discussed in chapter 2, it is therefore important to think about what makes them consider certain things as difference and not others. For example, why was not saying "please" considered mere rudeness that is the same anywhere instead of "cultural difference" in the way politeness is expressed? Was the perception of rudeness because of an ethnocentric assumption that everyone in the world expresses politeness in the same way? Was it because of host parents' ignorance about Korean "cultural" practices? Was there a stereotype about Koreans not being polite that led to the interpretation of rudeness? Or was there a stereotype about Koreans being polite so that not appearing to be polite comes off not as cultural difference but as an aberration that highlights the perceived impoliteness of that particular student even more? To stimulate this type of thinking in students, we can modify and ask them the questions in series 2-B (see chapter 2) on the mutual construction of difference between the student's home and host societies.

Meanwhile, study abroad students should be aware of the paradoxical dynamics of how perceived difference makes people tolerant and how perceived sameness can lead to intolerance. Students thus need to clearly understand what certain acts of tolerance/intolerance mean and, if they are rooted in ignorance about cultural expectations, engage the doers of such acts in discussing how their own behavior is based on such expectations (see question series 5-G).

In sum, no host society is homogeneous, and no host family is a static, "authentic" representation of life in a host society that is fundamentally different from students' home society. Societies are diverse and dynamic. Diverse people participate in the host society's constant making by constructing what constitutes difference and what constitutes similarity, and their treatment of students abroad is based on those judgments. The students' critical understanding of common assumptions about home stay and their effects, along with their interpretation of the complexity of how their stay affects the host society and host family, can produce a critical understanding of more general issues, including their views of society and especially its diversity, changes in it, and their role in ongoing coproduction of the world. Active probing into students' experience throughout their study abroad experience and beyond helps accustom them to such reflections.

Recommended Readings

Cook, Haruko Minegishi. 2006. "Joint Construction of Folk Beliefs by JFL Learners and Japanese Host Families." In *Language Learners in Study Abroad Contexts*, ed. Margaret A. DuFon and Eton Churchill, 120–150. Clevedon: Multilingual Matters.
  Analyses of what happens in the host family space.
Iino, Masakazu. 2006. "Norms of Interaction in a Japanese Homestay Setting: Toward a Two-Way Flow of Linguistic and Cultural Resources." In *Language Learners in Study Abroad Contexts*, ed. Margaret A. DuFon and Eton Churchill, 151–176. Clevedon: Multilingual Matters.
  Analyses of what happens in the host family space. Common assumptions about host family are critically discussed.
Jorge, Ethel. 2006. "A Journey Home: Connecting Spanish-Speaking Communities at Home and Abroad." *Hispania* 89 (1): 110–122.
  Analyses of what happens in the host family space.
Kinginger, Celeste. 2008. "Language Learning in Study Abroad: Case Studies of Americans in France." *Modern Language Journal* 92 (S1): 1–124.
  Analyses of what happens in the host family space based on detailed case studies.
Knight, Susan M., and Barbara C. Schmidt-Rinehart. 2002. "Enhancing the Homestay: Study Abroad from the Host Family's Perspective." *Foreign Language Annals* 35 (2): 190–201.
  Analyses of what happens in the host family space.

Yashima, Tomoko, Lori Zenuk-Nishide, and Kazuaki Shimizu. 2004. "The Influence of Attitudes and Affect on Willingness to Communicate and Second Language Communication." *Language Learning* 54 (1): 119–152. *Analyses of what happens in the host family space.*

◖◖◖ Sample Questions

5-A: Co-construction of the Host Society by Diverse People

5-A1: How do you think you affected the daily life of the host society? If you compare how daily life was before your stay to how it is after, will anything be different? The same? The same is also an effect of your presence, if your presence supported the status quo. How might your presence have affected the (1) host family, (2) host institution, and (3) host society (e.g., would keeping the numbers of tourists up push them to keep relying on tourism)?

5-A2: How do you think the host family's life changed because you were living with them? Why do you think they changed their lifestyle because of you?

5-A3: Did people in your study abroad program encourage you to contribute to the life of the host society? How? What do you think they could have done better to allow you to contribute more?

5-A4: Did you ever feel like an outsider who did not affect life in the host society? When? How?

5-B: What Students Want to Get Out from the Study Abroad Stay

5-B1: How do you learn best? By talking with people who know a lot about the topic, listening to structured instruction like classes and lectures, learning with others who have had the same experience, learning by reading about it on your own?

5-B2: Would you feel more comfortable incorporated as a family member in a household setting with host parents and siblings, or rooming with other students in a dorm and acting independently?

5-B3: How much freedom do you want? Do you want to set aside time to spend with host family members? Or would you rather do things on your own (e.g., eating meals, doing things in the evening)?

5-C: On Understanding Difference

5-C1: If you encountered something "strange" to you in the host society, what would you do? How would you explain it—would you ask people there, ask your compatriot friends, ask teachers on the topic, Google it?

5-C2: Why do you think they do these things? How is it done back home? Is it done differently or similarly? How? What caused the differences/variations/similarities?

5-D: Questions to Host Families: About the Student's Knowledge
5-D1: How much did you think the student would know about the host society? How much do you know about the student's home society [a reminder that the host family may know as little about places abroad as students know about the host society]? How would you want to be treated if you were visiting the student's country and did not know much about it?
5-D2: How well do you think the student can speak the host society's predominant language? How well can you speak the language the student speaks in their home country [a reminder that a student's first language may be one the host family does not know]? How would you want to be treated when you spoke the student's first language?

5-E: Influencing Host Society's People's Views
5-E1: Do you feel that some of your views about the host society could be construed as stereotypes by the people there? If so, how would you want them to correct such views?
5-E2: Do you think your host family will have some stereotypes about you and your country? If so, how will you correct them?

5-F: On Host Family (changing the verb tense to reflect whether the questions are asked before, during, or after the study abroad stay)
5-F1: How common do you think things you will experience living with your host family are?
5-F2: How do you think the racial, socioeconomic, regional, and other backgrounds of the host family shape their daily life?
5-F3: Did you notice any difference between your host family's ways of living or thinking, and other families' ways? What do you think made the difference?
5-F4: How did your friends experience living with host families? What do you think made the difference?
5-F5: Where did you get your idea of how the host family lives? Study abroad promotional materials? Travel agency advertisements?
5-F6: What do you think would be the effect of considering your host family experience to be common and universal? What effect would that have on minority groups within the host society?

5-G: "Cultural" and Not "Cultural" Behavior
5-G1: Was there a time when you felt your host family was intolerant of your behavior?
5-G2: Do you think they did not tolerate it because they thought the behavior was based on cultural difference?

5-G2-X1: Whose view of the student's behavior and the reasons behind it do you think gets privileged? Why? What are that view's effects?
5-G2-X2: Whose view of the student's behavior and the reasons behind it do you think gets erased? Why? What are the effects of such erasures?

6

BORDER CROSSING

Do We Instead *Construct* Borders through Learning and Volunteering?

Study abroad excites us about encountering something new. It involves crossing borders—usually those of nations, but sometimes continents or a First or Third World border, as well as more invisible border of one's specific comfort zone—to experience a world that is new to us. Border crossing is understood to lead to learning about a new place and people, as well as ourselves. As these various types of border crossing are rarely experienced in the classroom setting, study abroad is considered a good opportunity to engage in such acts.

This chapter, however, questions this line of thought by reversing the viewpoint. If study abroad is about crossing borders to experience something new and different, are we not actually *constructing* borders by expecting something new and different beyond that border before even getting there? That is, insofar as the project of study abroad relies on the existence of borders to cross, do we inevitably focus on, or even seek out, difference rather than similarity among things we experience? If that is the case, is it a problem? Or is it just the way it works?

Discussing issues surrounding "minority students," the educational anthropologists Ray McDermott and Hervé Varenne (1995) urge us to shift our focus from the difference of these minority students to the process of differentiation, as we saw in chapter 2 with the example of deaf people, whose difference we would not notice if everyone used sign language. Out of myriad differences, they argue, the political, economic, and sociocultural environment pushes us to notice only some and not others. That is, "difference" that we highlight does not preexist; instead, we construct it by noticing this difference instead of another. And the border becomes constructed accordingly. Activities that celebrate border crossing—study abroad but also volunteer/service activities, as will be described—are conducive to creating such borders.

It is worth noting here that there are borders that are stable, as they are constructed institutionally, such as nation-state borders. Most individuals must manage such institutional borders, though often in different degrees of difficulties depending on one's citizenship and sometimes class and race (Glick Schiller and Salazar 2013). Study abroad tends to be based on but also further constructs such borders to be crossed because the nation-state ideology makes us imagine homology between people, nation, and culture (see chapters 1 and 2).

This chapter discusses three ways in which study abroad relies on the existence of difference/border: as an "adventure" dependent on novel experiences; as a disorienting experience offering cognitive dissonance, which supposedly produces a particular sensibility; and as an immersion experience in which noticing difference is inherent in learning. This chapter also discusses volunteer/service learning, the merit of which is increasingly seen as lying in providing students with border crossing experiences (J. Taylor 2002) and which are increasingly incorporated in study abroad programs as a way to engage students with the community in their study abroad destination (Plater et al. 2009) and a way to give back to the community (Lewin and Van Kirk 2009).

Study Abroad as Adventure: Difference as Fascinating

Advertisements (Zemach-Bersin 2009) and guidebooks (Doerr 2012b) for studying abroad often feature the discourse of adventure, which stokes students' fascination with "difference." They portray study abroad as "an adventure of a lifetime" that produces "incredible adventure stories" (Oxford 2005: 96, 5); at times, it is even called "an adventure abroad" (Loflin 2007: x). Study abroad can "quench [students'] thirst for adventure, exploration, personal challenges, and, of course, fun!" (3). Exciting discourse like this can attract students who would not otherwise have ventured out of their comfort zone and encourage them to learn by opening up a new world to them. Passion for adventure can open many doors and help students gain new knowledge on the way.

This fascination with difference takes various forms with specific implications dependent on the destination, as discussed in chapter 2 in terms of two different concepts of "culture." Studying abroad in Europe—often called a "traditional" study abroad destination—is often framed with admiration for the destination, reminiscent of the Grand Tour of European cities in which aristocratic youths studied to finish their classical education (Lewin 2009b). Europe's "high" culture and its historical legacies are often celebrated in study abroad programs.

In contrast, studying abroad in Africa, Asia, and Latin America, which are often called "nontraditional" study abroad destinations, is often framed in terms of exoticism. Exoticism frames people from "faraway places" as cultural Others, who are viewed more as characters from exotic novels and films that evokes fantasies, fears, and desire in us than people we would associate daily. They serve as a mirror against which to define who "we" are (Fusco 1995). Also, a study abroad program that includes volunteer/service work in the destination can, while eliciting humanitarianism, mix it with voyeurism of poverty and a paternalistic sense of charity, Michael Woolf (2010) argues. Though there are increasing numbers of students with diverse ethnic backgrounds studying abroad, some going to their ancestral homeland ("heritage" study abroad students), this general framework persists.

This discourse of adventure also can construct problematic images. Talya Zemach-Bersin critiques this discourse for its portrayal, and thus positioning, of the American student as "explorer and adventurer, bravely penetrating the depths of other lands to discover new knowledge" (2009: 307). This discourse portrays host countries as passive and open to being explored by American students, like amusement parks. The discourse of adventure also depends on the existence of stark difference between study abroad students' home and host societies. If these societies are similar to each other, visiting one from another does not constitute an "adventure" (Doerr 2012b). That is, viewing study abroad as adventure implies that it is about crossing a border from one society to another, quite different one. This is conducive to pushing us to notice certain differences by highlighting if not constructing them out of myriad differences and thus borders.

Study Abroad as Learning from Cognitive Dissonance in a Disorienting Environment

The discourse of immersion discussed in chapter 4 often suggests that study abroad is a unique opportunity to learn more outside the classroom than inside—a claim reliant on the existence of difference that students can experience but that is not available in their home country (see Doerr and Suarez 2018). Even while outside classroom, the discourse of immersion encourages students to go further, out of their comfort zone. What awaits in such space outside the comfort zone is cognitive dissonance, which is said to provide students with opportunities for developing an "ability to fail" and learning to navigate unknown environments (Brockington and Wiedenhoeft 2009). Researchers say that cognitive dissonance also allows students to confront their personal anxieties and limitations, which often leads to self-awareness, self-confidence, increased adaptability, persistence, risk-taking, empathy with others, knowledge of another "culture" as well as their own, and ability to shift their perspectives (Cushner 2009).

In most cases, however, life in the destination is far from disorienting because there exist many layers of intermediaries: study abroad providers offering orientation and advice and local study partners and host family who would explain to them reasons behind certain behaviors and situation that may appear "different" to the student. Thus, drawing on Vygotsky's theory that social interaction is crucial to learning, Megan Che and colleagues suggest that study abroad offers a unique opportunity in which the "more capable" locals in the destination mediate cognitive dissonance, resulting in "a higher likelihood of the construction of an authentic, deep space or zone for development and transformation" (2009: 104).

In short, the discourse of immersion prevalent in study abroad suggests that crossing a border into the unknown, outside one's comfort zone, disorients students and thereby helps them learn, but with some support. In this understanding of study abroad, students' learning relies on disorienting difference—another way that a discourse of study abroad highlights and may even construct differences and the border. Here, the border is constructed at the edge of comfort zone, dividing the area of learning (outside comfort zone) and area of not learning (comfort zone).

It is worth noting here that, though the above is a common understanding of how students learn while studying abroad, "heritage" study abroad students who study in their ancestral homeland and minority immigrant students relate to the destination differently. "Heritage" study abroad students may encounter expectations that they should know fully the language and practices in their study abroad destination/ancestral homeland and be treated negatively if they are perceived to lack the knowledge (Moreno 2009; Riegelhaupt and Carrasco 2000). Minority immigrant students who study abroad in countries other than their ancestral homeland often draw on their existing cultural resources and experience of traveling to their own ancestral homeland to relate to the people and practices in the study abroad destination, treating them as variations of what they are familiar with rather than starkly "different" experience that would give them cognitive dissonance (see Doerr 2018).

Study Abroad Learning as Recognizing Difference

Students learn through "immersion" in various ways, but the common thread is learning experience centered on *noticing difference*, which implies that the student has experienced something new. In the framework of immersion, where learning activities are not clearly designated, acknowledging a particular act as learning involves a recognition of difference that can become an act of border construction (for detail, see Doerr 2017b).

One American study abroad student in France whom I interviewed reported a learning experience of fitting into the host society that involved recognizing the difference between French and American ways in people's mannerisms (e.g., French women swinging their arms while strutting versus American women walking slouched over) and clothes (e.g., French wearing flats and long pants versus Americans in sneakers and shorts) and emulating the former. The existence of "Americans" constructed as distinct from "French" therefore helped the student "act French" by providing someone concrete to contrast with and dissociate from. In short, her learning was predicated on this construction of French-American difference, and her becoming French was sustained by her dissociation from fellow Americans. This "learning" is an act of othering—positioning French as different from herself (American) in order to cross that border.

Another American study abroad student whom I interviewed described her learning in Spain as bridging two separate "cultures." Her awareness of learning derived from successfully acting as a translator, that is, connecting two different languages. Only when she intelligibly translated Spanish into English and vice versa for someone else—which was not about communicative competence but about being a bilingual *bridge* between Spanish and English—did she acknowledge her newly acquired Spanish skills. Thus, it was necessary to highlight the difference between Spanish and English, which she stood between in order to connect them.

Yet another study abroad student in Spain reported learning in two ways—*from* and *through* her fellow American study abroad students— by recognizing their difference from herself. From her friends, she learned the difference among various US states—for instance, that some students wear cowboy boots to go out—saying, "I'm learning about my own country while I'm here [studying abroad in Spain]." Here, her learning derived from realizing her difference from fellow Americans. Through her American friends, she reported, she learned what Spanish culture is. Her Latin American background and familiarity with both Hispanic and Anglo-American cultures made it difficult for her to recognize what Spanish culture is. Therefore, recognizing *difference* between her own reactions and those of her American friends (e.g., frustration with the slow pace of service in Spanish stores) allowed her to recognize American and Spanish difference and thus *learn* "Spanish culture" (and "American culture").

These three students learned in diverse ways while studying abroad, and all the learning involved othering or constructing "difference" or a border. Recognition of difference and learning occurred simultaneously, both constructing and supporting each other's existence. If differences between French and American appearance and behavior (first student), between Spanish and English language (second student), among Americans from various regions in terms of how they dress (third student), and between Spanish and American ways of acting (third student) had not been recognized and highlighted, there would have been no learning (for details, see Doerr 2017b). As mentioned earlier, McDermott and Varenne (1995) suggest that even though differences are myriad, our socioeconomic and cultural environment influences us to notice only certain difference as meaningful. What occurs, then, besides there being difference that pushes students to learn, is that students notice, identify, and recognize the difference, and *perceive* the experience as learning. This is the third way in which study abroad narrative constructs the "difference" or border.

Going beyond the Difference-as-a-Given Model

Above I have discussed three ways in which study abroad encourages the border by highlighting particular difference through the discourses of adventure, cognitive dissonance, and learning through immersion. Difference fascinates us and encourages us to learn something new. There is nothing wrong with having differences: we are surrounded by differences (and similarities) at many levels. What is important is to acknowledge that such differences are constructed when we are pushed to notice certain differences over others as meaningful in particular setup (McDermott and Varenne 1995).

The particular setup of study abroad pushes the students to notice differences between their home and host societies. Being aware of that process, rather than assuming that a difference already exists as the only meaningful difference, is the key realization I encourage in students. To that end, we can ask students what circumstances pushed them to notice certain difference and who is advantaged/disadvantaged by those conditions (e.g., the predominance of oral communication disadvantages deaf people), as will be elaborated later. We can then understand study abroad experience not as necessarily border-crossing experience but as learning in various ways as I discuss throughout this book while being in the host society, whose setup has some difference but similarity and which is filled with people who may act differently but also in similar ways to study abroad students.

Doing Volunteer/Service Work to Learn: Border Crossing as Learning

Border crossing has increasingly come to be considered the main merit of doing volunteer/service work[1] for students, as border crossing is seen as leading to a meaningful learning experience. Volunteer/service work is sometimes framed in the metaphor of a military campaign, as in the Peace Corps and the "war on poverty" (J. Taylor 2002) or as charity—religious acts of missionaries and their flocks, or "the well-off doing service to the poor if and when they feel like it, and then only on their terms" (Morton 1995: 25)—or civic engagement, conceived as "a duty of free men and women whose freedom is itself wholly dependent on the assumption of political responsibilities" (Barber 1994: 86). What is becoming more common, though, is the framework of border crossing as pedagogy. Border crossing as a learning process is said (J. Taylor 2002) to have been inspired by Gloria Anzaldúa's (1987) notion of "borderland," which sees borders as setting up artificial binaries and instead celebrates hybrid qualities within individuals, and by the "border pedagogy" of Henry Giroux (1992: 28) who, inspired by Anzaldúa, views borders as "forged in domination" that needs to be challenged and redefined.

Whereas Anzaldúa and Giroux stress that the border is constructed, the discourse of border crossing in volunteer/service work treats it as preexisting and thus as something students cross in doing volunteer/service work, which then supposedly pushes them to develop better understanding of and empathy toward people who are different from them (Chesler et al. 2006; Green 2001; Hayes and Cuban 1997; Rhoads and Neururer 1998; J. Taylor 2002). Joby Taylor (2002) suggests that service learning creates opportunities to cross three kinds of boundaries: physical boundaries, met when students leave the classroom to enter communities; socially constructed boundaries such as race, class, age, and religion; and epistemological and pedagogical boundaries, whose transgression creates space for new ways of knowing and learning. Through these crossings, service learning answers Giroux's call to recognize those living on epistemological, political, cultural, and social margins; create pedagogical conditions in which students become border crossers to understand otherness on its own terms;

and highlight the strengths and limitations of borderlands (Hayes and Cuban 1997; J. Taylor 2002).

Thus, many view volunteer/service work as aimed at bridging different groups (Chesler et al. 2006). Service learning is therefore seen as "deliberate encounters with diverse cultures": "through service, a divide based on social class and, in this context, a racial divide was somewhat mitigated" (Rhoads and Neururer 1998: 112, 109) because "despite the differences in age, race, social class, educational level, and cultural values, students learned from residents that perhaps people are not so different from one another" (111). Service is said to also raise students' awareness of different perspectives, especially that of white students who take their privilege and invisibility for granted (Green 2001).

Volunteer/service work in study abroad is framed variously. It can be offered as part of a study abroad program or positioned somewhat separately as International Service Learning (ISL) (Bringle et al. 2011). William Plater (2011: 38) argues that, while ISL can be described as almost always study abroad, there is some fundamental difference: "study abroad is *of* the community (and maybe some of it is even *in* the community) while ISL is *through* and *with* the community. These are substantive distinctions—not semantic." Increasingly, volunteer/service work is incorporated into study abroad programs primarily as a way to engage students with communities in the host society. For example, Plater and colleagues (2009: 489) argue that service work in study abroad "inherently calls upon participants to reflect on the differences and similarities of locale and on their own sense of civic identity in a comparative, if not collective, framework."

Some do put the community's needs first; however, they ultimately return to the benefits for students. Ross Lewin and Greg Van Kirk (2009: 544) argue that a study abroad program that incorporates service learning and puts the community's needs first (not the student's) "is paradoxically the most effective way to realize the development of students intellectually, morally, and civically." In sum, volunteer/service work is a way of incorporating border crossing into study abroad from another angle.

Critiques of Border Pedagogy

The discourse of border crossing that prevails in volunteer/service-learning literature (Jones et al. 2011; J. Taylor 2002) has not escaped critique. First, it highlights and thus perpetuates the difference between those serving and those being served. As mentioned, we notice, out of many differences, only the ones that our sociocultural environment pushes us to notice (McDermott and Varenne 1995). Someone's helpful and uncompensated work for others could simply be called "individuals working together with other individuals" or "supportive work for others in one's own society." But calling it border crossing highlights difference rather than similarity between these individuals and thus (re)creates the border itself. For example, the work of college students tutoring children in schools in the nearby community can be framed as college students helping children in the same town, or as white, middle-class students crossing sociocultural and economic borders by helping poor nonwhite children (as border-crossing discourse often assumes, as will be discussed later).

Second, the accentuated difference in the context of volunteer/service work implies hierarchy: those who can afford to provide "help" versus those who are helpless and dependent on outsiders' assistance (Sin 1999). Compared with other ways of framing volunteer/service work—for example, as the civic duty of citizens (Barber 1994)—the border-crossing framework highlights the hierarchy between the servers and the served.

Third, the focus on the border reinforces the inaccurate assumption that students who do volunteer/service work are white and middle class and those they help are nonwhite and lower class (Butin 2006; Doerr 2017a; Doerr and Suarez 2013). This is not always the case, yet the situation is often discussed as such: sometimes the discourse of border crossing pulls data analyses into this polarized positioning of the server and the served, even when the one serving comes from the same community as those served (see Hayes and Cuban 1997; for further analysis, see Doerr 2017a).

Fourth, the assumption that individuals who volunteer/serve are white and middle class erases the volunteer/service work done by minority students without affluent socioeconomic backgrounds. This has the performative effect of keeping minority students from disadvantaged socioeconomic backgrounds from being visible role models as volunteer/service workers. Fifth and finally, this assumption marginalizes and delegitimizes, or even erases, volunteer/service work done in one's own community without crossing borders (Coles 1999). That is, it suggests that helpful work done without leaving a community does not count.

Going beyond Border Pedagogy

This section introduces two views of volunteer/service work as alternatives to border-crossing discourse. First, service work can be collaborative work that does not involve differentiation of two groups. Sue Ellen Henry and M. Lynn Breyfogle (2006) argue that, instead of buying into the binary of server and served, each with a separate goal (e.g., service learning students may aim to learn something from the experience while the people being served want to improve their living conditions), people can work together to achieve the same goal, such as ending racism in the given society. The program is then assessed according to whether that common goal was achieved, rather than whether students learned from the experience or the community gained something from it.

In the study abroad context, this perspective can be applied as students and community members together think through their path to a common goal and work to that end, without framing it as students crossing a border to gain some learning experience. That way, even if students and community members have different national and ethnic backgrounds or are rooted in different countries or communities, such difference is not the key to the project. Students and community members can draw on diverse resources for achieving the common goal, and bridging the difference or "learning the difference" is not the aim (though it may happen).

Second, we can not only stop using the framework of border crossing but also stop identifying certain work as "volunteer" or "service work." These labels themselves create borders between those who serve and those who receive service as mentioned. For example, consider an act such as teaching a child how to do a math problem. Depending on whom you do it for—your own sibling, your friend, your neighbor's child, someone in an after-school tutoring program—the act is called by a different name; here, probably only the last case would be called volunteer/service work. The same goes for cooking meals—doing it for your own family or friends is not called volunteer/service work, but doing it at the soup kitchen is. This indicates that what we call volunteer/service work is something done for people perceived as socially less proximate to the doer. Calling a particular helpful act volunteer or service work is thus a performative act of constructing the helped as the helper's "other," differentiating and distancing them by constructing an us-them distinction and thus a border. The border between the volunteer and the helped then is not preexisting, as literature on volunteer/

service work tends to suggest, but rather constructed through calling the act of helping certain people volunteer/service work (Doerr 2015c). That is, we construct borders not only through the explicit framework of border pedagogy but also by the selective naming of certain helpful acts as volunteer/service work. Realizing this is key to stopping the construction of these borders. We can instead think of such work as merely working to support the community and call it that. In this way, we achieve a sense of camaraderie without separating ourselves from others or highlighting the border.

Implications and Suggestions

The discussion above shows that the difference we recognize is constructed through our own actions: framing study abroad as adventure, expecting to learn from cognitive dissonance, identifying the encounter with difference as the moment of learning, and calling an act of helping volunteer/service work. By talking about, framing, and setting up situations as crossing a "border," we actually construct that border. It is therefore important that we teach students to notice these moments and understand the dynamics of construction of difference.

I introduce example questions at the end of the chapter. The tense of these questions can be modified for asking before, during, or after the study abroad stay questions. Questions about (W) subject positions, (X) power relations, (Y) how these have changed and how we can change them, and (Z) mutual construction of difference between various societies can be asked in relation to any of the questions below, as mentioned in the introduction. We can also get students to discuss what it means to notice "difference" by explaining the ideas of McDermott and Varenne (1995) and then asking question series 6-A at the end of this chapter. Alternatively, we can ask more general questions, which may look like the following:

Study abroad practitioner: What difference did you notice?
Study abroad students: My Japanese host mother tells me what to do.
Practitioner: Is this because she is Japanese? Or because she is the type of person who wants to become a host mother, or because of her social class, et cetera?
Students: Probably the type of person she is—maybe it's a Japanese middle-class thing.
Practitioner: What makes you notice this particular difference (race/culture) and not others? Japanology? Media? Nation-state ideology?
Students: I guess a stereotype of "Asian tiger mom" in the United States?

Practitioner: Who is marginalized or advantaged by this perception?
Students: I'm not sure . . . Maybe Japanese mothers who don't tell their children what to do—maybe they are seen as not really Japanese?

Another alternative would be to preface the questions with an explanation of how difference is constructed:

> We only notice deaf people when we talk to each other, that is, when oral communication is predominant. If we all used sign language all the time, we wouldn't even notice who was and who was not deaf—deafness would not make deaf people "different." That is, the social circumstances make us notice certain "difference." Using this understanding of difference, what do you think about the difference you noticed while you studied abroad? What kind of circumstances do you think made you notice these differences? Why do you think there are such circumstances? Who is advantaged by those circumstances? Who is disadvantaged? What type of circumstances would hide the difference you noticed? Who would such circumstances advantage or disadvantage?

When engaging students in volunteer/service work in or out of the study abroad context, we can ask questions about what is considered volunteer/service work and what effects study abroad promotional materials have, as introduced in question series 6-B.

With these questions, I hope to engage students in thinking about their own taken-for-granted othering practices. Once they understand processes of constructing borders, they can start thinking about how and why we perceive the differences and effects such practices create. Students can then use this understanding to inform their practice of relating to people—from various places and backgrounds—they encounter in the destination as they create and recognize difference and similarity. This then can be applied to their daily life after studying abroad.

Recommended Readings

Anzaldúa, Gloria. 1987. *Borderlands / La frontera*. San Francisco: Aunt Lute Books.
  Discussion of the notion of borderland and hybrid spaces.
Boyte, Henry C. 2003. "Putting Politics Back into Civic Engagement." In "Service-Learning and Civic Education," summer special issue, *Campus Compact Reader*: 1–9.
  Discussion of civic engagement with a macro-level focus.
Coles, Roberta L. 1999. "Race-Focused Service-Learning Courses." *Michigan Journal of Community Service Learning* 6 (1): 97–105.
  Discussion of service work done by minority students.

Giroux, Henry. 1992. *Border Crossings: Cultural Workers and the Politics of Education.* New York: Routledge.
Discussion of border crossing and pedagogy based on border experiences.

Heath, Shirly Brice. 2007. "Widening the Gap: Pre-university Gap Years and the 'Economy of Experience.'" *British Journal of Sociology of Education* 28 (1): 89–103.
Analyses of gap-year experiences and the power politics around them.

Henry, Sue Ellen, and M. Lynn Breyfogle. 2006. "Toward a New Framework of 'Server' and 'Served': De (and re)constructing Reciprocity in Service-Learning Pedagogy." *International Journal of Teaching and Learning in Higher Education* 18 (1): 27–35.
Critical discussion of service learning and the notion of border.

Sin, Harng Luh. 2009. "Who Are We Responsible To? Locals' Tales of Volunteer Tourism." *Geoforum* 41: 983–992.
Discussion of power relations in volunteer works.

Taylor, Joby. 2002. "Metaphors We Serve By: Investigating the Conceptual Metaphors Framing National and Community Service and Service-Learning. *Michigan Journal of Community Service Learning* 9 (1): 45–57.
Categorization of rhetoric of volunteer/service work.

✺ Sample Questions

6-A: On Recognizing a Border

6-A1: Do you feel that study abroad is an adventure? What makes something an adventure? Does it have to involve something/someone different from you?

6-A2: Do you feel you will be disoriented when you are studying abroad? Do you feel that such disorientation would be a meaningful learning experience? How? Why?

6-A3: Do you think you can learn something that is not new to you? How?

6-A4: What sociocultural environment do you think made you notice a particular difference?

6-A5: What sociocultural environment do you think would have made that difference irrelevant?

6-A6: List something that you felt was different from your own society. Then think of reasons (other than host society–home society difference) why you felt it was different, pointing, for example, to difference between (1) individual subject positions of students and other people, (2) social classes, (3) regions, (4) positions within the group/family, (5) contexts, and (6) types of interactions. Why did you settle on the first reason you gave as the reason for the difference? What influenced that view? Who is advantaged or marginalized by that view?

6-B: Effects of Labeling an Act Volunteer/Service Work

6-B1: Would you call work you do for family members volunteer/service work? Why (not)? What does that tell you about the relationship and the social distance between you and them?

6-B2: Would you call work you do for your friends volunteer/service work? Why (not)? What does that tell you about the relationship and the social distance between you and them?

6-B3: Would you call work you do for your school volunteer/service work? Why (not)? What does that tell you about the relationship and the social distance between you and people at school?

6-B4: Would you call work you do for people in your community volunteer/service work? Why (not)? What does that tell you about the relationship and the social distance between you and them?

6-B5: Would you call work you did for your host family volunteer/service work? Why (not)? What does that tell you about the relationship and the social distance between you and them?

6-B6: Would you call work you did for other students volunteer/service work? Why (not)? What does that tell you about the relationship and the social distance between you and them?

6-B7: Would you call the work you did for your study abroad program volunteer/service work? Why (not)? What does that tell you about the relationship and the social distance between you and the people the program catered to?

6-B8: If calling an act of volunteering/service creates distance between you and the people you are working for, how do you think you can connect to these people?

6-B9: Do you feel that the promotional materials for volunteer/service work define what work is volunteer/service work and what work is not? How? How it can be changed?

Note

1. "Volunteer" and "service" carry different connotations, but here I use them as a single term for readability.

7

SELF-TRANSFORMATION

Do Assessing and Talking about Self-Transformation Involve
Power Politics?

A participant in a study abroad trip to Mexico refused to write a journal entry about the group's visit to an impoverished town because of
the possibility that strong emotions evoked by the visit could lead to
a "fake epiphany" whose insights would soon be forgotten (Menard-
Warwick and Palmer 2012: 122). Was this student being insightful? Or
too cynical? Is this something we should face squarely and discuss with
students? This chapter unpacks these and other issues and explores the
question of what it means to talk about self-transformation.

As mentioned in chapters 2 and 6, the type of study abroad I have
been discussing derives from two historical models of travel—the
Grand Tours of European aristocratic youth (the "traditional" study
abroad model) and imperial travel by Europeans to their nations' colonies (the "nontraditional" study abroad model)—that served as rites
of passage. For that reason, discourses of study abroad reference self-
transformation as a major outcome of the experience. But why do we
talk about self-transformation through study abroad in the ways we
do? Many activities can be transformative: meeting someone interesting, reading a great book, watching a film or show, starting at a new
job or school, and so on. Why are the ways we talk about, examine, and
celebrate self-transformation via these experiences so much less systematic than they are in the case of study abroad? If self-transformation
does not happen during study abroad, is the experience a failure? Is
talking about self-transformation an attempt to prove that study abroad
is a worthwhile endeavor? What kinds of students are we imagining
when we talk about self-transformation through study abroad in general? How do students who have already traveled extensively and are
comfortable with diverse settings transform themselves by studying
abroad? What kinds of power politics are involved in viewing study
abroad as self-transformative experience?

Self-transformation through studying abroad is typically talked
about in two ways. The first concerns assessment of learning outcomes

using various tools of measurement. In this chapter, I ask what we are really assessing when we assess learning outcomes of study abroad—students? Programs? Study abroad itself as an endeavor? Or is assessment not actually about assessing these things but about something else altogether? Drawing on educational studies, I argue that such assessments perpetuate structures of dominance by basing what is (and what is not) worth knowing, and thus worth testing, on the worldview of the dominant group and imposing it on all (Bourdieu and Passeron 1977).

The second way of discussing self-transformation is to introduce and examine narratives of study abroad students themselves. Some researchers contend that these narratives often merely repeat catchphrases, such as gaining "global competence" or "cultural sensitivity," and that students, when explicitly questioned, cannot explain what they mean by these catchphrases (Kortegast and Boisfontaine 2015). Does that mean students were not really transformed? Or do they just not know how to articulate it? Or were they just saying what they thought educators wanted to hear?

These questions lead to deeper questions about the act of narrating. What does it mean to talk about one's own experience and feelings? Is there really a "true self" we can talk about? How do the vocabulary and frameworks available to people relate to their actual experience? Do the former shape the latter, or vice versa? Does introducing new vocabulary and frameworks to use in talking about experience the same as imposing ways of looking at and experiencing the world? Who has the right to make such introductions or impose them? Who gains advantage through that process, and who is disadvantaged? I will tackle these questions by introducing theories on how "truth" gets constituted and the role of narratives in that process, as well as the power politics involved.

This chapter also revisits in two ways discussions about students' transformation through studying abroad measured by outcome assessment and students' own narratives. First, the discussions tend to assume that study abroad students are monocultural, monolingual, white, middle-class students who have not traveled abroad and are unaware that they are privileged. That is why the topics of gaining "global competence" and becoming aware of their privilege are set for students in outcome assessments and sought in their narratives of self-transformation: if they are already used to traveling abroad and aware of their privilege, or do not have privilege, relatively speaking, studying abroad will not be a special experience to gain these. Meanwhile, this assumption ignores the existence of students who are multicultural, multilingual, aware of their privilege, or relatively more marginalized than privileged, and limits the ways they can articulate their experience and their gains from studying abroad.

Second, our focus on study abroad as the main source of self-transformation can be revisited as the result of our paying special attention to study abroad by framing it as the rite of passage. Building on my earlier suggestion to focus on daily life in the same way as we do for study abroad period (see introduction and chapter 4), I suggest paying attention to self-transformation in daily life.

In what follows, I will first introduce the two ways of discussing study abroad—first, learning outcome assessments and educational studies that interpret such assessments of outcomes, and second, research on study abroad students' narratives of self-transformation and literature on the "truth" of self and the act of narrating. I then revisit these discussions of self-transformation by focusing on the assumptions about the student body and highlighting of self-transformation through study abroad. I then suggest some questions we can ask students before, during, and after their study abroad trips to create and increase their understanding of these issues.

Learning Outcome Assessment in Study Abroad

What needs to be learned, as well as what *can* be learned, has changed throughout history. Regarding changing ideas of education and the "educated subject," Lynne Fendler (1998) offers the example of medieval Christian belief that the soul could be educated separately from the body. In modernity, a distinction arose between "subjective" and "objective" knowledge. And currently, we focus on educating our "soul" (e.g., love for learning, will for social justice). What gets tested thus changes according to the shifting views and goals of education. Looking at these changes allows us to understand that what is considered "knowledge," "skill," "intelligence," or "competence" is not universal but arbitrary, dependent on particular historical contexts.

Our understanding of how to assess degrees of learning also changes throughout history. In the late twentieth century, outcome-based curricula became prominent, and education came to be organized around the question of whether a desired outcome is achieved after a period of education. Outcome-based curricula stipulate the goals and outcomes at the outset and then develop the procedures. Here, the objective is not the result but the target. Therefore, there is no room for unexpected results. Teaching procedures are evaluated only on how effective they are in achieving these goals (Fendler 1998).

This is also the case for study abroad learning outcome assessments. Ross Lewin and Greg Van Kirk (2009) describe how, until recently, assessment in study abroad tended to focus on foreign-language proficiency or the effectiveness of students' immersion in the host society. These foci were what educators wanted to know about, what they believed study abroad should produce, and what was important for students to gain at the time. More recently, knowledge, skills, and attitudes (e.g., "global awareness," "intercultural sensitivity," and "cross-cultural adaptability") were added to the list of things to be assessed, reflecting new goals in general higher education (e.g., the American Council on Education's 2003 report on internationalization, which discusses "global knowledge," "global skills," and "global attitudes") (Lewin and Van Kirk 2009).

What is being tested also reflects what is considered learning and how it should be done. As the role of faculty has shifted from the "sage on the stage" to the "guide on the side" (Deardorff 2009: 355), learner-centered approaches to assessment have come to prevail in higher education. Darla Deardorff (2009: 355) argues that this approach "(1) promotes high expectations for learning, (2) respects diverse talents and learning styles, (3) engages students in learning, (4) promotes coherence in learning, (5) synthesizes experiences, fostering ongoing practice of learned skills, and integrates education and experience, (6) provides prompt feedback, (7) fosters collaboration, and (8) depends on increased student-faculty contact." She sees this learner-centered approach as encouraging students' development of "global citizenship."

Evidence by which to assess "global citizenship development and intercultural learning" can be collected from multiple perspectives using multiple methods, direct and indirect, according to Deardorff (2009: 357). Direct methods measure what a student has learned or how the student performs (e.g., in supervised internships; community-based projects and comprehensive capstone projects; portfolios; observations by supervisors, faculty, and host families; and research papers, essays, and exams). Indirect methods rely on perceptions of learning or factors that predict learning as seen in surveys, self-reporting tools, interviews, focus groups, retention data, and job placement data (Deardorff 2009; see also Plater et al. 2009).

Indirect methods include various types of surveys, which I briefly review below, and self-narratives, which I will discuss in a later section. The Intercultural Development Inventory (IDI), developed by Milton Bennett and Mitch Hammer based on the Developmental Model of Intercultural Sensitivity, is a comprehensive assessment tool for identifying individuals' "intercultural sensitivity." It locates individuals on a continuum from highly ethnocentric (comprising three stages: denial, defense, minimization) to highly ethnorelative (also comprising three stages: acceptance, adaptation, integration). IDI asks subjects to respond to statements by selecting the best one of five response options and provides results in numeric and descriptive form for actual and self-perceived scores. IDI is also used before and after the trip to measure a student's development (Berg et al. 2009; Cushner 2009).

The Global Perspectives Inventory (GPI) aims to comprehensively assess a student's overall growth in terms of "intercultural competence" and maturity. Students respond to statements in three learning dimensions: (1) the cognitive, concerning knowledge and understanding of what is important knowledge; (2) the intrapersonal, concerning awareness of one's values and "identity" and their integration into one's personhood; and (3) the interpersonal, concerning how willing a person is to interact with and accept people of different sociocultural backgrounds, and how comfortably that person relates to others. GPI is a quantitative method that integrates with qualitative approaches to allow for expanded responses within the GPI categories (Doyle 2009).

Other assessment tools include the Global-Mindedness Scale (GMS) of thirty statements, each of which the subject answers with a number on a five-point Likert scale (from "strongly agree" to "strongly disagree") (Kehl and Morris 2007); the Cross-Cultural Adaptability Inventory (CCAI), which assesses subjects' effectiveness in "intercultural interaction and communication"; the Intercultural Adjustment Potential Scale (ICAPS), which identifies elements contributing to "intercultural adjustment"; the International Education Survey (IES), aimed at assessing how an international experience impacts personal and intellectual development; the Global Awareness Profile (GAP), which assesses the extent of a person's recognition and appreciation of the size, complexity, and diversity of intercultural experiences, as well as his or her formation of an integrated worldview; the Beliefs, Events and Values Inventory (BEVI), which, based on the level of agreement with various belief-value statements, seeks to assess a number of characteristics related to "intercultural competency," such as openness, tendency to stereotype, and receptivity (Rexeisen et al. 2008); and the Global Engagement Survey (GES), which tracks long-term outcomes of study abroad in terms of civic engagement, knowledge production, philanthropy, and social entrepreneurship (Redden 2010).

Linguistic proficiency, which many combine with linguistic and other "cultural competence" (see Carlson et al. 1990), can be assessed by the Oral Proficiency Interview (OPI) or the Simulated Oral Proficiency Interview (SOPI). The former requires a qualified rater who personally interviews each student. The latter does not; instead, recordings guide the student to carry out oral tasks while referring to a booklet. The student's oral responses are recorded, and upon completion of the test, a rater scores the results using oral proficiency guidelines developed by the American Council on the Teaching of Foreign Language (ACTFL) (Berg et al. 2009).

The attributes these assessment tools measure (e.g., "global awareness," "intercultural sensitivity," "cross-cultural adaptability") come under the umbrella of "global knowledge," "global skills," and "global attitudes" (Lewin and Kirk 2009). As for linguistic proficiency, "native speaker speech" is typically considered the model in these assessments (Doerr and Kumagai 2009) as discussed in chapter 3. In the next section, I introduce theories from educational studies regarding what this assessment and its goals mean and how they affect relations of power in the society that extend to study abroad projects.

Relations of Power: Educational Theories

Archer et al. (1973) show the relationship between what is considered knowledge and relations of power in an article parodying an intelligence test called OTIS (Archer et al. 1973). The test is given in Aotearoa/New Zealand, where New Zealanders of European decent (called Pākehā) constitute the dominant group, and indigenous Māori people are marginalized along with other Pacific Island and Asian populations there. Parodying an Aotearoa/New Zealand intelligence test, OTIS, they created Māori-OTIS, MOTIS. The questions in MOTIS are based on things that most Māori students would know from daily experience but Pākehā students would not, with the outcome that Māori students perform much better than Pākehā students.

For example, multiple-choice questions ask, "What is a waka?" with four choices—bird, horse, storm, and canoe. The answer is canoe. A Māori legend says Māori migrated to Aotearoa/New Zealand in a canoe, so waka is a commonly used word that almost all Māori students (and increasingly more Pākehā students, since the time of writing) would know. Another question, "Which one of these four words is most unlike the others?" offered answer choices of puha (a leafy green vegetable), pipi (a type of shellfish), tuna, and kina (sea urchin). All but tuna are Māori names for food commonly eaten by Māori people, so most Māori students would know the answer, whereas Pākehā students would not necessarily. Here, knowledge acquired at home helps answer these test questions. By showing how difficult answering these questions would be for someone unfamiliar with Māori daily life, the article seeks to demonstrate the cultural bias of "intelligence" tests in general (which disadvantage minority students) by pointing out how bias is usually overlooked by the dominant population, whose own intelligence tests likewise overlap with knowledge its members gain at home (Archer et al. 1973).

This work was published in the 1970s at a time when public outcry over "Māori underachievement" at school was blaming Māori communities and families for not providing what it takes to succeed in mainstream Aotearoa/New Zealand. Archer et al. put the blame instead on the biased nature of what is considered "achievement," if not "intelligence," which left Māori students at a disadvantage. That is, whereas OTIS may be considered a culturally neutral, objective test of intelligence, just as many IQ tests seem to be, it is biased in favor of the viewpoint of whoever made the test—typically, members of the dominant group. MOTIS challenged this façade of neutrality by parodying it with a Māori-centered test.

This way of thinking arose from arguments made by Pierre Bourdieu and Jean-Claude Passeron, who argue that the dominant group's "cultural arbitrary"—things commonly known to them—becomes the only legitimate "knowledge," and thus "cultural capital," through schooling. By accepting the legitimacy of the dominant group's knowledge, dominated classes devalue what they know, rendering themselves "ignorant." For example, knowledge of Europe-derived classical music is valued more than that of hip-hop music in school and beyond, though this may be changing. The dominated groups provide "a market for . . . symbolic products of which the means of production (not least, higher education) are virtually monopolized by the dominant classes" (1977: 42). Education systems also function as smokescreens for the connection between educational qualifications and the cultural capital that dominant-class children inherit. The logic of meritocracy on which the education system is based masks the fact that much of what is considered legitimate knowledge at school is actually gained in family upbringing through familiarization, not in what is taught at school. By disadvantaging those whose upbringing does not give them what the school values, relations of dominance reproduce themselves through schooling (Bourdieu and Passeron 1977).

MOTIS is another example of how what is considered "intelligence" differs from community to community and from historical period to historical period. In ancient Japan, being able to respond in a poetry face-off was considered intelligence; in Māori society, the ability to recite long genealogy contextually to create connections to the audience in oratory was the mark of intelligence. Both examples differ from what is regarded as intelligence in the United States today.

Likewise, study abroad and volunteer/service work researchers assessing results of students' transformation via these experiences look not for objective qualities but for the cultural arbitrary of the dominant group, as is evident from the preferred kinds of transformation. For example, Sandi Kawecka Nenga (2011) talks about four ways in which upper-middle-class students are transformed by doing service work among people of low socioeconomic status by focusing on how they treat their own privilege: they (1) refuse to acknowledge class difference; (2) consider poverty a matter of luck, which leads to discomfort being with people of low socioeconomic background and thus withdrawal into their wealthy bubble; (3) position themselves as potential victims of misunderstanding and withdraw from interacting with those they help; or (4) forge connections across class lines, rethink their idea of class inequality, and work for social justice. Nenga views only the fourth outcome as desired from service work, as the first three do not push students to challenge their privilege and work toward social justice. Though I concur that the fourth is the kind of transformation students should go through in this context, it is important to acknowledge that what Nenga views as desired outcome is based on her view of what these students should become through service work as well as what constitutes "social justice," which may differ from others' criteria. That is, to assess students' transformation with particular desirable transformations in mind is to impose our cultural arbitrary and thus reproduce structures of dominance by privileging our view over others. We should be aware of this aspect of assessment and discuss it openly with students.

That said, it is still imperative that educators equip students with what is valued by the wider society—including the professors who grade students, and employers—even though it is cultural arbitrary of the dominant group. The important part, then, is to be aware of the mechanism through which these relations of power get perpetuated even when we let students go along with it *for the time being*. That is, we need to challenge the processes that perpetuates relations of power by demanding at the macro level that "legitimate knowledge" be more inclusive, while also assuring that all students can access the "culture of power" or the legitimized knowledge (Delpit 1995). Awareness of this power-laden process is also important for the institution that is assessing what students have learned.

It is also worth noting that assessment of learning outcomes is also needed to show the effectiveness and thus legitimacy of study abroad endeavors in general. Because the uniqueness of study abroad is said to lie in experiential aspects summed up as "immersion in another culture," it is necessary to show how this immersion leads to tangible learning outcomes. This helps show study abroad's credibility, how it is on par with more conventional classroom-based education.

In sum, we need to be aware that what we assess is what we value, not something neutral. We then must always ask ourselves who gets to decide "what *we* value," because values are central to the power struggles among groups. The same argument applies to thinking about students' narratives of their own transformations: what changes are valued above others, and who decides this? I will give some concrete examples of this approach at the end of the chapter. In the next section, I focus on a specific aspect of narratives, pointing out that it is socially constructed (rather than articulating the "true" self) and analyzing how ways of talking about experience also shape the experience itself, involving relations of power.

Studies in Student Narratives of Self-Transformation

Student narratives apparently allow researchers to analyze what caused the students' transformation and how it happened. Some researchers argue that it stems from encountering a catalyst—such as individuals with different living conditions and life stories—though how it is interpreted is key to whether they transform themselves (Menard-Warwick and Palmer 2012). Others see being put in the position of visitor as a possible cause of the transformation of a student's views. Norris Palmer argues, as mentioned in chapter 4, that the unique contribution of study abroad is its inversion of the subject and object of study, as the object shifts from "culture different from students'" to "students' own culture." Being noticed by others in the study abroad destination, students are pushed to question their own assumptions. This separates visiting immigrant communities in one's own neighborhood from studying abroad: the former is "to visit the strange amidst the familiar," while the latter is "to become the strange within a recalibrated familiar" (2015: 67).

Yet others view transformation as resulting from a student's intentional act, such as changing their communication style and behavior to adapt to the host society's norms, seen as helping them gain "intercultural competence." This focus adds personal agency in self-transformation to the discourse of immersion that often renders students passive (Covert 2013). Such intentionality can be solicited through structured activities that are conducive to it. For example, Leeanne Chen (2002) suggests that students can transform their attitudes through a dialogic process of articulation: by writing about what they noticed as different in the host society for a readership of people of the host society, which allows them to better reflect on their own cultural assumptions. Explaining their views to the people of the host society forces them to frame their comparisons in less ethnocentric ways, to keep from sounding arrogant. Doing this also affects how they actually feel, in due course.

Researchers also analyze in different degrees student narratives of self-transformation to identify what is missing from, if not how to improve on, study abroad programs. For example, Julia Menard-Warwick and Debrah Palmer (2012) analyze students' transformations and critique how they have changed. Regarding encounters with people during study abroad as catalysts of students' transformation, they refer to what students hear in such encounters as "testimonials." Testimonials of individuals' experiences engage listeners by providing examples of the effects of larger social issues; as such, they place the listener under an ethical obligation to stand in solidarity with them. However, Menard-Warwick and Palmer report, most students viewed a particular person's experience as the feat of a heroic individual, not as an example of wider issues; therefore, they were not inspired to embrace solidarity with the collectivity of that struggling individual. These individualized interpretations, rather than steering students toward larger issues affecting groups of individuals, only led students to recognize their own privilege—"how lucky we are"—without seeing structural issues. They did not come to see themselves as agents of change, either.

Though Menard-Warwick and Palmer do not point it out, the outcome that the educators hoped for might have been reached by bringing in facilitators who could assist students in understanding structural causes and guide discussions so as to create a sense of solidarity—a step suggested by Carrie Kortegast and M. Terral Boisfontaine (2015) when they conclude that meaningful learning outcomes could result from post–study abroad opportunities for students to discuss their experiences. This suggestion sprang from their observation of aforementioned students who talked about their study abroad experience in superficial, stereotyping, reductionist ways, using catchphrases like "globally aware" and "culturally sensitive" without being able to explain what was meant by them.

Kortegast and Boisfontaine do not say what this post-trip discussion should look like and cover, but Elizabeth Root and Anchalee Ngampornchai (2012) do, suggesting that students incorporate their knowledge into ways of communication. They show that students self-report transformation through study abroad in three areas—cognitive, behavioral, and affective—but tend to keep it at a superficial level, describing, for example, getting used to certain foods or gaining the ability to speak the language, cook local meals, or use public transportation—observations similar to those remarked on above. They make several recommendations in this regard, encouraging students to (1) cultivate awareness of their own cultural biases, worldviews, and values, (2) understand where their subject positions stand within relations of power and how those relations shape their views, and (3) learn theoretical notions—ethnocentrism, cultural relativism, stereotyping, prejudice—and models of narrating, to better articulate what they have learned and how they were transformed.

At the heart of these suggestions is the understanding that narratives are related to how we think and that students can change how they think if we provide them with the tools of narratives: vocabulary and frameworks. However, such vocabulary and frameworks also reflect the cultural arbitrary (Bourdieu and Passeron 1977) I discussed earlier and as such could be perceived as an imposition of ways of thinking and experiencing; thus, students need to be alerted to this aspect of using these tools. Next I will introduce some theoretical discussions that unpack this aspect more.

Self-Narrative as a Social Construct

When thinking about descriptions of our own behavior—whether expressed in multiple-choice questions on a survey or in narrative form—we need to be aware of what it means to describe, or use language to talk about, ourselves. Researchers argue that there is no core "truth" about oneself that one can disclose to the world; rather, "truth" is constructed, articulated, and legitimized through various "techniques of truth." As Michel Foucault (1972: 131) argues:

> Each society has its regime of truth, its "general politics" of truth: that is, the types of discourse which it accepts and makes function as true; the mechanisms and instances which enable one to distinguish true and false statements, the means by which each is sanctioned; the techniques and procedures accorded value in the acquisition of truth; the status of those who are charged with saying what counts as true.

For example, different academic disciplines accept different "evidence" to support an argument or make a statement "true." Cultural

anthropology accepts data from interviews and participant observation with a small number of individuals as supporting the "truth,"
whereas the findings of multiple-choice surveys administered to thou-
sands of individuals are not accepted because they are seen as over-
looking important aspects of human experience. In the field of study
abroad, though, the reverse is often the case because in-depth, holistic,
qualitative data is considered ungeneralizable. This difference in what
methods are trusted shows different ways of establishing the "truth" of
human experience.

Narrative is seen as a way to establish the "truth" about one's personal,
inner self. Yet a closer look discerns that narrative is constructed socially.
Ken Plummer (1995) argues that by telling stories about ourselves, we
turn ourselves into "socially organized biographical objects" — "socially
organized" because we produce our stories by drawing on pieces of
others' stories. Besides providing us with the grammars, vocabularies,
and sequences of our own stories, existing narratives offer recipes for
structuring our experience and directing our lives.

Meanwhile, a description of our own experience in someone else's
narrative assures us that our experience is not anomalous but has a
name. It turns fragmented parts of our life into a coherent story and
creates bonds among those who share the story, making, for example,
LGBTQ coming-out stories empowering (Plummer 1995). Narratives
of self-transformation via study abroad work in a similar way, assuring students that their positive and negative experiences—frustration,
confusion, inspiration—are shared by others.

Coaxers in Study Abroad Narratives

Stories are produced not only by storytellers but also by coaxers, who
elicit stories by asking particular questions and guiding the responses
in a certain way. The trial lawyer, the therapist, and the ethnographer
are such coaxers (Plummer 1995). In daily conversations, any interlocutor can be a coaxer, given that utterances are formed dialogically, that
is, particular audiences we have in mind shapes what we say and how
we say it (Bakhtin 1981).

In study abroad, a quick search online for student testimonials
shows how narratives are constructed by a particular coaxer, reflecting
(though not always) a perceived desired outcome of study abroad. Next,
I introduce three kinds of coaxers: commercial study abroad providers
combined with future potential study abroad students as customers
to be enticed; service rating systems combined with future potential

study abroad students as consumers making provider choices; and educational institutions combined with future potential study abroad students as learners.

Coaxers: Commercial Study Abroad Providers and Future Potential Study Abroad Students as Customers to Be Enticed

Commercial study abroad providers' websites post student testimonials in order to draw customers / study abroad students. Both the people presenting the narratives (the study abroad provider) and the audience (future customers / study abroad students) act as coaxers of these narratives.

One example by a student who studied abroad in the Netherlands via the commercial provider is entitled "Gain a new Perspective on Life":

> At first, I was extremely nervous about going abroad. I've always been a bit of a control-freak and I knew that while studying abroad in The Netherlands and traveling throughout Europe there would be so much out of my control. But, it was such an important opportunity for me to get out of my comfort zone. It put many things from my life in the States in perspective for me—relationships, careers, friendships. When I was abroad, I learned to go-with-the-flow more, which has truly made my post-abroad life easier. If you worry too much, you'll miss out on the amazing sights and experiences. I've taken that mentality back home with me and it truly is the best souvenir." (StudyAbroad.com 2011)

This follows the linear self-transformation narrative—from "a control freak" to a "go-with-the-flow" person. Her being pushed out of her comfort zone, putting things in her life in perspective, and changing her attitude about life to worry less are common narratives of study abroad discussed in chapter 4 (regarding "comfort zone") and earlier in this chapter (regarding the perceptions, attitude, affect) (Fendler 1998; see also Doerr and Taieb 2017b). Though it was *study* abroad trip, the benefit of it is talked about in terms of attitudinal change, not gaining knowledge of the subject area. What is considered desirable—something the students gained—here is to be relaxed and have amazing experiences. The addressee "you" indicates the coaxer is potential future study abroad students, to whom this testimonial portrays her experience as positive, self-transformative, and desirable—something the addressee should also pursue.

Another testimonial from the same website that reports about her study abroad experience in England is entitled "Become Global-Minded" and states:

Studying abroad adds another level to your college experience. It takes you out of your element and places you in a place where you are less comfortable, enabling you to learn in a new way. Experiencing other cultures around the world broadens your knowledge base and teaches you to think and live differently. It is so important, today, to have a solid understanding of different cultures, and I think sending students abroad is an easy way to set up our generation to be a more globally-minded society.

In this also linear transformation narrative, the mention of being put outside the comfort zone as the catalyst and a new way of learning—through experiencing "different cultures"—resonate with the discourse of immersion discussed in chapter 4, pointing to the existing vocabulary they draw from. What is learned is knowledge about another "culture" and ways of thinking and living, which is summarized as "global-minded." Again, content area of the study is not mentioned, and attitude change is emphasized, besides knowledge of the "culture" of destination. With the coaxer of future study abroad students in mind, this narrative is structured with a common vocabulary and with desired outcome of study abroad in mind.

Both testimonials talk about self-transformation as the outcome of study abroad. They followed the same path of linear self-transformation: being out of their comfort zone pushed them to grow in terms of their attitude with no mention of subject content area they studied in classes. This almost identical narrative structure suggests the specific setup (study abroad programs to be promoted) and audience—future study abroad students (i.e., customer) looking for changes in their perspectives and attitude by doing something different.

Coaxers: Service Rating Systems and Future Potential Study Abroad Students as Consumers Shopping around

Another type of testimonial appears in a social media page of commercial study abroad providers and serves as reviews of the program, rating it for other consumers (i.e., potential future study abroad students). Apparently not filtered and thus sanctioned by the providers featured on the page, the testimonials there focus on the quality of service provided by the study abroad program: "[Program name] is a great study abroad program at a great price with great excursions, [friends], and directors. You are going to change as a person, meet a lot of people that are different than you, and grow" (Sol Education Abroad 2018). Here, we can see the quality of the program is rated by the degree by which the desired outcome of study abroad—self-transformation and meeting "a lot of people"—can be achieved. This is an example of how shared vocabulary and goals of study abroad is used in particular way to reach one of the coaxers, the audience.

It could be quite negative regarding the providers' service: "Had problems related to the accommodation. None of the people I talked to when I called [program provider] helped me at all. . . . I felt completly [*sic*] alone and hopeless." It could also be about the program's political viewpoint: "The whole damn program is loaded with liberal program 'leaders' who are often times, full of shit and busy preaching their propaganda views. . . . I simply wanted to focus on [destination] without having to feel ostracized because of some pussy 'leaders' who demonize people who aren't like them." Here, the mention of viewpoint narrows down the intended audience of the testimonial to those who are not "liberal" thus agree with his view. Depending on the audience, it could work to put off or encourage future "customers."

These testimonials appeared in the provider's Facebook page as page reviews (CIEE Study Abroad 2018b). Coaxers are social media setups that can work as a rating system of a program and the potential audience—future study abroad students viewed as consumers looking for a good study abroad service providers—whom may be imagined differently by those who posts, as the second post suggests.

Coaxers: Educational Institutions and Future Potential Study Abroad Students as Learners and Career Seekers

In college study abroad program websites, student testimonials take a different form. They discuss more in detail their homestay, learning, and travel experience, as well as their effects for their future careers (UCI Study Abroad Center 2006). A student who studied abroad in Australia states:

> As soon as I got to my homestay, my homestay mom immediately welcomed me into her home. . . . I was amazed at how friendly everyone in my program was and how welcoming the Australians were. The rest of the program seemed to be a blur of incredible experiences and fun times. I was participating in the Marine Biology and Human and Terrestrial Ecology at University of Queensland, of which field research was a requirement. Every couple of weeks, I would be able to travel to research stations all over the Eastern coast to design and execute independent research projects and then write scientific papers on them. The workload may have been more intense than I was used to in [home institution], but everything was so much more engaging. As soon as we would learn about the different fish that occupy a specific bay, we would all go out for a beach walk and actually see them. . . . When I applied to medical

schools last summer, I knew I had something worthwhile to write about in my applications and personal statement. I asked both of my Australian professors for letters of recommendation because we had gotten to know each other so well throughout the program. Even on interviews, my interviewer would ask me about my experience abroad, and I would talk about how amazing it was. Not only did it give me something to bond over with my interviewer, it is something that I genuinely love talking about, so I would immediately feel less nervous.

This shows familiar vocabulary of study abroad—meeting new people and "fun times"—but also focuses on the subject matter of the study as well as its pedagogy and the study abroad experience's implication to her career opportunities, which did not exist in the first two types of testimonials. The audience is potential study abroad students, but they are framed in this narrative as learners and ones who are seeking careers after graduation. The description focuses less on her overall linear attitudinal transformation than on experiences and their specific effects.

All narratives on this site show similar tendencies that contrast starkly with those in the other two setups, suggesting some cues given to the students in writing them, if not students following models provided by others. This shows the contrast not only in the featured programs but also in how they are written depending on the coaxer—who is providing the space to post these narratives and who the intended audience is.

Reframing Study Abroad Student Narratives

The above examples show how study abroad narratives of self-transformation can be understood as socially constructed, shaped by particular coaxers—settings and audience—that may have different desired outcomes in mind. While all the student testimonials targeted the audience of future potential study abroad students and while all programs must have some educational component as they are *study* abroad program, they were framed differently. The commercial study abroad providers framed them as customers looking to transform themselves in terms of their attitude and have a good time. The social media page about commercial study abroad providers framed them as consumers who are shopping around for a provider that can give them good-quality service. The educational institution's study abroad page framed them as learners and career seekers interested in things and ways in which they can learn during study abroad and how beneficial they are to their career development opportunities.

What this suggests in terms of our future actions is threefold. First, it suggests a need to take student narratives not as a window to their "true" experience but as something socially constructed with the available vocabulary and coaxers. This understanding allows researchers and practitioners to avoid making inaccurate conclusions about study abroad experiences that may ignore this constructed nature of the narratives. Instead, we can situate these narratives as something that is formed with particular audience in mind with its specific emphasis and biases, as no narratives are "neutral" and "true," while still using them as important source to see how students chose to express themselves in these particular settings of narration.

Second, this suggests a need for awareness that, when researchers call for providing students with theoretical concepts and frameworks (Root and Ngampornchai 2012) or an audience (Chen 2002), that act itself is a performative act of creating new narratives and perceptions shaped by them. That is, although these calls are made to deepen and enrich students' reflections and understandings, we need to avoid seeing them as neutral. Instead, we need to still step back and see what we offer as our way of transforming their narratives, like other ones we saw above, so that it remains an object of scrutiny for the purpose of further improving it.

The act of suggesting vocabulary itself resonates with a wider process of imposition of a way of thinking on individuals. Louis Althusser (1971) argues that to use categories is to be subjected to the society's ideology, as mentioned in chapter 2. Ideology works through the interpellation—the positioning of individuals as subjects—within systems of categories based on race, class, gender, sexual orientation, and so forth, which differ from society to society (e.g., "Asian" tends to mean Chinese/Korean/Japanese people in the United States, whereas in South Africa it means Indian/Pakistani/Bangladeshi) and can change historically (e.g., the new nonbinary gender categories in US discourse). People experience the world through categories, and categories structure their practices. In turn, individuals' behavior and language articulate perceived differences amongst people, thereby materializing ideology.

Here, an individual is a subject in a double sense, on the one hand being subject to systems of difference by being hailed or interpellated into them, while on the other hand having a sense of free will and acting as a subject who is the author of, and responsible for, their actions. That is, individuals are interpellated as subjects who subject themselves "freely" to a system of difference (Althusser 1971; see also Hall 1985). As briefly mentioned in chapter 2, Judith Butler further develops this framework by suggesting the notions of performativity and citationality. She uses the notion of performativity "not as the act by which a subject brings into being what she/he names, but rather, as that reiterative power of discourse to produce the phenomena that it regulates and constrains" (1993: 2). With the notion of citationality, she suggests that by being cited as the norm, certain systems (she calls them "matrices") of difference become naturalized and materialized as meaningful sets of categories in which to classify people.

In this framework, then, to provide students with vocabulary and structures for talking about their study abroad experience and self-transformation is to interpellate them into certain categories and impose on them these ways of thinking about their experience. This is inevitable, as thought relies on language and categories; what is important is that students be aware of this process and its effects, which is my next point.

Third, I suggest we let students be aware of this process—how the narratives are socially constructed, and how gaining new vocabulary and framework to construct them is a process of coming to think differently. As calling for new frameworks to narrate mentioned above is tantamount to imposing particular ways of thinking on students, we must also caution students that this process itself reproduces relations of power. I will suggest some ways to do this at the end of this chapter.

In the next two sections, I discuss two issues that pertain to both discussions of assessment and student narratives: assumed study abroad student body and the specific highlighting of study abroad as a site of self-transformation.

The Assumed Student Body of Study Abroad

The discussions of outcome assessment and the pattern of transformation have so far been silent about the assumed traits of the study abroad students themselves. These assumptions can be seen in what "coaxers" ask them—for example, survey questions that test "global competence" and "intercultural sensitivity" before and after study abroad experience—and coaxers' (i.e., researchers') critiques of narratives of self-transformation in which students focus merely on being lucky (Menard-Warwick and Palmer 2012), view their privilege uncritically, or do not want social justice (Nenga 2011). Such assumptions suggest that study abroad students are monocultural (and often monolingual), parochial, lack "intercultural experience," and are of privileged backgrounds racially and socioeconomically; otherwise, the coaxers would not expect these types of transformation to result from study abroad experience. As discussed in chapter 6, study abroad students tend to be seen as white and middle class. Questions about self-transformation add more traits to that background.

These assumptions are problematic in two ways. First, the assumption that most study abroad students are white and middle class has especially prompted calls for greater participation by minority students, whose situation has been framed problematically as a lack of "global competence" that needs to be remedied by gaining experience through study abroad. This view ignores the fact that many minority students have "crossed cultural borders" and competently adapt to and negotiate with people of different backgrounds, mainly because they have already experienced the need to adjust to not only mainstream life at school and elsewhere, but also, if they are immigrants or descendants of immigrants, to US mainstream life and their ancestral homeland's (see Doerr 2012a, 2017c, 2018).

A second problem with these assumptions is that the narrative structure of self-transformation via studying abroad excludes many students who do not fit in that structure, potentially causing them to have to reframe their experiences in ways that do not reflect how they really felt about them, robbing them of ways to talk about their experience, delegitimizing their experience, and erasing their experience—especially if there is no way to talk about it. For example, minority multilingual and multicultural students find it difficult to say that study abroad experience itself "allowed them to cross cultural borders" and "become culturally sensitive," or that they "learned to negotiate different cultures," when they have already gained such skills and competencies from having had to adjust to mainstream society. If students are already accustomed to such cultural adjustment, then nothing will have changed after their study abroad experience, so the outcome assessment may be that they did not learn anything, although they might have learned something else that was not asked about. Likewise, if students are already aware and conscientious about social justice, study abroad with a service work component may not change their views very much or change in different ways than just becoming "aware," which again makes their study abroad experience appear unworthy of favorable assessment.

Though researchers have not talked about this problem, it is important that questions for assessment, as well as narrative structures and vocabulary, acknowledge that study abroad students may be multicultural, multilingual, and already experienced in various lifestyles and group differences. They may already know the language of the destination when their compatriot students do not, as is often the case for

Hispanic American students fluent in Spanish who travel to Spanish-speaking countries (see Doerr 2015a). In order to recognize the experience of students outside of the mainstream, it is important to suggest new "learning outcomes" from study abroad and new ways of talking about their experience.

Regimes of Experience

What is considered meaningful self-transformation depends on what our sociocultural environments push us to notice as meaningful transformation, just as such environments push us to notice certain difference as more meaningful than others (McDermott and Varenne 1995), as discussed in chapters 2 and 6. For example, self-transformation via studying abroad is celebrated and almost expected, whereas self-transformation via reading books or attending a college lecture is not talked about much, though it does happen. I once asked about thirty students in my class to share with the class whatever they have done for the first time in the past twenty-four hours. Each one of them had done something new—went to a new restaurant, ate new food, read something new, tried a new game, put on a new clothing item, talked to someone new. Yet they had not even noticed it until they were asked to identify it. A small experiment like that shows that we do something new all the time, which may change ourselves in some way but we just do not have an opportunity to reflect on it, let alone think how that may have transformed us. Even when we recognize such transformation ourselves, we tend not to have occasions to express them unless given an opportunity (Many of my students reported that having to stop playing their favorite sport because of injury as a major self-transformative experience), as mentioned in the introduction.

I call it "regime of experience." Just like "regime of mobility" (Glick Schiller and Salazar 2013) celebrates mobility of the upper class who are often called "global citizens" while treating mobility of the lower class with suspicion, often even hindering their movement (see discussions in chapter 1), "regimes of experience" treat the experience of transformation that occur in various contexts differently. As study abroad derives from a rite of passage and is celebrated as the main medium to nurture "global competence" to create "global citizens," self-transformation that occurs through study abroad is celebrated. Backgrounding is the current valorization of "border crossing" as a way to learn (see chapter 6), which also celebrates experience of self-transformation via volunteer/service experience.

In this backdrop, acknowledging self-transformation that occurs in other contexts—including moving out from your own neighborhood, interaction with people with different socioeconomic background by attending new school or joining new workforce, as well as experience of immigrants that involves crossing ethnic "borders" to the mainstream or to the ancestral homeland—leads to challenging the regimes of experience and celebrating the experience and skills gained from it that have been marginalized (Doerr 2012a, 2017c, 2018).

Study abroad is meaningful in that it pushes us to focus on our daily life during that period. If we actively incorporate more rigorous analyses of our daily experience as reflecting structural issues and relations of power rather than static manifestation of "cultural difference" as suggested in the introduction and chapter 4, and if we consider talking about it is socially constructed with particular coaxers in mind, as discussed in this chapter, it provides us with a good model of thinking about our life as shaped by wider forces, which we participate in (re) producing.

In the introduction and chapter 4, I suggested examining our daily acts and experiences with the same rigor as we do during study abroad and becoming aware that mundane experiences in our daily life are effects of wider structural arrangements. Here, in a similar vein, I further suggest expanding things that transform us from happening in daily practices only during study abroad to daily practices anywhere. It not only allows us to pay closer attention to how we are constantly developing but also urges us to investigate how and why such transformations occur. Such understanding is important in thinking about how to create social changes regarding certain social issues—racism, sexism, classism, ageism, homophobia, and so on—because it allows us to analyze what makes us feel in certain ways and how we can change it. In this light, study abroad can be a practice not merely of "global competence" but of what I call "social competence" that is necessarily in any occasion.

Implications and Suggestions

In the field of study abroad, assessment of whether and how students have been transformed through their study abroad experience is used not only to understand the effects of studying abroad but also to improve the programs. Assessment also works to justify the need for study abroad in higher education, given the current agenda of "globalizing" education as well. Furthermore, the assessment process involves relations of power: it imposes what are considered desired knowledge and skills and assumes that students lack them. Given that students' own narratives of self-transformation are socially constructed based on the society's "regime of truth" and an assumed student body, more sophisticated and inclusive vocabulary and frameworks are needed to process the diversity of their experience, even though such guidance itself imposes a worldview whose mechanism needs to be made clear to the students as discussed.

Questions that could be asked to alert students to these issues before, during, and after their study abroad experience (with the tense of the questions to be changed accordingly) are listed at the end of the chapter. These questions should be accompanied by questions about (W) subject positions, (X) power relations, (Y) how things around us have changed and how we can change them, and (Z) mutual construction of difference between various societies, including study abroad students' home and host societies. (These questions are combined and included in the series of questions for particular topics discussed below.)

Self-Transformation

What does it mean that we care about whether students have transformed themselves via study abroad? We can ask students about various topics to prompt discussion of whether we have to transform ourselves, and why (see question series 7-A). We can also ask students why we care about whether we transform ourselves via study abroad (see question series 7-B).

Politics of Assessment

We have looked at various assessment tools and analyzed how the items in the assessment show what knowledge and skills are considered important, which is based on dominant group's values. In discussing this aspect of assessment with students, we can ask questions about which knowledge and skills are measured (question series 7-C1), who decides what is desired and who benefits from what is desired (question series 7-C2), and what it means to measure these things (question series 7-C3).

Narratives of Transformation

Student themselves also narrate how they were transformed by studying abroad. We can ask the types of questions listed as 7-D1 to let them reflect on what it means to narrate one's own experience as a transformation, as well as about intentional adaptive changes in behavior. Regarding how they would recount their experience to the people of the host society versus their compatriots and why, we can ask questions such as ones introduced as series 7-D2. Examples of providing students some theoretical vocabulary to talk about their experience, we can ask questions listed in series 7-D3.

As to whether students recognize the structural origins of what they saw, we can ask students the questions listed in chapter 2 (series 2-A and 2-C) and in chapter 4, as well as the ones labeled as 7-Z, and address theoretical vocabularies and frameworks by asking questions labeled as 7-D4.

Assumed Student Body of Study Abroad Students

To make students aware of the assumptions of the study abroad student body—white, monolingual/monocultural, middle-class students—in the existing assessment and narrative structure, we can ask questions that touch on the students' subject positions as listed as 7-W.

Regime of Experience

As to discuss what special attention we give to study abroad as a rite of passage pushes us to highlight self-transformation via study abroad and further draw students' attention to their daily activities, we can ask question series listed as 7-E. The Daorba Yduts activity (see chapter 4) also helps create awareness in students how they are being transformed in various ways in their daily life in their own home country. It can be followed by debriefing of the experience, making sure the point of the activity is understood.

* * *

Assessing learning outcomes and listening to students' narratives about their own transformations are important steps in understanding the impact of study abroad and improving the programs offered. Students, however, will benefit further from knowing how these practices also involve relations of power and social constructions of "truth" about themselves. Discussions prompted by some of the example questions can enhance students' understanding and awareness of what is happening around them before, during, and after their studies abroad: in their daily life. We can then suggest they engage in the investigations of the daily life.

Recommended Readings

Kortegast, Carrie. A., and M. Terral Boisfontaine. 2015. "Beyond 'It Was Good': Students' Post–Study Abroad Practices for Negotiating Meaning." *Journal of College Student Development* 56 (8): 812–828.
Critical analyses of students' narratives of their study abroad experience.

Menard-Warwick, Julia, and Debrah K. Palmer. 2012. "Eight Versions of the Visit to La Barraca: Critical Discourse Analysis of a Study-Abroad Narrative from Mexico." *Teacher Education Quarterly* 39 (1): 121–138
Critical analyses of students' narratives of their study abroad experience.

Nenga, Sandi Kawecka. 2011. "Volunteering to Give up Privilege? How Affluent Youth Volunteers Respond to Class Privilege." *Journal of Contemporary Ethnography* 40 (3): 263–289.
Analysis of how volunteer work changed students in various, not necessarily positive, ways.

Plummer, Ken. 1995. *Telling Sexual Stories: Power, Change and Social Worlds.* London: Routledge.
Analyses of narratives and how they are socially constructed.

Root, Elizabeth, and Anchalee Ngampornchai. 2012. "'I Came Back as a New Human Being': Student Descriptions of Intercultural Competence Acquired through Education Abroad Experiences." *Journal of Studies in International Education* 17 (5): 513–532.
Critical analyses of students' narratives of their study abroad experience.

◖◖◎ Sample Questions

7-A: On Self-Transformation

7-A1: Do you feel you will be changed by studying abroad? If yes, why do you think so? How do you think you will be transformed?

7-A2: Do you think you are supposed/encouraged to transform yourself? Why?

7-A3: What will happen if you are not transformed by your study abroad experience? Will that mean you have failed? Why?

7-B: Why We Care about Self-Transformation

7-B1: What made you think self-transformation is important? Study abroad promotional materials? Peers? Teachers? Parents?

7-B2: Why do you think they portray self-transformation as important?

7-B3: Do you feel that the legitimacy of study abroad rests on its transformation of students?

7-C: On the Politics of Measuring

7-C1-1: What do you think administrators of the program want to assess about you?

7-C1-2: Why do you think they would be interested in that aspect of your learning? What does that tell you about the administrators' interests?

7-C2-1: Who do you think decides what should be measured?

7-C2-2: Do you think aspects of other fields of study are measured in the same way? If not, what standards would they be measured by? Why? Why are there differences? What does that tell you about measuring things?

7-C3-X1: Who do you think benefits from these measurements?

7-C3-X2: Whose worldviews are represented in the assessment questions? Why do you think that is?

7-C3-X3: Do you think the fact of asking the given questions in the assessment advantages some people and not others? How?

7-D: Narratives of Transformation

7-D1-1: Do you think your behavior will change when you are in the host society? If yes, how will you learn how to act there?

7-D1-2: Do you think everyone will be acting and doing things differently to adjust to the host society? If not, who will and who won't? What do you think will make a difference?

7-D1-3: Do you think study abroad providers would want you to change your behavior in order to adapt to the host society? How do you know—did they say so explicitly?

7-D2-1: If you felt something in the host society was different from what you were familiar with, how would you talk about it with your compatriot friends?

7-D2-2: How would you talk about it with people in the host society?

7-D2-3: Would there be any difference in the way you talk about your experience with each of these two groups? How? Why?

7-D3-1: Do you know what ethnocentrism means? Can you give an example of ethnocentrism you have experienced?

7-D3-2: Do you know what cultural relativism mean? Can you give an example of cultural relativism you have experienced?

7-D3-3: Do you feel the above questions and vocabulary have changed how you think about things and act? Some people say your vocabulary and frameworks shape your views and experiences of the world. Do you feel you are led to think in certain ways because of that?

7-D3-4: Were any vocabularies and frameworks suggested not helpful in describing your experience? For example, if your parents are from Peru and you studied abroad in Peru, you may already have been familiar with the lifestyle of the study abroad destination. What does that tell you about the assumptions of study abroad program providers?

7-E: Self-Transformation in Daily Life

7-E1: What are the moments that you felt have changed you throughout your life? When did you find new aspects of yourself? How?

7-E2: Has starting this school [starting a new sport, moving to a new neighborhood, starting a new work, living in a new place, making a new friend or meeting a new partner, reading a book, seeing a film] changed you? In what way?

7-E3: How are you different compared to five years ago? Three years ago? One year ago? What made you change?

7-E4: Have you had a chance to talk about these changes? When and where? How?

7-E5: What are the differences in the ways you talk about changing yourself via study abroad and via other activities? Opportunities to talk about it? Read-audience? Why do you think there is such difference? What are the effects of such difference?

7-W: Assumed Student Body of Study Abroad Students

7-W1: What if your background makes you already familiar with life in the host society? Would you find it difficult to talk about self-transformation in the way assessors expect you to talk about it? What does that tell you about the assessors' assumptions?

7-W2: What kind of questions allows you to speak more about your own experience, if you feel existing questions do not allow you to talk about your experience?

7-Z: Structural Causes of Difference and Transformation

7-Z: What do you think caused the differences you noticed—cultural difference? Economic conditions? History? How do you know?

7-Z: If you notice something as different, what do you think are the causes of that difference? Cultural conditions? Economic conditions? History?

7-Z: How do you think the United States is involved in the formation of such difference? For example, if people view communism as good, do you think the US has any influence on that? How? Vice versa?

7-Z: Do you think the US has had any influence on policies in the host society? How? Vice versa?

Conclusion and Departure
New Frameworks for Study Abroad

Study abroad provides a unique learning experience, but it is not, as is often claimed, the nurturing of "global competence" or creation of "global citizens" or provision of opportunity to "immerse" oneself in the host society via a host family in order to learn another "culture" and language. In this book, I have pointed out various assumptions and effects produced by these notions, which are based on ideologies of nation-state, globalism, the "native speaker," countable language, standardization, immersion, host family, border crossing, and self-transformation. To keep using these notions in the way they are now is dangerous, I argued, because it would perpetuate these ideologies. In each chapter, I drew on current theoretical debates to carefully examine various key terms of study abroad and explore ways to move away from these notions. I suggested possible questions to ask to engage study abroad students in deep thinking about these issues with concrete examples in each chapter.

In chapter 1, I focused on ideologies around the linked notions of the global (i.e., the ideology of globalism, which valorizes global flows and regimes of mobility that celebrate mobility for only certain people—mainly, the white, upper middle class) and the national (i.e., the ideology of the nation-state as a bounded unit of internally homogeneous people with corresponding "culture" and language marked by unequivocal national borders): the global depends on the existence of national borders to be crossed. The result of this link then is a paradoxical reinforcement of the nation-state ideology through the encouragement of "global" activities.

To alert students to challenge this nation-state ideology, I suggested asking them questions about how "national/cultural difference" gets constructed through relationships among various nation-states on the one hand, and questions to stimulate recognition of the diversity within the nation-state on the other. As to the notion of the global, I encouraged involving students in discussion of the effects of globalism, particularly its double standard (i.e., regimes of mobility) that values the "global movement" of individuals from only some racial and socio-economic backgrounds. I suggested a workshop activity that highlights this double standard and bring to light the value of those whose mobility and its effects are under-celebrated. Overall, I called for using the prominence of the global in study abroad as a good starting point from which to engage students in understanding the ideologies of the nation-state and globalism.

Chapter 2 examined the notion of "culture." I reviewed five frameworks for understanding "culture"—culture-as-problem, culture-as-division-to-be-ignored, culture-as-safe-difference, culture-as-political-resource, and culture-as-constructed-difference—and encouraged involving students in discussion of how "cultural difference" is constructed in relations of power. I suggested this be done by showing students how the image of "culture" as a homogeneous and bounded unit of difference is a construction influenced by the aforementioned ideology of the nation-state; how we participate in the process of construction by using the concept of "culture" (i.e., citing a system of difference based on "culture"); how we are positioned in multiple intersecting systems of difference—race, class, gender, age, political vision, and so on—that then lead us to relate to various individuals through difference/similarity; how internally complex the students' home and host societies are as various "differences" derive from and come to be noticed through particular socioeconomic conditions, institutions and infrastructures, and government policies; how "cultural" difference then is one out of many "differences" that are constructed, yet we are guided to notice it for particular reasons; and how the host and home societies of study abroad students connect to shape each other's social organizations and conditions. In short, I urged study abroad professionals to help students understand that "culture" is one way to frame differences among people—a process that itself needs to be investigated as something produced in relations of power, not as a neutral term to think about relationships among people.

Chapter 3 discussed the notion of "native speakers," among whom study abroad students supposedly learn the language of the destination best. I first observed that the notion rests on three problematic assumptions—"native speakers" speak the national language of the host society, language is a homogeneous system, and "native speakers" have intrinsic competence in their language—and presented critiques of them. I then suggested engaging students in understanding the notion of language in terms of the diversity within what is assumed to be "one language" by asking how various linguistic varieties are positioned hierarchically according to the status of their speakers rather than linguistic qualities, and how the hierarchy is perpetuated by the ideology of standardization and the notion of linguistic competency, which creates a hierarchy of "native" and "non-native" speakers. That is, through understanding these issues in study abroad, students can understand wider issues of language and learning language.

In chapter 4, I revisited the notion of immersion, the key concept of study abroad. I focused on effects of the discourse of immersion: construction of the host and home societies as fundamentally different and internally homogeneous (relating to the ideologies of the nation-state and "culture"), and the creation of a hierarchy of study abroad experiences in relation to tourists, various non-immersive study abroad experience, classroom learning, and learning in the home society. I then suggested viewing host societies as diverse places where "locals" and visitors/sojourners intermix and co-construct the life. I also introduced analyses of the effects of labeling particular experiences "immersion." Describing a student as "living like a local" is not a neutral act but a loaded performative act that tells us how the labeler perceives the student doing the immersion, the people among whom the student is immersed, and the relationships between them.

Encouraging students to think critically about these effects of the notion of immersion, I further suggested capitalizing on that notion's focus on daily life to engage students in contemplating and analyzing their daily practices and connecting their lived experience to social structures, thereby gaining the understanding needed to be an active agent in changing social orders that privilege some and marginalize others, both during study abroad and in general. I suggested questions to ask, as well as a workshop activity, for this purpose. With this reframing, study abroad can be considered an important occasion for students to develop this important skill.

Chapter 5 focused on the notions of the host society and host family. Challenging the common view that a host society is homogeneous and that a host family represents the host society, I pointed to discussions that show that host family experience is diverse because host families are diverse (and not representative of the host society) and that a student's experience with a host family is not "authentic" as claimed, because the family members change their daily routine to accommodate the study abroad students they host. Therefore, staying with a host family is not an encounter between two distinct "cultures" because it is not about a study abroad student with a particular "cultural" background joining a new, static, homogeneous "cultural" lifestyle in a host society represented by a host family. Instead, staying with a host family is about the student joining in the ongoing production of the host society's life by the diverse people there, including visitors like students studying abroad. I suggested creating this awareness in students so that they can understand their life anywhere as a diverse, constantly changing co-construction in which they also participate. Involving students in this discussion would help them challenge not only ideologies about the host society and host family but also social changes and their roles in that process.

Chapter 6 offered discussions on the notion of border crossing in study abroad and on the volunteer/service work that is increasingly incorporated into study abroad experience. Crossing borders is celebrated by framing study abroad in various ways: as "adventure," as a disorienting experience that pushes one to gain certain skills, and as education through immersion, which assumes the host society is different from the home society. Volunteer/service work in domestic contexts and during studying abroad is increasingly framed as border crossing experience and lauded as nurturing students' empathy for the less fortunate. Yet framing study abroad and volunteer/service work this way, I suggested, actually constructs difference by focusing on and searching for it. Instead of making the newness and difference of the host society the only and necessary reason to enjoy the experience, we can frame study abroad as just experiencing diverse life of the host society. Volunteer/service work can be reframed as working together toward the same goal rather than crossing borders.

In chapter 7, I examined how students' learning outcomes and transformations are measured and discussed. Bringing in the issue of relations of power that determine what should be learned and how students should transform themselves from what, I suggested alerting students to the meaning of assessing certain knowledge and competence. I also illustrated the ways narratives are constructed—through the setups and the perceived audiences' interest—and "truth" are recognized as such so that we are more critical of narratives as a social construct. Pointing out the "regimes of experience"—the same experience is celebrated more than others depending on the context, such as transformative experience during study abroad being celebrated more than that in daily life—I referred back to the activity suggested in chapter 4 to focus on daily actions in the same way as they do about study abroad experience and relate them to wider social arrangements. I then suggested new learning goals and narrative structures that are more inclusive and reflective of the diversity of the student body abroad and the goals of its members.

Urging students to be aware of and analytical about these existing notions and their ideological underpinnings helps them develop skills to understand and further challenge reproductions of such notions. Study abroad is a unique area of education that focuses on the daily interactions as the source of learning. While it can perpetuate various ideologies as discussed in this book, it can also—if students are equipped with critical and rigorous theoretical frameworks to analyze ideological and constructed aspects of various concepts and how they continued to be perpetuated—become even more fruitful opportunity to understand how the world works. Its sociocultural, economic, and political structures shape our daily lives, and understanding their workings allows us to be an active agent in further shaping and changing it.

New Frameworks for Study Abroad

Having considered these critiques of existing notions and ideologies, this book suggests reframing study abroad in new ways. Next, I summarize four ways of reframing study abroad based on the discussions throughout the book.

Understanding and Challenging the Construction of "Homogeneity" Frameworks

As discussed in this book, the predominant vocabulary and frameworks for understanding study abroad imply the internal homogeneity of a nation, "culture," and language. We can not only criticize these notions as historically constructed but also challenge them by using different ways to understand them. That is, we need to view these terms as "folk terms" to be investigated, not as neutral terms used to understand and adjust to situations.

Recognizing its constructed nature means unmasking the process of homogenization, which, though oppressive, is often considered desirable or "natural" in the name of unity, harmony, or "propriety." Examples include forced assimilation and standardization of language through imposition of "the norm" based on the dominant group's ideals. Education of "legitimate knowledge" (often merely called "desired skills" and "competence") through certain methods (e.g., immersion) based on the dominant group's worldviews is another example. We can also urge students to challenge these notions by using alternative notions. For example, instead of using the notion of immersion to mean "living *like* a local" with an assumption of homogeneous local people, we can urge students to view immersion as "living *with* locals," who are diverse and flexible in their practices as they accommodate the students.

Study abroad practitioners can mention this when students are deciding on their accommodation arrangement and discuss this in orientation sessions with students. This awareness allows students to frame the situation not as their slipping into the host family's life but as working together to make the living arrangement comfortable for all. That would make students view their own behavior in a more active light with responsibility in co-constructing the homestay experience. Though students do need to position them as visitors in the host family's house, they can also appreciate more the effort the host family is making to accommodate their needs.

Instead of telling students to avoid spending time with fellow compatriot students, which implies that these students are all the same, urge them to engage in conversation about diverse experience and perceptions among fellow compatriots and what caused that diversity. For study abroad programs, this would mean creating more occasions for study abroad students themselves to discuss their own experience (for its importance, see Talburt and Stewart 1999; Woolf 2007) and highlight that as an important learning experience. Study abroad students can then think of their time with fellow compatriots not merely as staying in comfort zone but also meaningful interaction, which may have lasting effects after they go back home. Recognizing diversity within what is usually considered homogeneous is important. However, it must be done rigorously and critically; otherwise, it would reproduce the same "homogeneity" concept only at the different scale, such as at the scale of region, ethnic group, or class, as will be discussed in the next subsection.

Diversity and Difference

It is important to understand what is usually considered homogeneous — nation, "culture," language, as well as host society and study abroad students themselves — is diverse within. However, changing the scale at which we recognize the diversity is not good enough, as mentioned earlier.

It is also important to point out the complex relationships between the notion of diversity and difference in the context of study abroad. Here, while the concept of "diversity" implies the lack of homogeneity that may defy categorization and thus domestication, the concept of "difference" in the study abroad context implies the existence of bounded units, such as that between study abroad students' home and host societies, that works as the raison d'etre of study abroad, as discussed in chapter 1. That is, just like the global-national relationship, talking about "difference" implies homogeneity within each of these "different cultures and nations." Therefore, we need to be critical of this notion of difference celebrated in study abroad for "adventure," cognitive dissonance, and immersion experience.

There are several alternative ways to frame this celebrated "difference." First, we can urge students to frame study abroad not as "adventurous encounter with exotic difference" but just as experiencing the life of the host society regardless of their similarity or difference. This would discourage students from creating stereotypes by focusing only on the part that contrasts themselves and allow them to also analyze similarities and variations. For example, study abroad students in Spain often mention the difference in time that Spaniards eat dinner. This can be pushed to focus also on the similarity in how they eat dinner and who they eat with and consider any underlying similarity as to how they relate to family and friends through eating dinner together.

Second, we need to avoid framing the difference between students' home and host societies as preexisting. Instead, we should urge the students to view that construction of that difference occurred *in relation to* each other influenced not only by sociocultural perceptions but also by international agreements and regulations, government policies in each society, and commercial enterprises in and across these countries, as discussed in chapters 2, 4, and 7. Therefore, when study abroad students observes "different culture" in their destination, we need to urge them to see how the policies, practices, and ideologies of their home and host societies mutually influenced the development of that "difference" — for example, as mentioned in the introduction, poverty in Guatemala needs to be understood in context of the aftermaths of its long and devastating civil war that emerged out from the CIA-led military coup of their democratically elected president in the height of the Cold War. That is, what they observe in study abroad destination is not an independent "interesting difference" but potentially something we may be responsible for through past and ongoing relationships between our and their countries' government policies and practices.

This means that more research needs to be done on the part of the study abroad program as well as students because most study abroad program do not offer discussions on such in-depth relationships between the home and host countries. However, such knowledge would help students understand deeply what they observe during the stay. Furthermore, because many people in the destination may not be aware of such structural relationships between the countries, study abroad students becoming aware of them would benefit the people in the destination they interact with as well.

That is, we need to see "difference" as something that is arranged and categorized variously for particular purposes and effects, intentionally or unintentionally, as McDermott and Varenne (1995) argue: we are different from each other in myriad of ways, yet we are pushed to recognize only certain differences influenced by sociocultural and economic environments. Categorization helps us understand and operate in our daily lives, but we need to be aware of these mechanisms and effects that often mask oppressive practices that are involved. That is, we need to urge students to realize that such arrangements often benefit some and marginalize others, especially when some groups are forced to change their behavior and lifestyle to fit the "norm" and the legitimated "knowledge" based on the dominant group's worldviews and practices.

In study abroad context in particular, we can urge students to recognize diversity within host society as well as home society. We can start with encouraging students to have a solid understanding of diversity within their home society because students would be more familiar with the complexity and diversity within their own society that nonetheless need to be discussed explicitly so the students are aware of them. They can also be made aware of how stereotypes and simplistic view of their home society are developed despite the complexity due to various reasons. Recognizing and firmly understanding the complexity within the home society—particularly by understanding how this diversity is created in relations of power, and how it may be ignored or masked, with what effects—helps students understand that any country may be similarly diverse and complex (though the specifics may differ) despite an appearance of homogeneity. This aids in pushing students to seek understanding of the complexity in other parts of the world, including their host society.

This understanding of diversity also encourages students to view fellow study abroad students as diverse, whereby they can come to understand study abroad students' experience as based on their subject positions and related to how various people in the host society view them differently. This, in turn, can push them to understand the diversity within the host society as well as the complexity of encounters between individuals of various backgrounds.

Relations of Power

Relations of power permeate both daily life and study abroad experience in several different ways. First, relations of power influence the construction of the appearance of homogeneity or difference, as some people have to change themselves to look the same as the dominant group, and/or serve as a foil by appearing different as designated "others." "Cultural assimilation" and standardization of language are some examples of the former. For the study abroad program to point out this process specific to that country to students would be helpful for them to deepen the understanding of the society. For example, learning how much the immigrant communities there are encouraged to assimilate to the host society and how their cultural practices are received would deepen the students' understanding of the study abroad destination and situate how they themselves are treated there—for example, though study abroad students and immigrants may both act differently from the mainstream in the host society, they may be treated differently by the local population. This type of understanding helps study abroad students become aware of the similar processes in their home country, especially if they are not the one strongly affected by them and/or not aware of them.

Second, set goals—"global competence," "global citizenship," "native-like fluency in the language"—that are expected to be achieved by studying abroad are also part of the working of relations of power, because the dominant group's worldview determines what is these desired outcomes are. Such desired outcomes also assume the student body, often ignoring minority students who may already have these desired outcomes and are aiming at something else as outcomes of studying abroad, thus limiting ways their outcomes can be articulated and celebrated, as discussed in chapter 7. Making these desired outcomes more inclusive and flexible, less prescriptive, and more reflective of diverse populations would help challenge this process. Interviewing students about their own goals before their study abroad experience would make such desired outcome more flexible and fitting to each student's goals.

Third, relations of power are also brought to bear in labeling practices. What is considered "global" and thus celebrated is only half of a double standard that views white, upper-middle-class mobility as desirable and nonwhite, lower-class mobility as dangerous and illicit, as the notion of regimes of mobility suggests (Glick Schiller and Salazar 2013). This often results in a view that "global competence" can be gained only through studying abroad, whereas it can be gained through various experience of diversity through immigrating or moving between communities, as is often the case for minority students who have to survive in the mainstream (Doerr 2012a, 2017c, 2018).

Home universities can challenge this effect of regime of mobility by celebrating study abroad as well as diverse cultural background and knowledge students bring in from their upbringing and experiences through immigration or being minority (see chapter 4 for a possible activity; see also Doerr 2018). Study abroad programs can celebrate students with extra assets—linguistic and cultural—through various events and encourage group works through which some students can, though should be voluntarily, share their extra linguistic and cultural knowledge and skills with their peers. Because of the prevalent perception and discourse that study abroad is the main way to achieve "global competence" because of the regimes of mobility, many students with immigrant and/or minority backgrounds do not realize their own assets in dealing with diversity. Activities mentioned at home institutions as well as study abroad programs will bring awareness and confidence in such assets to the students themselves and others.

Finally, students are situated in relations of power through their own subject positions. Throughout the book, I urged that students be asked questions about their own positionality—that is, about how their subject positions influence their perceptions and experiences of the world as well as how others view and treat them. These subject positions are usually located in relations of power that need to be discussed and challenged, if needed (Talburt and Stewart 1999). Study abroad programs can intentionally create occasions in which students can discuss this in a safe, trusting environment. This analysis can be useful even after they return to their home country.

The relations of power manifested in study abroad practices can be examined and challenged by way of what may be the most prevalent notion in study abroad: immersion. Though immersion can perpetuate relations of power, as discussed in chapter 4, it is possible instead to capitalize on its focus on daily life by helping students connect their daily experiences to broader socioeconomic and other structures, enabling them to understand how relations of power affect and challenge them. Study abroad programs as well as home institutions can create occasions to reflect this through various activities (see chapters 2 and 4) and classroom discussions, as suggested by critical pedagogy advocates influenced by Paulo Freire (Giroux and McLaren 1989).

Participating in Ongoing Changes

Many things—including "culture" and language—are considered not only homogeneous but also static. However, everything changes. It is crucial to alert students that this is so and that they are part of making change happen. We all participate in processes of change in many ways. We do so by citing (Butler 1993) particular systems of difference as meaningful categories by which to divide and thus conceptualize the world. We do so by labeling certain acts as immersion, thus performatively positioning people involved as legitimately belonging to the host society, for instance, or as socially proximate to us or not, owing to the implications the word immersion holds for them, as discussed in chapter 4. We participate in the construction of what we see at home and abroad by citizens who vote for politicians that support certain legislations, consumers who "vote by money" by purchasing particular things instead of others, by activists marching on the street and posting information and viewpoints on the internet. That means we are responsible for what is happening in the world to various degrees (Doerr and Suarez 2013).

It is also important that students realize they are part of the production of the host society's daily life. This includes understanding that host families alter their daily routines to accommodate them and that hence what they see is not quintessential "host society life" but a life modified by their stay in the home. This will dispose students to understand study abroad not as an encounter of two separate "cultures" but as their joining the host society in its construction of life there, along with other visitors. This perspective also helps convey to them that the host society is not homogeneous but consists of diverse people, including various travelers and sojourners like themselves. This awareness would make students pay more attention to the effects of their actions on the host society as its coproducer—especially on the life of the host family while they are there. Study abroad program can have occasions to discuss the effects of their presence and contributions that they can make in the host society.

Summary: New Frameworks to View Study Abroad

Listed below for clarity and succinctness, this book suggests viewing study abroad:

- not as uniform experiences for all study abroad students but as specific experiences to each student shaped by the subject positions of the study abroad students and of those whom they interact with in specific contexts (introduction)

- not as an experience of static "culture" of someone else but as an experience of changing effects of international regulations, government policies, and commercial enterprises as they affect the specific context of the destination (chapters 1, 2, and 4)
- not as learning the language of destination by interacting with its ideal speakers—"native speakers"—but as an occasion to be exposed to diverse linguistic varieties that may differ from what they were exposed to in their language classroom (chapter 3)
- not as an occasion to "live like a local" but to "live *with* locals" (chapter 5)
- not as an encounter of two separate "cultures" but as the study abroad students joining the host society in its construction of life there, along with other visitors (chapter 5)
- not as "adventurous encounter with exotic difference" to have cognitive dissonance but as experiencing the life of the host society regardless of their similarity or difference (chapter 6)
- not as the only way to gain "global competence" but as one of many ways to do so (chapter 7)
- not as an activity to gain "global competence" as defined and measured in competency tests to show its validity in somebody else's terms but as experience that can be interpreted and reinterpreted in various ways as resources to draw on as the students grow and encounter various situations throughout their lives: "social competence" in general (chapter 7)
- not as the occasion for life-changing self-transformation but as another set of new experiences that change students along with other sets they experience even in their most mundane practices at their home society (chapter 7)

Tips for Developing Critical Student Engagement: Four Steps

In this book, I have attempted to draw attention to various key terms in study abroad that can be revisited and revisioned in light of current theories in related fields of research. There are and will be more key terms and notions that can be revisited in study abroad and beyond, as social conditions and practices continue to change. I invite the study abroad practitioners to involve study abroad students in continuing to examine such notions and explore new solutions and possibilities. For this purpose, I suggest four steps for engaging students in this section. The goal is for students to form a habit of asking these questions themselves, regarding any issue they may encounter.

The first step is to identify a notion to examine. To this end we can ask students what they think about particular concrete things, such as the image of the study abroad destination, how they learned the language, and what differences they noticed between their home and host societies. (We can also ask these questions before their departure as what they expected to encounter while studying abroad.)

The second step is to determine what conditions made them think the way they do or did, and to follow up by asking why they thought as they did and what influenced them to think that way. This spurs them to identify the sources of their thinking, acknowledge the constructedness of various notions, and link their daily activities to wider social structures. The notions at play in "culture," images of the host society and host family, and language competence can all be questioned in these ways.

The third step is to be aware of power relations in terms of who benefits and who suffers from a given arrangement. It is often helpful to ask what wider structural forces are at play in that arrangement. We can also ask students such questions about various notions under discussion to show how what is considered "normal," "proper," or "desirable" is often not neutral but conducive to perpetuating relations of power. The habit of asking these questions in various contexts can be nurtured through study abroad, if students approach it in this way.

The fourth step is to alert students to always consider their role in changing things for the better. Critical investigation and awareness are not only mere interesting intellectual exercises; rather, they are further actions to change what needs to be improved. Praxis—the cycle of reflection and action (Freire 1997)—is what I believe education is for. Again, this is a useful habit on any occasion.

Study Abroad and Beyond

Study abroad is a memorable, special occasion for many. It is often a time set aside to do things differently from the way we do in our "regular life at home." We pay attention to things that we usually do not, and thus we notice things that we usually do not. We think about and talk about things that we usually do not. And we get tested for things that we usually do not. Though we may experience new things and we may transform ourselves throughout our lives, these are the things that are unique about studying abroad—our perception that it is a special time, which then affects how we act. We have various key terms that help us frame this special time. This book examined them in light of current research in various disciplines and explored alternative ways to frame study abroad experiences.

I suggested that study abroad students analyze their daily experiences during their stay in light of larger structural forces that shape them and how our perceptions of "differences" are created in relations of power so that they can become agents of change. Such skills gained through studying abroad can then be used to analyze their daily life "back home." In short, I argued that study abroad can offer a good opportunity to nurture students' observational and analytical thinking from its special emphasis on daily experiences. That can become a special contribution study abroad makes for the field of education, equipping students with skills that are useful in diverse types of situations.

Study abroad can transform you. And, as we expand our theoretical rigor and broaden analytical horizon, we can continue transforming study abroad endeavor.

References

Aalbers, Manuel B. 2014. "Do Maps Make Geography? Part 1: Redlining, Planned Shrinkage, and the Places of Decline." *ACME: International Journal for Critical Geographies* 13 (4): 525–556.

ACTFL (American Council on the Teaching of Foreign Language). 2012. *ACTFL Proficiency Guidelines*. Alexandria, VA: ACTFL.

Akmajian, Adrian, Richard A. Demers, Ann K. Farmer, and Robert M. Harnish. 1995. *Linguistics: An Introduction to Language and Communication*. Cambridge, MA: MIT Press.

Althusser, Louis. 1971. *Lenin and Philosophy and Other Essays*. New York: Monthly Review Press.

Amin, Nuzhat. 1999. "Minority Women Teachers of ESL: Negotiating White English." In Braine 1999b: 93–104.

Amit, Vered. 2010. "Student Mobility and Internationalisation." *Anthropology in Action* 17 (1): 6–18.

Ammon, Ulrich, ed. 1989. *Status and Function of Languages and Language Varieties*. Berlin: Walter de Gruyter.

Anderson, Benedict. 1991. *Imagined Communities*. London: Verso.

———. 1994. "Exodus." *Critical Inquiry* 20 (2): 314–327.

Andreotti, Vanessa de Oliveira, and Lynn Mario T. M. de Souza, eds. 2012. *Postcolonial Perspectives on Global Citizenship Education*. London: Routledge.

Anzaldúa, Gloria. 1987. *Borderlands / La frontera*. San Francisco: Aunt Lute Books.

Appadurai, Arjun. 1990. "Disjuncture and Difference in the Global Cultural Economy." *Public Culture* 2 (2): 1–24.

Archer, Dane, R. S. Oppenheim, Timoti. S. Karetu, and R. S. George. 1973. "Intelligence and the Pakeha Child." In Webb and Collette 1973: 238–241.

Bakhtin, Mikhail. 1981. *The Dialogic Imagination: Four Essays*. Austin: University of Texas Press.

Baldwin, James. 1984. "On Being 'White' . . . and Other Lies." *Essence* (April): 90–92.

———. 1985. "Introduction: The Price of the Ticket." In Baldwin 1985: ix–xx.

———, ed. 1985. *Price of the Ticket: Collected Nonfiction, 1948–1985*. New York: St. Martin's Press.

Balibar, Etienne. 1988. "The Nation Form: History and Ideology." In Balibar and Wallerstein: 86–106.

———. 1994. *Masses, Classes, Ideas: Studies on Politics and Philosophy Before and After Marx*. New York: Routledge.

Balibar, Etienne, and Immanuel Wallerstein, eds. 1988. *Race, Nation, Class: Ambiguous Identities*. London: Verso.

Barber, Benjamin. R. 1994. "A Proposal for Mandatory Citizen Education and Community Service." *Michigan Journal of Community Service Learning* 1 (1): 86–93.

Barnick, Heather. 2010. "Managing Time and Making Space: Canadian Students' Motivations for Study in Australia." *Anthropology in Action* 17 (1): 19–29.

Barth, Fredrik. 1969. *Ethnic Groups and Boundaries*. London: Allen & Unwin.

Bauman, Richard. and Charles L. Briggs. 2000. "Language Philosophy as Language Ideology: John Locke and Johann Gottfried Herder." In Kroskrity 2000: 139–204.

Bayart, Jean-Francois. 2007. *Global Subjects: A Political Critique of Globalization*. Cambridge: Polity.

Belich, James. 2001. *Paradise Reforged: A History of the New Zealanders from the 1880s to the Year 2000*. Honolulu: University of Hawaii Press.

Benedict, Ruth. 1989. *Chrysanthemum and the Sword*. New York: Mariner Books.

Bennett, Neville. 1998. *Asian Students in New Zealand*. Wellington, NZ: Institute of Policy Studies.

Bernstein, Basil. 2003. *Class, Codes and Control*. London: Routledge.

Bex, Tony, and Richard J. Watts, eds. 1999. *Standard English: The Widening Debate*. London: Routledge.

Bhatt, Rakesh M. 2001. "World Englishes." *Annual Review of Anthropology* 30: 527–550.

Block, David. 2007. "The Rise of Identity in SLA Research, Post Firth and Wagner (1997)." *Modern Language Journal* 91 (S1): 864–876.

Block, David, and Deborah Cameron, eds. 2002. *Globalization and Language Teaching*. London: Routledge.

Bloomfield, Leonard. (1933) 1984. *Language*. Chicago: University of Chicago Press.

Borneman, John. 1992. *Belonging in the Two Berlins: Kin, State, Nation*. Cambridge: Cambridge University Press.

Bourdieu, Pierre. (1977) 1991. *Language and Symbolic Power*. Cambridge, MA: Harvard University Press.

———. 1989. "Social Space and Symbolic Power." *Sociological Theory* 7 (1): 14–25.

Bourdieu, Pierre, and Jean-Claude Passeron. 1977. *Reproduction in Education, Society and Culture*. London: Sage.

Boyte, Harry C. 2003. "Putting Politics Back into Civic Engagement." In "Service-Learning and Civic Education," summer special issue, *Campus Compact Reader*: 1–9.

Brading, D. A. 1985. *The Origins of Mexican Nationalism*. Cambridge: Cambridge University Press.

Braine, George. 1999a. "Introduction." In Braine 1999b: viii–xx.

———, ed. 1999b. *Non-native Educators in English Language Teaching*. Mahwah, NJ: Lawrence Erlbaum Associates.

Bringle, Robert G., and Julie A. Hatcher. 2011. "International Service Learning." In Bringle et al. 2011: 3–28.

Bringle, Robert G., Julie A. Hatcher, and Steven G. Jones, eds. 2011. *International Service Learning: Conceptual Frameworks and Research*. Sterling, VA: Stylus Publishing.

Broad, Kenneth, and Ben Orlove. 2007. "Channeling Globality: The 1997–1998 El Nino Climate Event in Peru." *American Ethnologist* 34 (2): 285–302.

Brockington, Joseph L., and Margaret D. Wiedenhoeft. 2009. "The Liberal Arts and Global Citizenship: Fostering Intercultural Engagement Through Integrative Experiences and Structured Reflection." In Lewin 2009a: 117–132.

Brustein, William. 2009. "It Takes an Entire Institution: A Blueprint for the Global University." In Lewin 2009a: 249–265.

Bunten, Alexis Celeste. 2008. "Sharing Culture or Selling Out? Developing the Commodified Persona in the Heritage Industry." *American Ethnologist* 35 (3): 280–295.

Burbules, Nicholas C., and Carlos Alberto Torres. 2000a. "Globalization and Education: An Introduction." In Burbules and Torres 2000b: 1–26.

——, eds. 2000b. *Globalization and Education: Critical Perspectives*. New York: Routledge.

Butin, Dan W. 2006. "The Limits of Service-Learning in Higher Education." *Review of Higher Education* 29 (4): 473–498.

Butler, Judith. 1993. *Bodies That Matter*. New York: Routledge.

Cadena, Marisol de la, and Orin Starn, eds. 2007. *Indigenous Experience Today*. Oxford: Berg.

Calvet, Louis-Jean. 1998. *Language Wars and Linguistic Politics*. Oxford: Oxford University Press.

Cameron, Deborah. 2002. "Globalization and the Teaching of 'Communication Skills.'" In Block and Cameron 2002: 67–82.

Canagarajah, A. Suresh. 1999. *Resisting Linguistic Imperialism in English Teaching*. Oxford: Oxford University Press.

——. 2007. "Lingua Franca English, Multilingual Communities, and Language Acquisition." *Modern Language Journal* 91 (S1): 923–939.

Carlson, Jerry S., Barbara B. Burn, John Useem, and David Yachimowicz. 1990. *Study Abroad: The Experience of American Undergraduates*. New York: Greenwood Press.

Che, S. Megan, Mindy Spearman, and Agida Manizade. 2009. "Constructive Disequilibrium: Cognitive and Emotional Development through Dissonant Experiences in Less Familiar Destinations." In Lewin 2009a: 99–116.

Chen, Leeann. 2002. "Writing to Host Nationals as Cross-Cultural Collaborative Learning in Study Abroad." *Frontiers: The Interdisciplinary Journal of Study Abroad* 8: 143–164.

Chesler, Mark A., Joseph A. Galura, Kristie A. Ford, and Jessica M. Charbeneau. 2006. "Peer Facilitators as Border Crossers in Community Service-Learning." *Teaching Sociology* 34 (4): 341–356.

Chieffo, Lisa, and Lesa Griffiths. 2004. "Large-Scale Assessment of Student Attitudes after a Short-Term Study Abroad Program." *Frontiers: The Interdisciplinary Journal of Study Abroad* 10: 165–177.

Chomsky, Noam. 1965. *Aspects of the Theory of Syntax*. Cambridge, MA: MIT Press.

CIEE (Council on International Education Exchange). 2018a. "College Study Abroad > January in Paris." Accessed 17 July. https://www.ciee.org/go-abroad/college-study-abroad/programs/france/paris/january-paris.

CIEE Study Abroad. 2018b. Facebook page reviews. Accessed 17 July. https://www.facebook.com/pg/cieestudyabroad/reviews.

Clifford, James. 1986. "Introduction: Partial Truth." In Clifford 1986: 1–26.

———. 1988. *The Predicament of Culture: Twentieth-Century Ethnography, Literature, and Art.* Cambridge, MA: Harvard University Press.

———. 1997. *Routes: Travel and Translation in the Late Twentieth Century.* Cambridge, MA: Harvard University Press.

———. 2007. "Varieties of Indigenous Experience: Diasporas, Homelands, Sovereignties." In Cadena and Starn 2007: 197–223.

———, ed. 1986. *Writing Culture: The Poetics and Politics of Ethnography.* Berkeley: University of California Press.

Cohen, Andrew D., R. Michael Paige, Rachel L. Shively, Holly A. Emert, and Joseph G. Hoff. 2005. *Maximizing Study Abroad through Language and Culture Strategies: Research on Students, Study Abroad Program Professionals, and Language Instructors.* Minneapolis: Center for Advanced Research on Language Acquisition, University of Minnesota.

Coles, Roberta L. 1999. "Race-Focused Service-Learning Courses." *Michigan Journal of Community Service Learning* 6 (1): 97–105.

Collier, Stephen J., and Aihwa Ong. 2005. "Global Assemblages, Anthropological Problems." In Ong and Collier: 3–21.

Comaroff, John. 1987. "Of Totemism and Ethnicity: Consciousness, Practice and the Signs of Inequality." *Ethnos* 52 (3–4): 301–323.

Comaroff, John L., and Jean Comaroff. 2004. "Criminal Justice, Cultural Justice: The Limits of Liberalism and the Pragmatics of Difference in the new South Africa." *American Ethnologist* 31 (2): 188–204.

Commission on the Abraham Lincoln Study Abroad Fellowship Program. 2005. *Global Competence and National Needs: One Million Americans Studying Abroad.* Washington, DC: Commission on the Abraham Lincoln Study Abroad Fellowship Program.

Conradson, David, and Alan Latham. 2005. "Transnational Urbanism: Attending to Everyday Practices and Mobilities." *Journal of Ethnic and Migration Studies* 31 (2): 227–233.

Cook, Haruko Minegishi. 2006. "Joint Construction of Folk Beliefs by JFL Learners and Japanese Host Families." In DuFon and Churchill 2000: 120–150.

Cook, Vivian. 1999. "Going beyond the Native Speaker in Language Teaching." *TESOL Quarterly* 33 (2): 185–209.

Covert, Hannah H. 2013. "Stories of Personal Agency: Undergraduate Students' Perceptions of Developing Intercultural Competence during a Semester Abroad in Chile." *Journal of Studies in International Education* 18 (2): 162–179.

Crenshaw, Kimberlé. 1992. "Whose Story Is It, Anyway? Feminist and Antiracist Appropriations of Anita Hill." In Morrison 1992: 402–436.

Crowley, Tony. 1989. *Standard English and the Politics of Language.* Urbana: University of Illinois Press.

Cummins, James. 2001. *Negotiating Identities*. Los Angeles: California Association for Bilingual Education.

Currier, Connie, James Lucas, and Denise Saint Arnault. 2009. "Study Abroad and Nursing: From Cultural to Global Competence." In Lewin 2009a: 133–150.

Cushner, Kenneth. 2009. "The Role of Study Abroad in Preparing Globally Responsible Teachers." In Lewin 2009a: 151–169.

Davies, Alan. 2003. *The Native Speaker: Myth and Reality*. Clevedon: Multilingual Matters.

Deardorff, Darla. 2009. "Understanding the Challenges of Assessing Global Citizenship." In Lewin 2009a: 346–364.

Delpit, Lisa. 1995. *Other People's Children: Cultural Conflict in the Classroom*. New York: New Press.

Dewey, John. 1938. *Experience and Education*. New York: Touchstone.

Doerr, Neriko Musha. 2009a. "Investigating 'Native Speaker Effects': Toward a New Model of Analyzing "Native Speaker" Ideologies." In Doerr 2009c: 15–46.

——. 2009b. *Meaningful Inconsistencies: Bicultural Nationhood, Free Market, and Schooling in Aotearoa/New Zealand*. London: Berghahn Books.

——, ed. 2009c. *The Native Speaker Concept: Ethnographic Investigations of "Native Speaker Effects."* Berlin: Mouton de Gruyter.

——. 2012a. "Producing American Citizens with 'Global Competence': Internationalization of Higher Education and the Unique Contribution of the Community College through English-as-a-Second-Language Education of Adult Immigrants," In *Community Colleges Worldwide: Investigating the Global Phenomenon*, ed. Alexander W. Wiseman, Audree Chase-Mayoral, Thomas Janis, and Anu Sachdev, 71–98. Bingley: Emerald Group Publishing.

——. 2012b. "Study Abroad as 'Adventure': Construction of Imaginings of Social Space and Subjectivities." *Critical Discourse Studies* 9 (3): 257–268.

——. 2013a. "Damp Rooms and Saying 'Please': Mimesis and Alterity in Host Family Space in Study-Abroad Experience." *Anthropological Forum* 23 (1): 58–78.

——. 2013b. "Do 'Global Citizens' Need the Parochial Cultural Other? Discourses of Study Abroad and Learning by Doing." *Compare* 43 (2): 224–243.

——. 2014. "Desired Learning, Disavowed Learning: Scale-Making Practices and Subverting the Hierarchy of Study Abroad Experiences." *Geoforum* 54: 70–79.

——. 2015a. "Learner Subjects in Study Abroad: Discourse of Immersion, Hierarchy of Experience, and their Subversion through Situated Learning." *Discourse: Studies in the Cultural Politics of Education* 36 (3): 369–382.

——. 2015b. "Standardization and Paradoxical Highlighting of Linguistic Diversity in Japan." *Japanese Language and Literature* 49 (2): 389–403.

——. 2015c. "Volunteering as Othering: Understanding A Paradox of Social Distance, Obligation, and Reciprocity." *Partnerships: A Journal of Service-Learning and Civic Engagement* 6 (2): 36–57.

——. 2016. "Chronotopes of Study Abroad: The Cultural Other, Immersion, and Compartmentalized Space-Time." *Journal of Cultural Geography* 33 (1): 80–99.

——. 2017a. "Discourses of Volunteer/Service Work and Their Discontents: Border Crossing, Construction of Hierarchy, and Paying Dues." *Education, Citizenship, and Social Justice* 12 (3): 264–276.

——. 2017b. "Learning as Othering: Narratives of Learning, Construction of Difference, and the Discourse of Immersion in Study Abroad." *Intercultural Education* 28 (1): 90–103.

——. 2017c. "Phantasmagoria of the Global Learner: Unlikely Global Learners and the Hierarchy of Learning." *Learning and Teaching* 10 (2): 58–82.

——. 2018. "'Global Competence' of Minority Immigrant Students: Hierarchy of Experience and Ideology of Global Competence in Study Abroad." *Discourse: Studies in the Cultural Politics of Education.* Published online 11 April. https://doi.org/10.1080/01596306.2018.1462147.

——. Forthcoming. "Sleepless in Albuquerque: Diversity, Learning through Service, and Pedagogy of Exploration." *Pedagogies: An International Journal.*

Doerr, Neriko Musha, and Hannah Davis Taieb. 2017a. "Affect and Romance in Study and Volunteer Abroad: Introducing our Project." In Doerr and Taieb 2017b: 3–34.

——, eds. 2017b. *The Romance of Crossing Borders: Studying and Volunteering Abroad.* Oxford: Berghahn Books.

Doerr, Neriko Musha, and Yuri Kumagai. 2009. "Towards Teaching Diversity in the Second Language Classroom." In Doerr 2009c: 299–317.

Doerr, Neriko Musha, and Kiri Lee. 2013. *Constructing the Heritage Language Learner: Knowledge, Power, and New Subjectivities.* Berlin: Mouton de Gruyter.

Doerr, Neriko Musha, and Richard Suarez. 2013. "The Allegory of Cold Showers and the Politics of Empathy: Production of Diverse Humanitarian Subjects." Paper presented at the Annual Meeting of the American Ethnological Society, Chicago, 11–13 April.

——. 2018. "Immersion, Immigration, Immutability: Regimes of Learning and Politics of Labeling in Study Abroad." *Educational Studies* 54 (2): 183–197.

Doyle, Dennis. 2009. "Holistic Assessment and the Study Abroad Experience." *Frontiers: The Interdisciplinary Journal of Study Abroad* 18. Retrieved 22 August from https://files.eric.ed.gov/fulltext/EJ883695.pdf.

DuFon, Margaret A., and Eton Churchill, eds. 2000. *Language Learners in Study Abroad Contexts.* Clevedon: Multilingual Matters.

Eriksen, Thomas Hylland. 2003. "Introduction." In Eriksen 2003: 1–17.

——, ed. 2003. *Globalization: Studies in Anthropology.* London: Pluto Press.

Fendler, Lynn. 1998. "What Is It Impossible to Think? A Genealogy of the Educated Subject." In Popkewitz and Brennan 1998: 39–63.

Fichte, Johann Gottlieb. 1968. *Addresses to the German Nation.* New York: Harper Torch Books.

Firth, Alan, and Johannes Wagner. 2007a. "On Discourse, Communication, and (Some) Fundamental Concepts in SLA Research." [Republication from *Modern Language Journal* 81 (1997): 285–300.] *Modern Language Journal* 91 (S1): 757–772.

———. 2007b. "Second/Foreign Language Learning as a Social Accomplishment: Elaborations on a Reconceptualized SLA." *Modern Language Journal* 91 (S1): 800–819.

Fishman, Joshua. 2001. "300-Plus Years of Heritage Language Education in the United States." In Peyton, Ranard, and McGinnis 2001: 81–97.

Fobes, Catherine. 2005. "Taking a Critical Pedagogical Look at Travel-Study Abroad: 'A Classroom with a View' in Cusco, Peru." *Teaching Sociology* 33 (2): 181–194.

Foucault, Michel. 1972. *Archaeology of Knowledge*. London: Harper Colophon.

———. 1977. *Discipline and Punish: The Birth of the Prison*. New York: Vintage Books.

Frankenberg, Ruth. 1993. *White Women, Race Matters: The Social Construction of Whiteness*. Minneapolis: University of Minnesota Press.

———. 1997. "Introduction: Local Whiteness, Localizing Whiteness." In Frankenberg 1997: 1–34.

———, ed. 1997. *Displacing Whiteness: Essays in Social and Cultural Criticism*. Durham, NC: Duke University Press.

Fredrick, Williams, ed. 1970. *Language and Poverty: Perspectives on a Theme*. Chicago: Markham Publishing.

Freed, Barbara F. 1995. "What Makes Us Think That Students Who Study Abroad Become Fluent?" In Freed 1995: 123–148.

———, ed. 1995. *Second Language Acquisition in a Study Abroad Context*. Amsterdam: John Benjamins Publishing.

Freire, Paulo. (1970) 1997. *Pedagogy of the Oppressed*. New York: Continuum.

Frekko, Susan. 2009. "Social Class, Linguistic Normativity and the Authority of the 'Native Catalan Speaker' in Barcelona." In Doerr 2009c: 161–184.

Friedman, Jonathan. 2003. "Globalizing Languages: Ideologies and Realities of the Contemporary Global System." *American Anthropologist* 105 (4): 744–752.

Fusco, Coco. 1995. *English is Broken Here: Notes on the Cultural Fusion in the Americas*. New York: New Press.

Gellner, Ernest. 1983. *Nations and Nationalism*. Ithaca, NY: Cornell University Press.

Giroux, Henry. 1992. *Border Crossings: Cultural Workers and the Politics of Education*. New York: Routledge.

———. 2001. *Theory and Resistance in Education: Towards a Pedagogy for the Opposition*. Rev. and expanded ed. Westport: Bergin & Garvey.

Giroux, Henry A., and Peter L. McLaren. 1989. "Introduction." In Giroux and McLaren: xi–xxxv.

———, eds. 1989. *Critical Pedagogy, the State, and Cultural Struggle*. Albany: State University of New York Press.

Glick Schiller, Nina, and Noel B. Salazar. 2013. "Regimes of Mobility Across the Globe." *Journal of Ethnic and Migration Studies* 39 (2): 183–200.

Goldberg, David Theo. 1994. *Multiculturalism: A Critical Reader*. Oxford: Blackwell.

Goldoni, Federica. 2013. "Students' Immersion Experiences in Study Abroad." *Foreign Language Annals* 46 (3): 359–376.

Gore, Joan Elias. 2009. "Faculty Beliefs and Institutional Values: Identifying and Overcoming These Obstacles to Education Abroad Growth." In Lewin 2009a: 282–302.

Gray, Noella J., and Lisa M. Campbell. 2007. "A Decommodified Experience? Exploring Aesthetic, Economic and Ethical Values for Volunteer Ecotourism in Costa Rica." *Journal of Sustainable Tourism* 1 (5): 463–482.

Green, Anne E. 2001. "'But You Aren't White': Racial Perceptions and Service-Learning." *Michigan Journal of Community Service Learning* 8 (1): 18–26.

Gutel, Heather. 2007. "The Home Stay: A Gendered Perspective." *Frontiers: The Interdisciplinary Journal of Study Abroad* 15: 173–188.

Haberly, David T. 1983. *Three Sad Races: Racial Identity and National Consciousness in Brazilian Literature.* Cambridge: Cambridge University Press.

Hall, Stuart. 1996. "Introduction: Who Needs 'Identity'?" In Hall and du Gay: 1–17.

Hall, Stuart, and Paul du Gay, eds. 1996. *Questions of Cultural Identity.* London: Sage.

Halliday, Michael. 1978. *Language as Social Semiotic: The Social Interpretation of Language and Meaning.* Baltimore: University Park Press.

Handler, Richard. 1985. "On Having a Culture: Nationalism and the Preservation of Quebec's *Patrimoine*." In Stocking 1985: 192–217.

Hanson, Allan. 1989. "The Making of the Maori." *American Anthropologist* 91 (4): 890–902.

Harvey, David. 1990. *The Condition of Postmodernity.* Cambridge, MA: Blackwell.

Hayes, Elizabeth, and Sondra Cuban. 1997. "Border Pedagogy: A Critical Framework for Service-Learning." *Michigan Journal of Community Service-learning* 4 (1): 72–80.

Heath, Shirly Brice. 2007. "Widening the Gap: Pre-university Gap Years and the 'Economy of Experience.'" *British Journal of Sociology of Education* 28 (1): 89–103.

Henry, Sue Ellen, and M. Lynn Breyfogle. 2006. "Toward a New Framework of 'Server' and 'Served': De (and Re)constructing Reciprocity in Service-Learning Pedagogy." *International Journal of Teaching and Learning in Higher Education* 18 (1): 27–35.

Henze, Rosemary, and Kathryn A. Davis. 1999. "Authenticity and Identity: Lessons from Indigenous Language Education." *Anthropology and Education Quarterly* 30 (1): 3–21.

Hobsbawm, Eric J. 1990. *Nations and Nationalism since 1780: Programme, Myth, Reality.* Cambridge: Cambridge University Press

Hobsbawm, Eric J., and Terence Ranger. 1992. *Invention of Tradition.* Cambridge: Cambridge University Press.

Hochschild, Arlie Russell. 1983. *The Managed Heart: Commercialization of Human Feeling.* Berkeley: University of California Press.

Holland, Dorothy, Debra Skinner, William Lachicotte Jr., and Carole Cain. 1998. *Identity and Agency in Cultural Worlds.* Cambridge, MA: Harvard University Press.

hooks, bell. 1989. "Representing Whiteness: Seeing Wings of Desire." *Zeta Magazine* 2 (3): 36–39.

———. 1992. *Black Looks: Race and Representation*. Boston: South End Press.

House, Julian. 2003. "English as a Lingua Franca: A Threat to Multilingualism?" *Journal of Sociolinguistics* 7 (4): 556–578.

Hovey, Rebecca, and Adam Weinberg. 2009. "Global Learning and the Making of Citizen Diplomats." In Lewin 2009a: 33–48.

Hovland, Kevin. 2014. *Global Learning: Defining, Designing, Demonstrating*. Washington, DC: NAFSA: Association of International Educators and the Association of American Colleges and Universities.

Hovland, Kevin, Caryn McTighe Musil, Ellen Skilton-Sylvester, and Amy Jamison. 2009. "It Takes a Curriculum: Bringing Global Mindedness Home." In Lewin 2009a: 466–484.

Howes, David. 1996. "Introduction: Commodities and Cultural Borders." In Howes 1996: 1–16.

———, ed. 1996. *Cross-Cultural Consumption: Global Markets Local Realities*. New York: Routledge.

Hunter, Bill, George P. White, and Galen C. Godbey. 2006. "What Does It Mean to Be Globally Competent?" *Journal of Studies in International Education* 10 (3): 267–285.

Ignatief, Noel. 1996. "Introduction: A Beginning." In Ignatief and Garvey 1996: 1–8.

Ignatief, Noel, and John Garvey. eds. 1996. *Race Traitor*. New York: Routledge.

Iino, Masakazu. 2006. "Norms of Interaction in a Japanese Homestay Setting: Toward a Two-Way Flow of Linguistic and Cultural Resources." In DuFon and Churchill 2000: 151–176.

Illich, Ivan. 1981. *Shadow Work*. Boston: Marion Boyars.

Irvine, Judith T., and Susan Gal. 2000. "Language Ideology and Linguistic Differentiation." In Kroskrity 2000: 35–83.

Jackson, Jane. 2009. "Intercultural Learning on Short-Term Sojourn." *Intercultural Education* 20 (1–2): 59–71.

Jenkins, Jennifer. 2006. "Current Perspectives on Teaching World Englishes and English as a Lingua Franca." *TESOL Quarterly* 40 (1): 157–181.

Jones, Susan Robb, Claire Kathleen Robbins, and Lucy A. LePeau. 2011. "Negotiating Border Crossing: Influences of Social Identity on Service-Learning Outcomes." *Michigan Journal of Community Service Learning* 17 (2): 27–42.

Jorge, Ethel. 2006. "A Journey Home: Connecting Spanish-Speaking Communities at Home and Abroad." *Hispania* 89 (1): 110–122.

Kachru, Braj B. (1982) 1992a. "Models for Non-native Englishes." In Kachru 1992b: 48–74.

———, ed. (1982) 1992b. *The Other Tongue: English Across Cultures*. Urbana: University of Illinois Press.

———. (1982) 1992c. "Teaching World Englishes." In Kachru 1992b: 355–366.

Kahne, Joseph, and Joel Westheimer. 2003. "Teaching Democracy: What Schools Need to Do." *Phi Delta Kappan* 85 (1): 34–66.

Keesing, Roger. 1989. "Creating the Past: Custom and Identity in the Contemporary Pacific." *Contemporary Pacific* 1 (1–2): 19–42.

Kehl, Kevin, and Jason Morris. 2007. "Differences in Global-Mindedness between Short-Term and Semester-Long Study Abroad Participants at Selected Private Universities." *Frontiers: The Interdisciplinary Journal of Study Abroad* 15. Retrieved 22 August 2018 from https://files.eric.ed.gov/fulltext/EJ878383.pdf.

Kincheloe, Joe L., and Shirley R. Steinberg. 1997. *Changing Multiculturalism.* London: Open University Press.

King, Michael 1985. *Being Pakeha: An Encounter with New Zealand and the Maori Renaissance.* Auckland: Hodder & Stoughton.

Kinginger, Celeste. 2008. "Language Learning in Study Abroad: Case Studies of Americans in France." *Modern Language Journal* 92 (S1): 1–124.

Knight, Susan M. and Barbara C. Schmidt-Rinehart. 2002. "Enhancing the Homestay: Study Abroad from the Host Family's Perspective." *Foreign Language Annals* 35 (2): 190–201.

Kolb, David A. 1984. *Experiential Learning: Experience as the Source of Learning and Development.* Englewood Cliffs, NJ: Prentice Hall.

Kortegast, Carrie. A., and M. Terral Boisfontaine. 2015. "Beyond 'It Was Good': Students' Post–Study Abroad Practices for Negotiating Meaning." *Journal of College Student Development* 56 (8): 812–828.

Kramsch, Claire. ed. 2002. *Language Acquisition and Language Socialization: Ecological Perspectives.* London: Continuum.

Kroskrity, Paul V., ed. 2000. *Regimes of Language: Ideologies, Polities, and Identities.* Santa Fe, NM: School of American Research Press.

Kubota, Ryuko. 2003. "Critical Teaching of Japanese Culture." *Japanese Language and Literature* 37 (1): 67–87.

Kumagai, Yuri. 2017. "Learning Japanese/Japan in a Year Abroad in Kyoto: Discourse of Study Abroad, Emotions, and Construction of Self." In Doerr and Taieb 2017b: 166–192.

Kymlicka, Will. 1995. *Multicultural Citizenship: A Liberal Theory of Minority Rights.* Oxford: Clarendon Press.

Labov, William 1970. "The Logic of Nonstandard English." In Fredrick 1970: 153–187.

Lambert, Richard. D. 1994. "Parsing the Concept of Global Competence." In Lambert 1994: 11–24.

——, ed. 1994. *Educational Exchange and Global Competence.* New York: Council on International Educational Exchange.

Larsen-Freeman, Diane. 1997. "Chaos/Complexity Science and Second Language Acquisition." *Applied Linguistics* 18 (2): 141–165.

——. 2002 "Language Acquisition and Language Use from a Chaos/Complexity Theory Perspective." In Kramsch 2002: 33–46.

Laubscher, Michael R. 1994. *Encounters with Difference: Student Perceptions of the Role of Out-of-Class Experiences in Education Abroad.* Westport, CO: Greenwood Press.

Lave, Jean, and Etienne Wenger. 1991. *Situated Learning: Legitimate Peripheral Participation.* Cambridge: Cambridge University Press.

Law, Andrew, and Susan Mennicke. 2007. "A Notion at Risk: Interrogating the Educational Role of Off-Campus Study in the Liberal Arts." *Frontiers: The Interdisciplinary Journal of Study Abroad* 15: 81–91.

Levine, Hal. 1991. "Comment on Hanson's 'The Making of the Maori.'" *American Anthropologist* 93 (2): 444–446.

Lewin, Ross, ed. 2009a. *The Handbook of Practice and Research in Study Abroad: Higher Education and the Quest for Global Citizenship*. New York: Routledge

——. 2009b. "Introduction: The Quest for Global Citizenship through Study Abroad." In Lewin 2009a: viii–xxii.

Lewin, Ross, and Greg Van Kirk. 2009. "It's Not About You: The UConn Social Entrepreneur Corps Global Commonwealth Study Abroad Model." In Lewin 2009a: 543–564.

Linnekin, Jocelyn. 1991. "Cultural Invention and the Dilemma of Authenticity." *American Anthropologist* 93 (2): 446–449.

Lindenberg, Lise. 2015. "International Student Programs in Ontario: An Examination of the Academic, Emotional, and Cultural Supports Offered to International Students in Ontario High Schools." Master's thesis, Queen's University Kingston.

Liu, Jun. 1999. "From Their Own Perspectives: The Impact of Non-native ESL Professionals on their Students." In Braine 1999b: 159–176.

Lisle, Debbie. 2006. *Global Politics of Contemporary Travel Writing*. Cambridge: Cambridge University Press.

Loflin, Stephen E. 2007. *Adventures Abroad: The Student's Guide to Studying Overseas*. New York: Kaplan Publishing.

Lott, Eric. 1995. *Love and Theft: Blackface Minstrelsy and the American Working Class*. Oxford: Oxford University Press.

Makihara, Miki. 2009. "Heterogeneity in Linguistic Practice, Competence and Ideology: Language and Community on Easter Island." In Doerr 2009c: 249–276.

Makoni, Sinfree and Alastair Pennycook, eds. 2007. *Disinventing and Reconstituting Languages*. Clevedon: Multilingual Matters.

Mann, Charles C. 2006. *1491: New Revelations of the Americas Before Columbus*. Vintage Books.

Mansilla, Veronica Boix, and Howard Gardner. 2007. "From Teaching Globalization to Nurturing Global Consciousness." In Suarez-Orozco 2007: 47–66.

Mashiko, Hidenori. 2000. *Tatakai no Shakaigaku: Hikigeki toshiteno Kyoso Shakai* [The sociology of struggle: The competitive society as a tragicomedy). Tokyo: Sangensha.

——. 2003. *Ideologii to shite no "Nihon": "Kokugo," "Nihonshi" no Chishiki Shakaigaku* ["Japan" as an ideology: Sociology of knowledge of "national language," "Japanese history"]. Sangensha: Tokyo.

Massey, Doreen. 2005. *For Space*. London: Sage Publications.

Maurer, Evan. M. 2000. "Presenting the American Indian: From Europe to America." In West 2000: 15–28.

May, Stephen. 2001. *Language and Minority Rights: Ethnicity, Nationalism and the Politics of Language*. Harlow: Pearson Education.

McClintock, Anne. 1995. *Imperial Leather: Race, Gender and Sexuality in the Colonial Contest*. New York: Routledge.

McDermott, Ray, and Hervé Varenne. 1995. "Culture as Disability." *Anthropology and Education Quarterly* 26 (3): 324–348.

Menard-Warwick, Julia, and Debrah K. Palmer. 2012. "Eight Versions of the Visit to La Barraca: Critical Discourse Analysis of a Study-Abroad Narrative from Mexico." *Teacher Education Quarterly* 39 (1): 121–138.

Mendelson, Vija G. 2004. "'Hindsight Is 20/20': Student Perceptions of Language Learning and the Study Abroad Experience." *Frontiers: The Interdisciplinary Journal of Study Abroad* 10. Retrieved 22 August 2018 from https://files.eric.ed.gov/fulltext/EJ891448.pdf.

Miller, Daniel, ed. 1995. *Worlds Apart: Modernity through Prism of the Local*. London: Routledge.

Milroy, Lesley. 1999. "Standard English and Language Ideology in Britain and the United States." In Bex and Watts 1999: 173–206.

Milroy, James, and Lesley Milroy. (1985) 1991. *Authority in Language: Investigating Language Prescription and Standardization*. London: Routledge.

Miner, Horace. 1956. "Body Ritual among the Nacirema." *American Anthropologist* 58 (3): 503–507.

Moreno, Kristin Heather. 2009. "The Study Abroad Experiences of Heritage Language Learners." PhD diss., University of Texas, Austin.

Morris-Suzuki, Tessa. 1998. *Re-inventing Japan: Time, Space, Nation*. Armonk: East Gate Book.

Morrison, Toni. 1992. *Race-ing Justice, En-gendering Power: Essays on Anita Hill, Clarence Thomas, and the Construction of Social Reality*. New York: Pantheon Books.

Munt, Ian. 1994. "Eco-tourism or Ego-tourism?" *Race and Class* 36 (1): 49–60.

Murphy-Lejeune, Elizabeth. 2002. *Student Mobility and Narrative in Europe: The New Strangers*. London: Routledge.

Murray, Garold, Xuesong Gao, and Terry Lamb, eds. 2011. *Identity, Motivation and Autonomy in Language Learning*. New York: Multilingual Matters.

Nash, Dennison. 1989. "Tourism as a Form of Imperialism." In Smith 1989: 37–53.

Nenga, Sandi Kawecka. 2011. "Volunteering to Give up Privilege? How Affluent Youth Volunteers Respond to Class Privilege." *Journal of Contemporary Ethnography* 40 (3): 263–289.

Nero, Shondel J. 2006. "Introduction." In Nero 2006: 1–18.

——, ed. 2006. *Dialects, Englishes, Creoles, and Education*. New York: Lawrence Erlbaum.

Ogden, Anthony C. 2006. "Ethnographic Inquiry: Reframing the Learning Core of Education Abroad." *Frontiers: The Interdisciplinary Journal of Study Abroad* 8: 87–112.

——. 2007. "The View from the Veranda: Understanding Today's Colonial Student." *Frontiers: The Interdisciplinary Journal of Study Abroad* 15. Retrieved 22 August 2018 from https://files.eric.ed.gov/fulltext/EJ878378.pdf.

Omi, Michael, and Howard Winant. 1994. *Racial Formation in the United States: From the 1960s to the 1990s*. New York: Routledge.

Ong, Aihwa, and Stephen J. Collier, eds. 2005. *Global Assemblages: Technology, Politics, and Ethics as Anthropological Problems.* Malden, MA: Blackwell Publishing.

Oxford, Stephanie M. 2005. *Study Abroad: Travel Vacation in College.* Friant, CA: Where In the World Publishing.

Palmer, Norris W. 2015. "Inverting the Object of Study: Recalibrating the Frame of Reference in Study Abroad Experiences." *Teaching Theology and Religion* 18 (1): 63–72.

Pashby, Karen. 2012. "Questions for Global Citizenship Education in the Context of the 'New Imperialism': For Whom, by Whom?" In Andreotti and de Souza 2012: 9–26.

Pennycook, Alastair. 1994. *The Cultural Politics of English as an International Language.* London: Longman.

———. 2004. "Performativity and Language Studies." *Critical Inquiry in Language Studies: An International Journal* 1 (1): 1–19.

———. 2007. "The Myth of English as an International Language." In Makoni and Pennycook 2007: 90–115.

Peterson, Chip. 2002. "Preparing Engaged Citizens: Three Models of Experiential Education for Social Justice." *Frontiers: The Interdisciplinary Journal of Study Abroad* 8: 41–82.

Peyton, Kreeft Joy, Donald A. Ranard, and Scott McGinnis, eds. 2001. *Heritage Languages in America: Preserving a National Resource.* McHenry, IL: Center for Applied Linguistics and Delta Systems.

Philips, Susan U. 2004. "The Organization of Ideological Diversity in Discourse: Modern and Neotraditional Visions of the Tongan State." *American Ethnologist* 31 (2): 231–250.

Phillipson, Robert. 1992. *Linguistic Imperialism.* Oxford: Oxford University Press.

Pike, Graham. 2000. "Global Education and National Identity: In Pursuit of Meaning." *Theory into Practice* 39 (2): 64–73.

Plater, William M. 2011. "The Context for International Service Learning: An Invisible Revolution is Underway." In Bringle et al. 2011: 29–56.

Plater, William M., Steven G. Jones, Robert G. Bringle, and Patti H. Clayton. 2009. "Educating Globally Competent Citizens through International Service Learning." In Lewin 2009a: 485–505.

Plummer, Ken. 1995. *Telling Sexual Stories: Power, Change and Social Worlds.* London: Routledge.

Popadiuk, Natalee. 2009. "Unaccompanied Asian Secondary Students Studying in Canada." *International Journal of Advanced Counselling* 31: 229–243.

Popkewitz Thomas S., and Marie Brennan, eds. 1998. *Foucault's Challenge: Discourse, Knowledge, and Power in Education.* New York: Teachers College Press.

Povinelli, Elizabeth A. 1998. "The State of Shame: Australian Multiculturalism and the Crisis of Indigenous Citizenship." *Critical Inquiry* 24 (2): 575–610.

———. 2002. *The Cunning of Recognition: Indigenous Alterities and the Making of Australian Multiculturalism.* Durham, NC: Duke University Press.

Pratt, Mary Louise. (1992) 2008. *Imperial Eyes: Travel Writing and Transculturation.* London: Routledge

Quirk, Randolph. 1985. "The English Language in a Global Context." In Quirk and Widdowson 1985: 1–6.

Quirk, Randolph, and Henry G. Widdowson, eds. 1985. *English in the World: Teaching and Learning the Language and Literatures.* Cambridge: Cambridge University Press.

Rampton, Ben. 1995. *Crossing: Language and Ethnicity among Adolescents.* London: Longman.

Raymond, Eliza Marguerite, and C. Michael Hall. 2008. "The Development of Cross-Cultural (Mis)understanding through Volunteer Tourism." *Journal of Sustainable Tourism* 16 (5): 530–514.

Redden, Elizabeth. 2010. "Academic Outcomes of Study Abroad." *Inside Higher Ed*, 13 July. http://www.insidehighered.com/news/2010/07/13/abroad.

Reimer, Kristin, and Lorna R. McLean. 2009. "Conceptual Clarity and Connections: Global Education and Teacher Candidates." *Canadian Journal of Education* 32 (4): 903–926.

Rexeisen, Richard J., Philip H. Anderson, Leigh Lawton, and Ann C. Hubbard. 2008. "Study Abroad and Intercultural Development: A Longitudinal Study." *Frontiers: The Interdisciplinary Journal of Study Abroad* 17: 1–20.

Rhoads Robert A., and Julie Neururer. 1998. "Alternative Spring Break: Learning through Community Service." *NASPA Journal* 35 (2): 100–118.

Riegelhaupt, Florencia, and Roberto Luis Carrasco. 2000. "Mexico Host Family Reactions to a Bilingual Chicana Teacher in Mexico: A Case Study of Language and Culture Clash." *Bilingual Research Journal* 24 (4): 405–421.

Rizvi, Fazal. 2000. "International Education and the Production of Global Imagination." In Burbules and Torres 2000b: 205–226.

Roberts, Celia, Michael Byram, Ano Barro, Shirley Jordan, and Brian Street. 2001. *Language Learners as Ethnographers.* Clevedon: Multilingual Matters.

Roediger, David. 1991. *The Wages of Whiteness: Race and the Making of the American Working Class.* London: Verso.

——. 1994. *Towards the Abolition of Whiteness.* London: Verso.

Romaine, Suzanne. 1997. "World Englishes: Standards and the new World Order." In Smith and Forman 1997: xi–xvi.

Root, Elizabeth, and Anchalee Ngampornchai. 2012. "'I Came Back as a New Human Being': Student Descriptions of Intercultural Competence Acquired through Education Abroad Experiences." *Journal of Studies in International Education* 17 (5): 513–532.

Ryan, Stephen, and Sarah Mercer. 2011. "Natural Talent, Natural Acquisition and Abroad: Learner Attributions of Agency in Language Learning." In Murray, Gao, and Lamb 2011: 160–176.

Sakai, Naoki. 1997. *Translation and Subjectivity: On "Japan" and Cultural Nationalism.* Minneapolis: University of Minnesota Press.

Saussure, Ferdinand de. (1916) 1959. *Course in General Linguistics.* New York: McGraw-Hill.

Seidlhofer, Barbara. 2001. "Closing a Conceptual Gap: The Case for a Description of English as a Lingua Franca." *International Journal of Applied Linguistics* 11 (2): 133–158.

Sheller, Mimi, and John Urry. 2006. "The New Mobilities Paradigm." *Environment and Planning A* 38 (2): 207–226.

Sin, Harng Luh. 2009. "Who Are We Responsible To? Locals' Tales of Volunteer Tourism." *Geoforum* 41: 983–992.

Sinclair, Keith. 1986. *A Destiny Apart: New Zealand's Search for National Identity*. Wellington: Allen & Unwin.

Sinervo, Aviva. 2011. "Connection and Disillusion: The Moral Economy of Volunteer Tourism in Cusco, Peru." *Childhoods Today* 5 (2): 1–23.

Skelly, James M. 2009. "Fostering Engagement: The Role of International Education in the Development of Global Civil Society." In Lewin 2009a: 21–32.

Skutnabb-Kangas, Tove, and Robert Phillipson. 1989. "'Mother Tongue': The Theoretical and Sociopolitical Construction of a Concept." In Ammon 1989: 450–477.

Smith, Larry E. 1982. "Spread of English and Issues of Intelligibility." In Kachru (1982) 1992b: 75–90.

Smith, Larry E., and Michael L. Forman, eds. 1997. *World Englishes 2000*. Honolulu: University of Hawaii Press.

Smith, Valene L., ed. 1989. *Hosts and Guests: The Anthropology of Tourism*. Philadelphia: University of Pennsylvania Press.

Sol Education Abroad. 2018. "Student Testimonials." Accessed 17 July. http:// www.soleducation.com/student-testimonials.

Sommer, Doris. 1991. *Foundational Fictions: The National Romances of Latin America*. Berkeley: University of California Press.

Spoonley, Paul. 1991. "Pakeha Ethnicity: A Response to Maori Sovereignty." In Spoonley, Pearson, and Macpherson 1991: 154–170.

Spoonley, Paul, David Pearson, and Cluny Macpherson, eds. 1991. *Nga Take: Ethnic Relations and Racism in Aotearoa/New Zealand*. Palmerston North: Dunmore Press.

Stocking, George W. Jr., ed. 1985. *Objects and Others: Essays on Museums and Material Culture*. Madison: University of Wisconsin Press.

Stoler, Ann Laura. 1995. *Race and the Education of Desire: Foucault's* History of Sexuality *and the Colonial Order of Things*. Durham, NC: Duke University Press.

Streitwieser, Bernhard T. 2009. "Undergraduate Research During Study Abroad: Scope, Meaning, and Potential." In Lewin 2009a: 399–419.

StudyAbroad.com. 2011. "Study Abroad Testimonials." Ed. Valeri Boyle. 25 July. https://www.studyabroad.com/resources/study-abroad-testimonials.

StudyAbroad.com. 2018. "France > Study Abroad > Undergraduate > Paris." Retrieved 17 July 2018 from https://www.studyabroad.com/in-france/ paris.

Suarez-Orozco, Marcelo M., ed. 2007. *Learning in the Global Era: International Perspectives on Globalization and Education*. Berkeley: University of California Press.

Suarez-Orozco, Marcelo, and Desiree B. Qin-Hillard. 2004. "Globalization: Culture and Education in the New Millennium. In Suarez-Orozco and Qin-Hillard: 1–37.

——, eds. 2004. *Globalization: Culture and Education in the New Millennium.* Berkeley: University of California Press.

Taguchi, Naoko. 2008. "Cognition, Language Contact, and the Development of Pragmatic Comprehension in a Study-Abroad Context." *Language Learning* 58 (1): 33–71.

Talburt, Susan, and Melissa A. Stewart. 1999. "What's the Subject of Study Abroad? Race, Gender and Living Culture." *Modern Language Journal* 82 (2): 163–175.

Taylor, Charles. 1994. "The Politics of Recognition." In Goldberg 1994: 75–106.

Taylor, Joby. 2002. "Metaphors We Serve By: Investigating the Conceptual Metaphors Framing National and Community Service and Service-Learning." *Michigan Journal of Community Service Learning* 9 (1): 45–57.

TESOL (Teachers of English to Speakers of Other Languages). 2005. *PreK–12 English Language Proficiency Standards in the Core Content Areas: An Augmentation of the World-Class Instructional Design and Assessment (WIDA) Consortium's English Language Proficiency Standards for English Language Learners.* Alexandria, VA: TESOL.

Tibaldo-Bongiorno, Marylou, dir. 2007. *Revolution '67.* Documentary film. 90 min.

Tomlinson, John. 1999. *Globalization and Culture.* Chicago: University of Chicago Press.

Train, Robert. 2009. "Toward a 'Natural' History of the Native (Standard) Speaker." In Doerr 2009c: 47–80.

Trask, Haunani-Kay. 1991. "Natives and Anthropologists: The Colonial Struggle." *Contemporary Pacific* 2 (1): 159–167.

Tsing, Anna. 2000. "The Global Situation." *Cultural Anthropology* 15 (3): 327–360.

——. 2005. *Friction: An Ethnography of Global Connection.* Princeton, NJ: Princeton University Press.

Turner, Terence. 1994. "Anthropology and Multiculturalism: What Is Anthropology That Multiculturalism Should Be Mindful of It?" In Goldberg 1994: 406–425.

Tylor, Edward B. (1871) 2016. *Primitive Culture.* New York: Dover Publications.

UCI Study Abroad Center. 2006. "Study Abroad Testimonials." http://www.studyabroad.uci.edu/yearofstudy/testimonials06.html.

Urciuoli, Bonnie. 1995. "Language and Borders." *Annual Review of Anthropology* 24: 525–46.

Vande Berg, Michael. 2009. "Intervening in Student Learning Abroad: A Research-Based Inquiry." *Intercultural Education* 20 (1–2): 15–27.

Vande Berg, Michael, Jeffrey Connor-Linton, and R. Michael Paige. 2009. "The Georgetown Consortium Project: Interventions for Student Learning Abroad." *Frontiers: The Interdisciplinary Journal of Study Abroad* 18. Retrieved 22 August 2018 from https://files.eric.ed.gov/fulltext/EJ883690.pdf.

Volosinov, Valentin N. 1973. *Marxism and the Philosophy of Language.* Cambridge, MA: Harvard University Press.

Walker, Ranginui. 1990. *Ka Whawhai Tonu Matou: Struggle without End*. Auckland: Penguin.

Warner, Sam L. No'eau. 1999. "Kuleana: The Right, Responsibility, and Authority of Indigenous Peoples to Speak and Make Decisions for Themselves in Language and Cultural Revitalization." *Anthropology and Education Quarterly* 30 (1): 68–93.

Webb, Stephen D., and John Collette, eds. 1973. *New Zealand Society: Contemporary Perspectives*. Sydney: John Wiley & Sons Australia.

West, Richard, ed. 2000. *The Changing Presentation of the American Indian: Museums and Native Cultures*. Washington, DC: University of Washington Press.

Whiteley, Peter. 2003. "Do 'Language Rights' Serve Indigenous Interests? Some Hopi and Other Queries." *American Anthropologist* 105 (4): 712–722.

Widdowson, Henry. 1994. "The Ownership of English." *TESOL Quarterly* 28 (2): 377–389.

Wiegman, Robyn. 1995. *American Anatomies: Theorizing Race and Gender*. Durham, NC: Duke University Press.

Wilk, Richard. 1995. "Learning to Be Local in Belize: Global Systems of Common Difference." In Miller 1995: 110–133.

Wilkinson, Sharon. 1998. "On the Nature of Immersion During Study Abroad: Some Participant Perspectives." *Frontiers: The Interdisciplinary Journal of Study Abroad* 4. Retrieved 22 August 2018 from https://files.eric.ed.gov/fulltext/EJ608215.pdf.

——. 2002. "The Omnipresent Classroom during Summer Study Abroad: American Students in Conversation with Their French Hosts." *Modern Language Journal* 86 (2): 157–173.

Williamson, Wendy. 2004. *Study Abroad 101*. Charleston, IL: Agapy Publishing.

Wimmer, Andreas, and Nina Glick Schiller. 2002. "Methodological Nationalism and Beyond: Nation-State Building, Migration and the Social Sciences." *Global Networks* 2 (4): 301–334.

Wolf, Eric R. 1994. "Perilous Ideas: Race, Culture, People." *Current Anthropology* 35 (1): 1–7.

Woolf, Michael. 2006. "Come and See the Poor People: The Pursuit of Exotica." *Frontiers: The Interdisciplinary Journal of Study Abroad* 13: 135–146.

——. 2007. "Impossible Things before Breakfast: Myths in Education Abroad." *Journal of Studies in International Education* 11 (3–4): 496–509.

——. 2010. "Another Mishegas: Global Citizenship." *Frontiers: The Interdisciplinary Journal of Study Abroad* 19: 47–60.

Wurdinger, Scott D., and Julie A. Carlson. 2010. *Teaching For Experiential Learning: Five Approaches That Work*. Lanham, MD: Rowman & Littlefield.

Yashima, Tomoko, Lori Zenuk-Nishide, and Kazuaki Shimizu. 2004. "The Influence of Attitudes and Affect on Willingness to Communicate and Second Language Communication." *Language Learning* 54 (1): 119–152.

Zemach-Bersin, Talya. 2009. "Selling the World: Study Abroad Marketing and the Privatization of Global Citizenship." In Lewin 2009a: 303–320.

Zuengler, Jane, and Elizabeth R. Miller. 2006. "Cognitive and Sociocultural Perspectives: Two Parallel SLA Worlds?" *TESOL Quarterly* 40 (1): 35–58.

Index

Lightning Source UK Ltd.
Milton Keynes UK
UKHW021038190920
369795UK00017B/336